Dessert
in half the time

Also by Linda West Eckhardt and Diana Collingwood Butts

Bread in Half the Time

✧

Dessert
in half the time

Use Your Food Processor and Microwave

to Make Great Desserts

in Less Time Than It Takes to Buy

a Pint of Ice Cream

✧

Linda West Eckhardt and *Diana Collingwood Butts*

Illustrations by Dolores R. Santoliquido

CROWN PUBLISHERS, INC., NEW YORK

To LHB
For always being there for me.
I love you very much.
D.C.B.

For JCAE
Again and forever.
Love, Love
L.W.E.

Copyright © 1993 by Linda West Eckhardt and Diana Collingwood Butts

Illustrations copyright © 1993 by Dolores R. Santoliquido

Published by Crown Publishers, Inc., 201 East 50th Street, New York, New York 10022. Member of the Crown Publishing Group.

Random House, Inc. New York, Toronto, London, Sydney, Auckland

CROWN is a trademark of Crown Publishers, Inc.

Manufactured in the United States of America

Design by Lauren Dong

Library of Congress Cataloging-in-Publication Data
Eckhardt, Linda West
   Dessert in half the time / Linda West Eckhardt and Diana Collingwood
Butts ; illustrations by Dolores R. Santoliquido. — 1st ed.
      p.   cm.
      Includes index.
      1. Desserts.   2. Food processor cookery.   3. Microwave cookery.
   4. Quick and easy cookery.   I. Butts, Diana Collingwood.
   II. Title.
   TX773.E33   1993
   641.8′6—dc20   93-2734
                                                                                 CIP

ISBN 0-517-58721-1

10 9 8 7 6 5 4 3 2 1

First Edition

CONTENTS

Acknowledgments

For loving dessert as much as we do, we thank our agent, Mildred Marmur, for steering us toward this sweet, sweet baby sister to *Bread in Half the Time*.

We thank our wise and chocolate-loving editor, Erica Marcus, who kept the project on track and made valuable suggestions that were not only lagniappe but became as basic as butter to cake.

Lauren Dong and Dolores Santoliquido did their usual glorious job with the design and illustrations. We especially wish to acknowledge the hard and dedicated work that sometimes spilled over into the nights and weekends for Kim Hertlein, the production editor, who wrangled this stallion out of the chute.

We also thank our friends in the business without whose help with supplies, equipment, and knowledgeable suggestions we could never have made the discoveries we did. Bob Cronon at Braun, who first showed us that we could successfully beat egg whites in a food processor. Susan Dumont-Parrish, who backed that up by offering us a Cuisinart food processor to prove this valuable workhorse could lift those egg whites right to the top of the work bowl. What a discovery! We thank you both. You've changed our egg white–whipping ways forever.

Lily Gruver at Black & Decker provided us with inspiration and equipment to make delectable dessert waffles and cakes. Ben Nomoto at Zojirushi and Paul Mizuki at Panasonic helped us perfect bread machine breads, and Lloyd Montgomery at White Lily, and the King Arthur folks, who proved once again that to get the best product, you should settle for nothing but the best flours.

To the people at Parrish Cake Decorating and Pans and CushionAire, we're sold on the quality of your baking pans. To the makers of Nielsen Massey vanilla, and American Spoon Foods dried cherries, we say thanks. Your products are so much better than what we buy in the supermarket.

And, finally, to all our friends and neighbors who acted as ancillary test cooks, tasters, and dishwashers, thanks, thanks, thanks.

Linda and Diana

Dessert

in half the time

INTRODUCTION

We admit it. We are obsessed with change. We just love to look at a recipe and see how we could make that recipe taste better, look better, and be easier and quicker to make.

It's gotten really crazy. How many women do you know who would get on the phone with each other shouting into the mouthpiece: Eureka! I just figured out why I never have to sift flour again.

That was the day we discovered we could aerate flour and other dry ingredients in the food processor and get better results than if we used a triple sifter. One more item for the garage sale, we said, placing the sifter in the back corner of the garage.

So we sat down that afternoon, over a bowl of Häagen-Dazs, and said to each other: Now just what all is a food processor good for?

- We already knew we could knead yeast dough in 1 minute.
- We'd just discovered we could aerate flour and didn't need a sifter.
- We knew if we tossed sticky fruits and oily nuts in flour first, we could successfully chop them in the food processor.

So we asked ourselves, Can we make a cake in the food processor? Can we beat egg whites? Can we whip cream? We were both eager to turn our kitchens into food labs to find out.

We also knew the microwave oven was good for more than heating leftovers. In the long, laborious task of writing *Bread in Half the Time,* we invented a new and glorious use for the microwave oven, raising yeast dough. Using the process we came to call Micro-Rise, we knocked that imprecise function down from an hour plus to 15 minutes flat. Initially there was a lot of resistance to this notion, since it violated all sorts of long-held beliefs. But once Julia Child tried it and began telling others that it worked, the naysayers stopped their grumbling and gave it a try.

In the process of testing for *Bread in Half the Time,* we got past fear-of-microwave cooking. We looked on this new-age tool as ours to be used. So what else could a microwave do besides raise dough?

- We both had successfully melted chocolate in the microwave.
- We knew we could toast nuts in it.
- We could make puddings and custards foolproof.

What all is the microwave good for? This question drove us in our quest.

We've come to call ourselves the half-time cooks and our kitchens the half-time kitchens, because that's all the time and energy we've got. We've learned that by figuring out new ways to make old favorites, we can have our cake and eat it too.

Four years ago, neither one of us would ever have guessed that we would soon routinely make the family's bread. But then for 2 years we worked on the Micro-Rise method for making yeast breads, and out of that came our first joint venture, *Bread in Half the Time*.

Now both of us make most of the bread either family needs, and with great pleasure.

Not that our lives have gotten any calmer. We're still rocketing along, lickety-split, trying to find time to do everything we want to do.

In fact, this subject arose out of our mutual complaint that we never had time to make desserts anymore.

But, we said to each other, if we could figure out a way to raise dough in the microwave oven in 15 minutes, surely we could improve on traditional dessert instructions.

And we both just love to tear into recipes. It's become our joint obsession.

To convince ourselves and you that dessert making is worth the trouble, we knew we had two desserts to best: that delicious bowl of Häagen-Dazs and a dish of just-picked raspberries. What could we make for dessert that would taste better than those? Plus, what wouldn't take two days and a course at the Cordon Bleu to accomplish?

There's chocolate, of course, and cake and pie and fruit. We had favorites in all those areas. But could we do them in half the time?

We had also discovered the thrill of low-fat desserts that not only taste good but don't pack the pounds on us. We particularly love low-fat frozen-yogurt desserts, and we knew we could make those in 15 minutes. We began picking through our flour-spattered recipe boxes. Soon, we had lots of choices.

Our goal always was to streamline recipes, heighten flavor, and make dessert making itself a delicious experience. We tried to pare down the process by using high-tech appliances so that you could create desserts as delicious as those you'd buy in a good bakery.

We rely on the food processor and microwave as the basis for the half-time kitchen. We try to make these two appliances work overtime. Always, these two appliances drive our voyage of discovery. And boy have we moved along fast.

So now, here we sit, with another subject area knocked into submission. We expect we'll hear screams of protest from our compatriots who like to resist change. Lots of people will say it can't be done. All we say to them is, Try it, please.

Once again, we've had to throw off old shibboleths. Who said you can't beat egg whites in the food processor? You can if you'll learn a new technique. Add a little lemon juice through the feed tube once the whites are foamy to stabilize them, and you can get egg whites to at least quadruple in volume.

Who said you can't whip cream in the food processor? The main risk here is that you'll make homemade butter, it whips up so fast. But we can teach you how.

We learned—as usual, through the process of testing for this book—just what we could and couldn't do. Melting chocolate, for example, is a snap in the microwave and offers a scientific control not possible when you're melting chocolate on top of the stove.

You can make a Quick Queen of Sheba cake using the food processor to grind the almonds and the microwave to melt the chocolate. You can make perfect piecrust in the food processor and be ready to roll in 30 seconds.

You can cut fruits using the food processor's slicing blade. You can make bread and cookie crumbs for specialty crusts as well. You can whip up a recipe of bar cookies in 3 or 4 minutes using the food processor, then bake them in the regular oven. You can make an almost-instant frosting by simply melting chocolate chips on top of brownies hot out of the oven.

We've learned, through necessity, how to make cookies a kid can take to the school Christmas party and have them ready to go before the kid gets on the school bus in the morning—even if the child only told us she'd need the cookies that morning at seven.

We've learned how to whip up a dessert when someone decides to drop in, and they'll be here in 15 minutes, by starting with some store-bought something, then adding our own homemade finish.

We learned what a friend to cornstarch the microwave is. Any sauce or pudding that's thickened with cornstarch works splendidly in the microwave. You don't have to stand at the stove and stir the stuff. You can just microwave it, uncovered, at 100% for a few moments, then whisk the mixture with a balloon whisk, and voilà—you'll have a thoroughly cooked, smooth, pleasant-tasting pudding or sauce.

In fact, we decided that just about anytime you see the words "Heat in a double boiler," you can translate that to "Place in the microwave."

We also learned that for our purposes, most microwave functions, with a few notable exceptions, could be done at 100% power and without a cover on the vessel.

Besides getting the satisfaction of quickly made desserts while testing for this book, we learned anew not to be reluctant to experiment with the food processor and microwave oven. They really are the cook's toys. We're addicted to them and always fooling around to see just what else we can make them do.

Used for what they do best, these two kitchen appliances can make your life easy. And you'll have fewer dirty dishes at the end, besides.

What we enjoyed most about the recipe testing for this book is that we were able to take some of our favorite old-fashioned American desserts and update the procedure so that we could offer them to our families just as our mothers and grandmothers had offered them to us—but in half the time.

What we learned we couldn't do in half the time were some complicated cakes, elaborate decorations that called for pastry tubes or spun sugar. There are no cutout cookies in this book. No elaborate decorated cookies either. No filled eclairs or real puff pastry.

What is here is a collection of desserts you can make quickly, easily, and with great pleasure. We've come to enjoy dessert making so much that we've even taken to entertaining with simple dessert parties. A made-in-half-the-time dessert, a cup of espresso, a collection of liqueurs—these make a satisfying party for people who have busy, overcommitted lives and who, if they had to create a whole dinner party, would just as soon forget the whole thing.

We know you'll soon be eating dessert first. Not only because life's so short, but also because dessert tastes good and is so much fun to make.

And if you discover a new use for our food processor or microwave oven, give a holler. There is nothing more fun to us than learning a new use for these half-time kitchen friends.

HOW TO USE THIS BOOK

Before you start cooking from this book, we encourage you to read the introductory material. The new techniques are easy as the proverbial pie, but they may be different from methods you've used before.

The basic premise of the half-time kitchen is that you can make your microwave oven and food processor begin working overtime. You'll need a 650- to 700-watt microwave oven and a heavy-duty food processor to begin cooking half-time. You'll learn new techniques and short-cuts to traditional methods using these two appliances that will make dessert making both fun and easy. Soon, we hope, you'll rely on your equipment the way we do.

You'll find the new techniques referred to again and again in the recipes. You'll learn how to make pastry in the food processor. How to beat (and not overbeat) a cake in the food processor. We'll teach you how to whip cream and egg whites in the food processor using the steel blade or a whisk attachment.

Soon you'll be micro-melting chocolate in the microwave for recipes in this and all other cookbooks. This technique in particular gives the cook as much scientific control as can be found in a commercial confectionary. Believe us, once you learn about micro-melting chocolate, you'll never do it any other way. Nor will you shy away from chocolate recipes that instruct you to haul out thermometers and other more arcane scientific devices. You have a microwave oven. That's all the control you need.

We'll teach you how to make cornstarch-thickened puddings and sauces in the microwave. How to rehydrate dried fruits quickly and toast nuts in a flash using the microwave.

You'll find instructions for the new methods in the section "Ingredients." Want to know how to beat egg whites in the food processor? Turn to "Eggs" in the "Ingredients" section. Want to learn to Micro-Rise yeast doughs? Turn to "Yeast."

In addition to the new techniques described in the introductory material, more detailed information can be found in the chapters themselves. Want to try your hand at food processor pastry making? Turn to the chapter on pies. Need help with using chocolate? Turn to the chapter "Chocolate."

Since the decision to place a recipe in a particular chapter can be rather arbitrary (i.e., even though we have a "Chocolate" chapter, you will find chocolate recipes scattered throughout the book), turn to the index to find a complete listing for any one category. We tried always to place a recipe in the chapter where it seems most available to cooks, but there are recipes that are a toss-up between two or more categories. We've tried to make a complete cross-reference system so that you can find what you want when you want it.

In the sidebars to recipes, we offer ancillary recipes, serving suggestions, and go-withs. We try to share with you the tips that have helped us improve our half-time performance. These recipes are also cross-referenced in the index. You can mix and match the recipes like a color-coordinated wardrobe. We encourage you to play with new combinations.

We tell you where to order specialty items by mail in the "Ingredients" section as well. And we offer tips sprinkled throughout the book that will help you make successful desserts.

Our final word on how to use this book is to say that you should approach dessert making as an adventure—an adventure where you can lick your fingers, have a great time, and play with the equipment in your kitchen.

And do remember that Perfection is the Enemy of Good. If your cake cracks, fill the hole with frosting. If your meringue weeps, just explain that even egg whites get the blues. If your chocolate seizes, be forgiving. Your neck goes into spasms, too, on bad days. It happens.

Please use this book to have fun. Learn some new techniques. Soon you'll be a world-class half-time cook, too. Life is short. Make dessert first.

EQUIPPING THE HALF-TIME KITCHEN

The heart and soul of the half-time kitchen is the food processor and microwave oven. Learn to use these, and you can clear the decks and the counters of your kitchen. No more stand mixer. No more hand-held mixer. You won't need a blender or a mandoline.

Put your double boiler in the garage sale. Throw that pastry cloth away. You're a new generation of cooks—no matter what your chronological age. Learn some half-time techniques and take a step into the future.

FOOD PROCESSORS

We have tested recipes using Cuisinarts new and old, a couple of Braun Multipractics, a Black & Decker ShortCut, and a Hamilton Beach we bought one day when all else failed. Here's what we've found.

If you're on a short budget and have never owned a food processor, you'll probably be happy with one of the following.

Hamilton Beach. It does, however, have a motor that sounds like a chopper taking off in a scene from a Vietnam movie. But for under 40 bucks, it's ok.

The Black & Decker ShortCut is well named. With its small-capacity bowl, its quiet motor, and its easy-to-use interchangeable disks, we like this processor a lot for little jobs. It also takes up less space in the dishwasher and is well suited to small families and small processing tasks.

The Cuisinart, which we've both owned and loved, is a workhorse. We especially love the whisk attachment that makes this machine as useful as a stand mixer.

The Braun Food Preparation Center 5-in-1 K-1000, well priced at about $100 and coming with all the attachments, is an excellent food processor. Good old German engineering shows. The motor is quiet. The base is solid so that it doesn't jump all over the cabinet. The infinite variable-speed 600-watt motor makes it versatile as all get-out. You can whip egg whites. You can mix cake batter without overmixing it by turning down the processor speed. Using the little bowl that comes with it and the teeny-weeny blade, you can chop nuts to an even dice. All bowls have sealed bottoms and won't leak. The big one holds 18 cups dry, the middle one 11 cups, and the little chopper bowl, 1 cup.

MICROWAVE OVENS

For best results with any microwave oven, rely on the desired result ("until mixture boils") rather than the time given in a recipe. Microwave ovens vary in wattage and power output, so your best bet is to use judgment and watch the food as it reaches the desired result named in the recipe.

We have settled on 650- to 750-watt medium- to large-capacity ovens for testing. All recipes in this book were tested either in a Panasonic or Quasar microwave in this power range. We use a carousel and microwave-safe containers.

Smaller microwave ovens, either in oven capacity or in wattage, are just too limited, and we do not recommend them. Those under-the-counter models get too hot. Those 400-watt off-on models aren't good for much besides heating a bowl of soup at the office. If you're in the market for a new microwave, for less than $200 you can get one with all the features you'll need.

If you're trying to figure out your microwave's wattage, look in the owner's manual or on the serial-number plate usually located on the front of the oven near the bottom left or on the back of the oven.

In this cookbook, unless otherwise noted, preparations are cooked *uncovered.* Mostly we cook at 100% power. If we mean otherwise, we'll tell you so.

We remind you that microwave nomenclature is not standard. In fact, this is one area that is rife with confusion. Some brands give you number settings. Others use percentages. Others tell you what wattage a certain setting is. Others just use words.

What may be called "medium" on one brand might be called "defrost" on another. Think of it this way: If your microwave has ten power settings, each level raises the power by

10%. In other words, level 5 will be 50% power, regardless of whether it's called "defrost" or "medium." If you can begin to think in percentage terms, you'll have a better chance of matching up your particular microwave's settings with those you find in a recipe in this or any other book.

MICROWAVE-SAFE MATERIALS

We have come to love certain kinds of microwave cookware for the things we do in this appliance. A nested Pyrex (or other microwavable ovenproof glass) measuring-cup set and batter bowl is an ideal way to begin. This gives you 1-, 2-, and 4-cup vessels, plus an 8-cup batter bowl. With these you can mix, microwave, and pour. The handles remain cool, and the deep sides usually keep the food in the bowl and not gurgling out to make a mess on the bottom of the microwave.

We use only microwave-safe crockery and glass for cooking and baking in the microwave oven. We never use dishes with metal fittings or glassware that's been glued back together.

Don't recycle plastic tubs that came with food from the grocery store as microwave cooking utensils. You don't want strange petrochemicals leaking into your food from a plastic container that wasn't meant to be used hot.

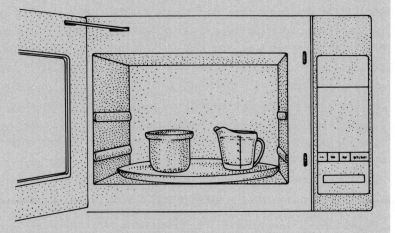

How to Test a Container for Safe Microwave Oven Use

Fill a 1-cup microwavable glass measure with water and place it in the microwave oven on or beside the dish you wish to test. Microwave on 100% (high) for 1 minute. If the water becomes hot, the dish is safe. If the dish becomes hot, it should not be used for microwaving.

Choosing the Right Size Container for Microwave Cooking

Microwavable containers should hold three times the volume of the food being cooked to ensure that a boil-over does not occur.

WAFFLE IRONS

We've had a lot of fun making heart-shaped dessert waffles with a Black & Decker waffle iron with a nonstick surface. We recommend it for a quick and to-the-point dessert.

OVENS

We still prefer electric ovens over gas for even heating and accurate temperature control. Even so, we keep an independent oven thermometer in each of our ovens and check the calibration against what's called for in a recipe to make sure we're baking at the "real" temperature called for. The good news about modern ovens with super heat cleaning is that the cleanability is enhanced, but the bad news is that the thermostat is compromised. If you are using a self-cleaning oven, you can rest assured that you should *never* trust the thermostat. It can be off by 100° F. And in baking, that could be fatal.

Unless otherwise noted, most baked goods cook best on the rack placed in the middle of the oven. This allows the maximum heat to flow around the food.

MEASURING UTENSILS

Measuring for baking and desserts is critical. Buy yourself a good set of nested dry measures and one for liquid measures. Avoid plastic because these measures are not as likely as glass or metal to be dead accurate. And that's why you're measuring in the first place.

Whenever a recipe calls for flour, you should dip the dry measuring cup into the flour bin, then level it off with a spatula before dumping it into the recipe. Don't pack the flour into the measure or use a liquid measure with a lip for this job or you are likely to add too much flour. In liquid measure, pour the liquid into a transparent glass measure then hold the cup at eye level (or lower your eyes to cup level) and check to see that you have added just what you need.

Jim Fobel taught us not to trust the accuracy of just any measuring cups. They can be off by a tablespoon or more. Jim bought a scientific beaker and cross measured against his own nested measures and liquid measures for accuracy, discarding any measuring cups that were inaccurate. Although you may not wish to go this far, we urge you to measure accurately using good-quality liquid and dry measuring cups, because in dessert making and baking, measuring accuracy is critical for best results.

BAKING GEAR

We use a lot of glass bakeware simply because we like utensils that can go freely between the microwave and the oven. For raised doughs, we use ovenproof glass sheets and loaf pans so that we can Micro-Rise the doughs (see page 25). However, we could remind you that glassware heats more quickly than metal, and you should begin baking foods in glassware by knowing you must start checking for doneness a few minutes before the suggested baking time given in the recipe. Be prepared to remove the pan from the oven a good 10 minutes before the time suggested in the recipe.

We agree with Rose Levy Beranbaum that dull aluminum pans make the best cake and cookie bakers because they conduct heat quickly and have a dull heat-absorbing finish. Stainless steel, shiny and a poor conductor, is the worst. Almost as bad are those popular black-finished pans that absorb heat so quickly they can overbrown or burn crusts.

So-called nonstick pans seem confusing to cooks. Do you have to grease and flour them? Yes. Are they better for baking? Not necessarily. A cake actually needs a slightly granular side to climb up for maximum lift. Think of walking up a hill that's covered with ice versus one that's covered with snow. Which is easier?

However, nonstick pans can be useful for angel food or other eggy chiffon-type cakes that will deflate in a greased pan.

Lately we've been baking a lot of pies in those spatterware porcelain pie pans. They conduct heat beautifully, give a glorious crisp brown crust, and present so nicely that we're happy to serve at the table.

Shiny, aluminum throwaway pans are useful when you plan to take a baked item somewhere and don't want to worry about getting the container home. But do remember the shiny bright aluminum doesn't give you the nice brown crust you'll get with other pans. So the dilemma becomes: Do you want to take your favorite pie and risk a soggy crust, or would you rather schlepp the pie pan home? You decide.

BASIC BAKING PANS

Whether you use ovenproof glass or dull-finished aluminum, here's our basic list:

5 cake pans: two 9 inch round, one 9 inch square, one 8 inch square, one 9 inch springform, and one 13 × 9 inch
2 fluted tart pans, 9 and 12 inches with removable bottom
2 loaf pans, 9 × 5 × 3 inch, preferably ovenproof glass
1 glass baking sheet, 12 × 10 × 1 inch
1 glass baking dish, 7 × 11 × 1½ inch
2 rimmed nonstick baking sheets, 18 × 12 × 1 inch
2 ovenproof glass pie pans, 8 and 9 inches
1 spatterware porcelain pie pan, 9 to 10 inches
2 muffin tins ½-cup capacity, 12 and 18 cups each
6 ovenproof ramekins, ¾-cup capacity
2 or more cooling racks

PAN PREPARATION

Parchment paper is an ideal addition to the right bakeware. Coat the bottom of the baking pan with cooking spray, then cut a round of parchment paper to fit the bottom, smooth the paper onto the bottom of the pan, then coat that paper with cooking spray. Dust lightly with flour or cocoa, and you're ready to bake.

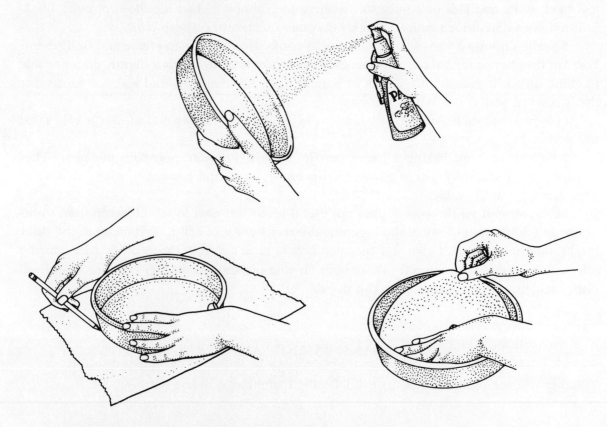

Cooking spray, which is nothing more than vegetable oil under pressure, not only is handy for spritzing on baking dishes, but also allows you to bake with less added fat.

Baker's Joy is another convenient addition to the baker's gear. This is simply vegetable oil and flour in an aerosol can. A quick spritz of this mixture on your cake pans, and you're ready to bake.

THE LITTLE STUFF

Who can walk by one of those doodad racks without stopping to see if there's one more kitchen gizmo you can't live without?

Here are the ones we adore.

APPLE SECTIONER: This is the round, metal cutter with a core circle and six spokes that will core any apple or pear and cut it into six pieces. The sectioner is sold wherever pears and apples are found; be sure and get a big metal one. The little plastic ones just don't get the job done. This tool works particularly well when you want to drop the pear pieces into the feed tube of a food processor fitted with a slicing blade for thin slices. It makes quick work of the whole job.

CHERRY PITTER: This tool makes it easier to prep sour or sweet cherries for a pie.

ICE CREAM SCOOP: A number 30 will help you make cookies as quickly as they are made at Mrs. Fields.

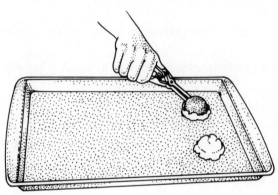

LEMON ZESTER: This little gem peels off tiny ribbons of citrus peel without one bit of the bitter pith. We use ours constantly.

LEMON REAMER: Likewise the lemon reamer, which makes it possible to get out every last bit of juice from citrus. This bullet-shaped device looks kind of like a morel mushroom.

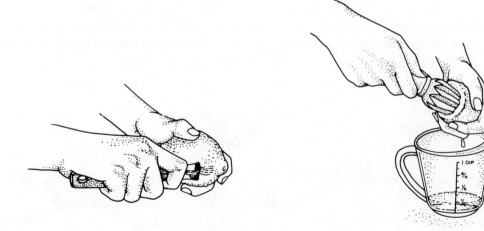

Nutmeg Grater: This cute little doodad gives you a place to store three or four whole nutmegs and a fine grater to grate with. You can even hang it on the wall.

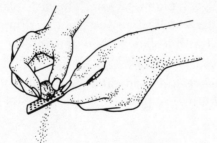

Oven Thermometer: To guarantee accurate temperature readings, a thermometer is an absolute must for ovens.

Pastry Scraper: A rectangular metal scraper in a wooden handle, this makes lifting pastry a breeze.

Pie Weights: Use dried beans or pie weights over foil or parchment when you're baking a piecrust blind (empty), and you'll avoid all those puffy places that make it difficult to fill later. Store the beans or weights in a jar and use them time and again, and don't worry about the discoloration you see. It won't affect the taste of the piecrust. The skins of dried beans flake off eventually. Then, you need to start over. Throw out old beans. Use new ones.

Pizza-Cutting Wheel: Use this with any cookie recipe that you want to zip through, instead of all that time-consuming figure cutting you did before you ran out of time.

Rolling Pins: Generally, the heavier the better. We like a French-style pin, which is one long cylinder tapered on both ends, as well as the more classic American style, which is fitted with ball bearings and, at six pounds, heavy enough to bean somebody.

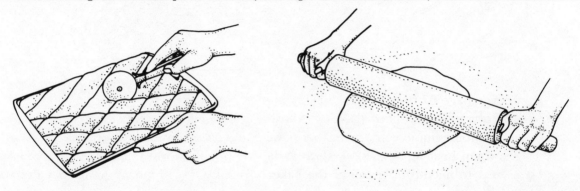

Spatulas: You'll need two types—rubber, spoon shaped, straight sided, and narrow, and a metal spatula for lifting cookies.

Wire Whisks: We can't say enough good things about wire whisks. For microwave puddings and sauces made in an ovenproof-glass batter bowl, there's nothing like the wire balloon whisk. Microwave the pudding, then whisk the mixture to a smooth cooked perfection. We like 10-inch or bigger sizes with wooden or stainless-steel handles and stainless wires. You can get a cheaper tin whisk, but acid foods will soon eat away the finish, and you'll get an off taste in the food products you beat with it.

Wooden Skewers: You can use wooden skewers to lift waffles off the iron and to test cakes to see if they're done. They're also handy for handling chocolate when you don't want to leave your fingerprints.

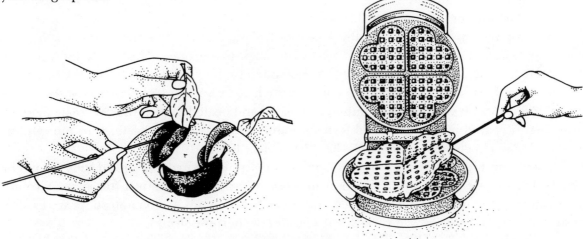

INGREDIENTS

Apples: See page 67 for the best cooking apples.

Baking Powder: Double-acting baking powder is what we mean, when the first rising takes place as you combine liquid with the baking powder and other dry ingredients and the second action starts when heat hits the food. Carbon-dioxide bubbles form in the presence of both liquid and heat to make this leavener the baker's friend. Old-fashioned baking powder was single action and began making carbon-dioxide gas the moment liquids were mixed with the dry. Old-fashioned cooks got their half-time experience by having to get the cake in the oven in half the time, otherwise it would deflate before baking had firmed up the lift.

If you'd like to play the pioneer, you can make single-action baking powder at home by combining 2 parts cream of tartar with 1 part baking soda. Use in the same amount called for in the recipe you're using. Now is your real chance to be the half-time cook. Once you've added the homemade baking powder—*hurry*. Pop that cake or quick bread into the preheated oven immediately. It works.

BAKING SODA: To use as a leavener, you must combine baking soda with an acid, such as buttermilk, yogurt, or molasses. Then it will form a carbon-dioxide gas that lifts baked goods. If you're out of regular milk at your house, you can sometimes improve on a baked good by using an equal amount of yogurt or buttermilk and adding ½ teaspoon of baking soda to each liquid cup of milk in the recipe along with any baking powder the recipe calls for in the first place.

BUTTER: Unsalted butter gives the best results in cooking and allows optimum control over the amount of salt in a recipe. However, in cases where we have not specified unsalted butter, we don't find there's much difference. Margarine can always be substituted if you're watching your cholesterol, but you will notice a compromise in flavor.

Measuring butter is easy. Each stick is ½ cup, or 8 tablespoons. A half stick is ¼ cup. If a recipe calls for softened butter, you can do this easily in the microwave. Place the refrigerated stick of butter on a dish and heat at 20% (low) for 10 seconds. Feel it. Softened butter should be malleable but not oily and slick looking.

CHOCOLATE: This Mexican standby is one of America's contributions to the world's cuisines, and when Cortez took the first chocolate back to Europe, it's possible even he was surprised at the Europeans' adoration for it. Harvested from tropical cacao trees, the beans are fermented a short while, then dried, cleaned, roasted, and winnowed, separating the shell from the nib. The nib, 50 percent cocoa butter, is crushed and heated to melt the chocolate liqueur. It is then prepared in all the myriad forms we know and love as chocolate. (For more information about chocolate, see pages 91–92, "Chocolate Basics.")

CINNAMON: From the bark of a tree, cinnamon is available ground and in stick form. For the best flavor, we like to grind our own in a coffee grinder we use just for spices. Ground cinnamon is used in cakes, pies, cookies, and other baked goods. Cinnamon sticks are used in syrups and make great swizzle sticks for sweet, hot, wintertime drinks.

CITRUS JUICE AND ZEST: Whenever we call for lemon juice or orange juice or grapefruit juice, we mean *fresh squeezed*. Man has never improved upon the natural container that these juices come in, and we do not recommend frozen reconstituted juices. The zest, or colored part of the skin, also adds an unmistakable citrus oil that boosts flavors. Use a lemon zester, a potato peeler, or a paring knife to peel off just the colored part of the rind. You can also scrape off the colored citrus rind using a grater. We don't recommend using the food processor for this job. Too much bitter white pith gets into the zest and can ruin the flavor of your dessert.

CLOVES: Ground cloves work well, but for the cloviest taste you can grind your own whole cloves in a coffee grinder reserved for spice grinding.

COCONUT: In most cases, we mean sweetened, shredded store-bought coconut.

If you make a white cake-mix cake, top it with food processor whipped cream, then finish it with your own home-grated fresh coconut; your reputation as a baker will be made.

One coconut will yield about 3¾ cups grated coconut. Store it covered in the refrigerator for about a week, or frozen up to a year.

COOKING SPRAY: Simply vegetable shortening in an aerosol can, we love it for spritzing the bottoms and sides of cake pans. It means we use less fat in the pan and in the final dish. All you have to do is dust the pan with flour after spritzing, and your pan is prepared. We also like Baker's Joy, which is a mixture of shortening and flour. Spray that in a pan, and you're ready to bake most batters that you'd normally have to grease and flour the pan for.

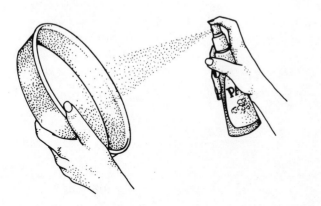

CORNSTARCH: A fine flour made from corn, this common thickener used for cream pies and sauces works admirably in the half-time kitchen once you learn to cook it in the microwave.

Cornstarch creates a silky, translucent gloss when micro-cooked. No more raw-as-wallpaper puddings or sauces when you cook cornstarch-thickened sauces in the microwave.

Food Processor Grated Coconut

If you'd like to make your own, we recommend knocking the eyes out of the coconut with hammer and nail and draining out the good coconut milk, then heating the coconut in a 400° F oven until the shell cracks (about 20 minutes). Slug that hot coconut with a hammer after it's out of the oven, and it will pop into two or three pieces. Separate the meat from the shell, using a sharp paring knife to pop the coconut out, then pare away the brown skin and use the fine shredding disk on your food processor to grate the coconut meat.

Toasting Grated Coconut

If you wish to toast the grated coconut, spread it one layer deep on a cookie sheet and bake it in a 350° F oven for about 10 minutes, until brown, or you can toast a cup of coconut in the microwave on a microwavable pie plate at 100% (high) for 4 minutes, stirring three times. Don't overdo it. The coconut will continue to brown even after you remove it from the microwave.

Microwave Cooking with Cornstarch

Combine cornstarch with the recipe's other dry ingredients in a batter bowl. Whisk in the liquid using a balloon whisk, then microwave the mixture uncovered at 100% (high) for a minute or so. Remove the bowl from the microwave. Whisk to mix the sauce or pudding, and examine it. If the mixture still looks thin and liquid, repeat, microwaving at 100% (high), whisking every 15 seconds or so, and soon you'll have a silky-smooth pudding or sauce that will taste thoroughly cooked and delicious. The microwave is a friend to cornstarch.

Do allow the mixture to reach a full rolling boil that you allow to cook no more than a minute before you start checking it. The microwave is blessedly fast.

If you wish to add cornstarch to a mixture that's already boiling, dissolve the cornstarch in a little cold water, then remove the primary mixture from the heat, spoon a little hot sauce from the primary mixture into the cornstarch and water, stir, then pour the now-warm cornstarch mixture back into the main hot mixture. Whisk vigorously. Now you can place it back in the microwave, raise it to a boil, and watch it turn into a glorious, shiny thick pudding or sauce right before your very eyes.

One word of warning. If you're using cornstarch along with acid, such as lemon juice or cherry juice, as in lemon pie or cherry pie filling, the mixture cannot be allowed to boil or it will break down and never thicken. You can control this as easily as it's controlled in an old-fashioned double boiler by simply turning the microwave power down to 70% (medium). Microwave for short intervals, whisking and checking the mixture until you see it begin to look shiny and thicker. Stop immediately.

If you've overheated a cornstarch-acid mixture, remove it to the refrigerator to cool completely, then try again, turning your microwave down to 50% to prevent overheating. Use the same intermittent cook-and-whisk technique.

▶ KEY TECHNIQUE

1. Remember microwave cooking is fast. Have everything ready. Cook the pudding or sauce in a glass measure or batter bowl at least three times bigger than the volume of the ingredients.

2. Place a balloon whisk on a saucer beside the microwave, handy for intermittent whisking every 15 seconds or so. Hold the whisk on the saucer, and you won't get drips on the counter.

3. Prevent overcooking. Stop microwaving the moment the sauce begins to thicken and gloss, because microwave cooking continues about 5 minutes after you've removed the mixture from the oven.

CREAM: *Heavy cream* and *whipping cream* are interchangeable terms. The richest cream you can buy, with up to 40 percent butterfat to prove it, whips easily in the food processor with the steel blade or whisk attachment. No more chilling the bowl and beaters unless your kitchen is exceptionally hot, more than 80° F. All you have to watch out for is not making butter. Within 30 seconds or so you'll have a perfectly whipped cream.

Sweeten whipped cream with granulated, powdered, or brown sugar or scent it with liqueurs, and you've made a dessert you could eat from the bowl with a spoon.

Half-and-half is just what it says: half milk and half cream. It can be used instead of "light" cream, but it will not whip.

Whipping Cream in the Food Processor

For every 2 cups of cream, use about 2 tablespoons of sugar and a teaspoon of vanilla.

Place the cream in the food processor bowl fitted with the steel blade or whisk attachment. Process until the cream begins to form droplets on the side of the bowl (about 15 to 20 seconds), then add sugar and vanilla through the feed tube. Continue processing a few seconds, then open the top and check the cream by lifting a spoonful. The mixture should be thick and creamy. A slight peak will form when you dip the spoon into the mixture and lift it.

If you've used the steel blade, the mixture won't be fluffy, but it will be stable enough to pipe onto desserts. If you've used the whisk attachment, it will take a little longer, but the cream will have increased in volume by about a third, and it will be both stiff and fluffy.

▶ *KEY TECHNIQUE*

1. When whipping cream in the food processor, don't add sugar or flavoring until the cream begins to cling to the side of the work bowl, after about 30 seconds. Open the top, scrape down the side, then continue

2. If you're using a whisk attachment and you begin adding sugar or flavoring through the feed tube, take care not to pour sugar onto the top of the whisk attachment instead of into the cream. That big flat top on the whisk attachment holds a lot of sugar. You may have to open the top and scrape it down into the cream.

3. Remember the food processor is fast. Overdo it, and you've made butter. If this happens, just call in the kids to see this wonder of nature, squeeze the butter together into a ball, and use it to butter bread. You can't unbutter an overbeaten cream.

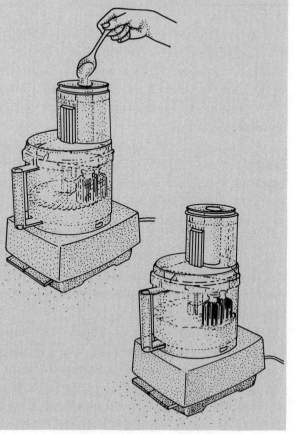

CREAM OF TARTAR: A by-product of wine making, this tart white powder has a slight acidity that helps stabilize beaten egg whites. We sometimes use it in addition to plain old lemon juice for our processor-whipped egg whites.

CURRANTS: The smallest fruits in the raisin group, currants add a tart, acidic taste that we like in sweet cookies and cakes.

DATES: We use supermarket dates that we can buy in bulk for baking: those sweet, sticky, moist plump whole dates with the best flavor. Chopped dates are dried and less flavorful and not recommended. Throw whole dates into the food processor after you've remembered to pull out the seed, and you can pulse to chop them. Toss them in a little flour first to prevent too much stickiness. Yes, they will still stick some to the steel blade. That's inevitable.

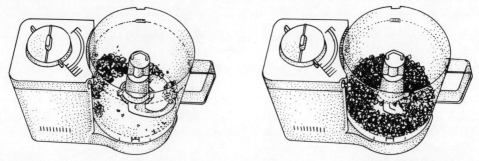

EGGS: With a few exceptions, we use large grade-A eggs for all our dessert making. Taking into consideration new information about salmonella, we do not recommend keeping eggs out of the refrigerator. To raise the temperature of egg whites to room temperature so that they'll beat up to their maximum lift, separate the eggs, then microwave the whites at 100% (high) for 2 seconds per egg, or until they're about 72° F. And we are careful to wash our hands after handling eggshells.

If using a recipe that calls for uncooked eggs, be sure to use clean, uncracked eggs. Because of the risk of salmonella, we would not recommend such recipes for persons in a high-risk group for contracting food poisoning. This group includes the elderly, the very young, the chronically ill, pregnant women, or others with a compromised immune system.

In recipes calling for either yolks or whites, you're likely to have some leftover. You can store egg whites in a covered jar in the refrigerator 3 or 4 days. Store up a dozen or so, and you can make an angel food cake. Yolks can store in the refrigerator 2 or 3 days. Cover them with plastic wrap that you fit down against the yolks so they don't form a hard skin. If you have no use for yolks, mix them with a little water and use them to fertilize your houseplants. We don't recommend freezing egg yolks.

Egg yolks are sometimes added to custards in addition to whole eggs, because they make the texture more creamy and sturdy, and they thicken the mixture. Egg-yolk mixtures will curdle if they get too hot, so take care when microwaving them to use the minimum times recommended, then whisk, look at the mixture, and repeat only if the mixture is still thin. Microwaved mixtures continue to cook for 4 to 5 minutes after they're out of the microwave oven, so keep that in mind as well. Don't overdo it—or you'll have an unwanted floating island.

Beating Egg Whites in the Food Processor

You can successfully beat from two to six egg whites in the food processor, using its whisk attachment or the steel or plastic blade. We're not pretending you'll get as much volume as you'd get using a copper bowl or even a KitchenAid with the whisk. But you can get a respectable four-volume lift in most cases. And in the spirit of the half-time kitchen, you won't have to get out another appliance.

In a perfect world, egg whites can be beaten to expand by sevenfold. But how high your egg whites lift depends on several factors, not all of them in your control.

Fresh egg whites won't beat up as high as older eggs. Neither will cold eggs. Both fresh and cold egg whites are too viscous to expand to their fullest potential.

You may not have much control over the age of egg whites you're using, but you can warm them up. Break the egg whites into a glass measure and heat them in the microwave a couple of seconds until they feel barely warm to the touch. Stick your finger in.

Then transfer the egg whites to the food processor bowl fitted with the steel blade or whisk attachment. If your processor has adjustable speeds, turn it to medium, and process the whites until they are foamy.

To stabilize the egg whites, now add ½ teaspoon lemon juice per egg white and process a few moments more.

Then raise the processor speed to high (if it's adjustable), and continue processing, adding sugar and flavorings through the feed tube, a teaspoon at a time, until the egg whites have reached that nice shiny stage where the peaks hold but the tops just tip over. Think of the top of a chocolate chip: a mountain, but with a peak that tips—that's what properly beaten egg whites look like.

When folding beaten egg whites together with other ingredients, remember that less is more. The less you handle the egg whites, the more volume you'll get in the final product. If you have transferred the beaten egg whites from the food processor bowl to a large mixing bowl, you can fold in the other ingredients using a rubber spatula, your bare hand, or a slotted spoon.

Sprinkle dry ingredients or batter over the beaten egg whites, about a third of the dry ingredients or batter at a time. Cut the dry ingredients down into the beaten whites, then turn the bowl a quarter, and fold again, repeating just until you can no longer see dry powder or batter separated from the beaten egg whites.

(continued)

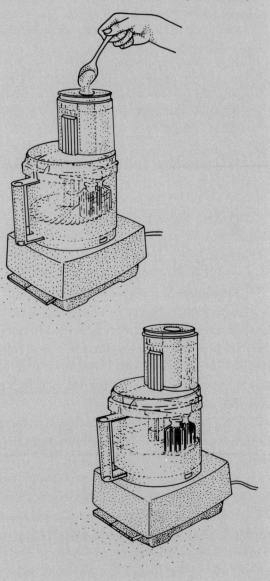

FLOURS: We learned in writing *Bread in Half the Time* what vast differences there are in flours. Now we use specialized flours for special purposes. One thing we don't buy is bleached all-purpose white flour. Since this product varies from region to region, we prefer to stick with flours with special, defined properties.

Bread flour is a high-protein, enriched, bromated white flour made from hard wheat that is high in gluten. For yeast doughs, it is our recommendation because it stands up to machine kneading in the food processor, and it makes an elastic, strong dough that will create a sturdy web to hold the carbon-dioxide gases released by yeasts, yielding the most volume to the dough. Breads made with bread flour will be flavorful, light, strong, and well risen. Bread flour has 14 percent protein compared with 10.5 percent found in all-purpose flour, so it's better for you too.

The potassium bromate that is added to bromated flour is what manufacturers call a dough conditioner. Machine-kneaded doughs have a better crumb and a finer grain when made with bromated bread flour.

Cake flour is a highly refined flour made from soft wheat. We recommend cake flour for tender cakes and in some other tender crumbed baked goods.

Unbleached all-purpose flour is a pale-tan flour milled from a combination of hard and soft wheat. This flour ages several months, during which time natural oxidation causes the flour to whiten. It has a slightly higher protein content than bleached all-purpose flour, plus it retains vitamin E, which makes it a healthier product.

Pastry flour is a soft wheat flour with less gluten than bread flour but slightly more than cake flour. It's hard to find where we live, so we sometimes blend 60 percent cake flour and 40 percent bread flour in recipes that call for pastry flour.

Plain all-purpose soft winter wheat flour, also known as light baking flour, is the best for biscuits, short paste, and piecrust. Every time we make a trip to the South, we smuggle back to the Northwest where we live sacks of our favorite White Lily flour. This aptly named pure-white, enriched flour is pliable, easy to handle, rolls out easy as pie, and makes cakes, shortcakes, biscuits, or piecrusts that melt in your mouth.

Instant-blending flour, sold in shaker cans, is made from flour that's been combined with water, then dried and pulverized into an instant-blending powder. Splendid for soups and sauces, it won't work for baked goods.

Self-rising flour, popular in the South where biscuits still reign supreme, is not used in recipes in this book, since it is actually a mix of all-purpose flour, baking powder, and salt.

Whole wheat flour is milled from the whole wheat kernel. Commercial whole wheat flour is a recombination of parts from milling: white flour, germ, and bran. Stone-ground whole wheat—which retains all the natural nutrients—is made by grinding the wheat berry between heavy stones. Stone-ground whole wheat flour is more perishable than chemically treated white flour. Buy only what you can use in a short time, and store it in a cool place, even the refrigerator or freezer in the summer. We're particularly taken with King Arthur flour's new *white whole wheat.* Although it doesn't look white, it has a splendid, nutty taste and is recommended in any recipe that calls for whole wheat flour.

Fʀᴜɪᴛs: Make a good diet dessert by microwaving cored, whole fresh fruits with a splash of wine or maybe some orange zest, covered. You'll get a concentrated fruit flavor without additional sugar. See chapter 9, "Fresh Fruit Desserts," for more information.

Dried fruits can be rehydrated easily in the microwave. For apricots, mixed fruit, prunes, or raisins, place the fruit in a microwavable dish. Add enough hot tap water to cover the fruit. Cover the dish and microwave at 100% (high) until the water boils. If you wish to add sugar, now's the time. If you wish to continue cooking the dried fruit, re-cover it, turn the microwave down to 30% (medium-low), and cook 2 to 5 minutes more, until the fruit is tender. Let it stand 5 minutes before further use. If you simply want to soften dried fruit, place it one layer deep on a plate, sprinkle it with water, cover it with microwave plastic wrap, and microwave at 100% (high) for 30 seconds. Raisins take about a minute and a half and work best if done in a glass measure.

You can make an ad-lib dried-fruit compote by mixing your favorite dried fruits, adding fruit juice or water, covering, then microwaving at 100% (high) for about 9 to 10 minutes. Remove the fruit from the oven, stir it, and set it aside for five minutes before serving.

Gɪɴɢᴇʀ: This spice comes fresh, crystallized, or powdered. For baking, the powdered product is most commonly used. It adds a spicy, hot snap to the taste of baked goods. Crystallized ginger, found in the Asian section of supermarkets, in Asian markets, or through mail-order sources, including Williams-Sonoma, is also a terrific addition to desserts. The very

Blanching Almonds, Hazelnuts, or Pistachios

Put shelled nuts into a microwavable measure. Cover them with water. Microwave at 100% (high) just until the water reaches a boil. Remove them from the microwave and let them stand a minute. Drain and pinch the skins off. Alternately, you can, of course, blanch nuts in a saucepan on the stove following the same procedure.

Toasting Nuts

Arrange a cup of pecans or almonds on a microwave pie plate and microwave them at 100% (high) for 4 to 5 minutes. Stir two or three times and don't overdo it. The nuts will continue to brown after you've removed them from the microwave.

best crystallized ginger comes from Australia, where it grows mild and fiber free. Use it in oatmeal cookies instead of raisins for a little pep. Add it to fruitcake, shortbread, and, of course, to gingersnaps and gingerbread. It's great in Katherine's Faux Truffles (page 102). To chop this and other sticky fruits in the food processor, dust the fruits with a little flour or confectioners' sugar before chopping and use the steel blade.

LARD: Loathsome old lard, long out of favor with the cognoscenti, is making a comeback now that we've discovered it is true what our grandmothers said: that lard makes the flakiest, tastiest piecrust. We like to mix it half-and-half with unsalted butter for the best-flavored, best-textured piecrusts. Those with cholesterol problems, please turn the page.

MILK: Homogenized milk gives you the richest taste in dessert recipes. However, if you're watching the fats in your diet, feel free to substitute 2%, 1%, or skim milk. The end result will be subtly changed, less silky, less rich.

NUTS: We've used pecans, walnuts, macadamia nuts, almonds, pine nuts, pistachios, just about every nut we can lay our hands on to improve the taste and textures of desserts. See sidebar, opposite for more information on chopping nuts in the food processor.

PEACHES: See page 229 for the best cooking peaches.

PEARS: See page 77 for the best cooking pears.

RAISINS: See discussion of dried fruits, page 21.

SALT: In our recipes, "salt" means plain old fine-grained non-iodized table salt. If you only have kosher salt around, use a third more.

SEEDS: You can add a nice crunch to desserts with seeds. Store them in a cool, dark place.

Anise tastes like licorice and is good sprinkled atop plain cake. In India, they combine this with other seeds, call it *cachou,* and pass it around for dessert in tiny dishes.

Fennel also tastes like licorice and is used in baked goods. Indians have a dessert made of fennel and fennel candy that they call *pan masala.* There's an easy dessert.

Poppy seeds are used in cakes, cookies, and breads. They will turn if kept too long. Take a taste before you begin.

Sesame seeds have a nice, nutty flavor that intensifies with toasting. Add them to shortbreads and cakes for their nutty properties. Like other nuts and seeds, they become rancid. Taste them first.

SUGAR AND OTHER SWEETENERS: *Granulated sugar* is by far our greatest ally in making dessert. Not only does sugar make foods taste sweet and good, it also tenderizes baked goods, caramelizes in the oven, and makes those gorgeous golden-brown finishes we love on cookies, cakes, and breads.

Confectioners' sugar is a powdered granulated sugar with a small amount of cornstarch added to prevent caking. Don't substitute it for granulated sugar. You can, however, make your own confectioners' sugar by whizzing up granulated sugar in the food processor using the steel blade. The powerful motor of the food processor will pulverize the sugar crystals into a fair approximation of the commercial product—and without the off taste you get from the cornstarch in the stuff you buy.

For good-looking tops on cakes, dust a little confectioners' sugar through a fine-meshed sieve directly onto the cake or, for even more glamorous results, over a pattern you've cut out—say a witch's hat for Halloween or a leaf for Thanksgiving—and you will achieve a stenciled effect.

Brown sugar is granulated sugar with molasses added. It comes as both light and dark. Unless otherwise noted, these two are interchangeable in our recipes. The dark is more intensely flavored. Store brown sugar in an airtight container so it will remain soft and moist. If it does get hard, place it in a tightly covered microwavable container with just a sprinkling of water and microwave at 20% (low) for 45 seconds. Stir and re-cover.

Turbinado sugar is a raw sugar crystal that tastes great and looks luscious on top of cookies or pies.

Chopping Nuts

In the food processor, the steel blade works well if you pulse to the count of five, open the lid, and scrape the big pieces off the sides, then continue. Don't overdo it, or you'll make nut dust. Dust oily nuts with flour and break up big pieces by hand before you begin.

Grinding Nuts

In the food processor using the steel blade you can effectively grind nuts to make nut flour. Pulse the machine, working with a small amount of nuts, until the nuts are chopped fine and dry. If you over-process them, they'll begin to clump up and release oils. If you have a small-capacity food processor, like the Black & Decker mini-processor or the insert for the Braun, you'll get the best results.

Vanilla Extract: Like chocolate, one of the profound American contributions to the world's cuisine, vanilla was first found in Mexico. When Cortez conquered the Aztecs, the Aztec emperor offered him a drink called *chocolatl,* made from—you guessed it—chocolate and vanilla. The rest is, as they say, history. For the best vanilla, we recommend Nielsen Massey vanilla, sold through Williams-Sonoma. Watch out for imitation vanilla flavor. It ain't the same. (See also page 86 for Diana's Homemade Vanilla Extract, which is as good as the vanilla beans you buy and a darn sight cheaper than any of the gourmet vanillas sold in stores or through mail-order catalogs.)

Vegetable Shortening: It's used in baking primarily for making piecrusts, but we still look for shortening that combines vegetable and animal fats for the flakiest piecrust. If you're watching cholesterol, you will want to hunt for pure vegetable shortening.

Yeast: We learned when writing *Bread in Half the Time* the value of 50 percent faster active dry yeast and now use that type yeast exclusively. Fleischmann's makes a reliable yeast that gets mixed with the dry ingredients before hot tap water or another hot liquid is added. Food processor knead the dough, then Micro-Rise it (see opposite), and you'll get sweet breads that are full flavored, fully risen, and very little trouble to make in half the time. For more information about micro-rising yeast dough, see the beginning of the "Sweet Breads, Pancakes, and Waffles" chapter.

How to Food Processor Knead and Micro-Rise Yeast Dough

Combine 50 percent faster active dry yeast with other dry ingredients in the food processor bowl. Pulse to aerate and mix. Then combine liquids in a glass measure and heat to 120° F in the microwave (about 30 seconds on 100% [high]). Pour the liquids through the feed tube to mix with the dry ingredients while the motor is running. Process until the dough forms a ball that rides the blade around.

Machine knead the dough 1 minute in the food processor to make a supple, elastic ball. Then remove the steel blade and dough from the bowl.

Punch a hole in the dough ball with your thumbs, forming a doughnut. Replace the dough in the food processor bowl. Cover with plastic wrap and place the bowl in the microwave.

Place an 8-ounce glass of water in the back of the microwave. Turn the power down to 10%.

Heat 3 minutes, rest 3 minutes, heat 3 minutes, and rest 6 minutes. That's a total of 15 minutes. The dough should be doubled in bulk.

▶ *KEY TECHNIQUE*

1. Remember the food processor is fast. It will release gluten in the dough within 1 minute, not the 15 minutes it takes to knead dough by hand. You will have a supple, satiny dough that forms a soft-as-baby-fat ball very quickly.

2. Flour is hygroscopic (takes up water). All recipe measurements therefore are approximate. You still must use your judgment in determining the precise flour-to-liquid ratio. If the dough is sticky and refuses to form a ball, add flour by the tablespoon through the feed tube. If the dough ball is hard as a cannonball, break it into four parts in the food processor bowl and sprinkle water by the tablespoon over it, processing until you have a smooth-as-satin ball.

3. What if the dough doesn't rise in the microwave? If after the first 15 minutes of micro-rising you take the dough out of the microwave and discover the dough has not risen and is too hot to handle, you know you've killed the yeast with a too-hot oven. Not to worry. Simply dissolve another package (2½ teaspoons) of yeast in water with a little flour and sugar. Stir to make a smooth paste, then reprocess it with the dough ball. Lower your microwave setting by 5% and drop the heat time back a minute at each intermittent stage and repeat. In other words, instead of micro-rising 3–3–3–6, heat 2 minutes, rest 4 minutes, heat 2 minutes, and rest 7 minutes. It's still 15 minutes, and now you should have a nice light dough.

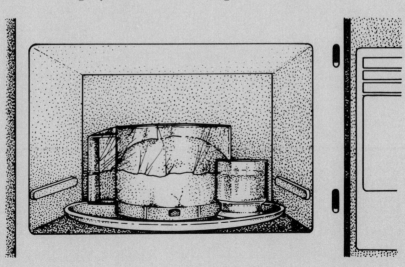

1
NO-FRILLS CAKES

e thought, for a good while, that you couldn't mix up a cake in the food processor. When we first tried it, all we got were these awful sponges that looked like something you should use to polish your shoes.

The problem—which we've encountered before—is that the food processor is so fast, it can overmix a cake if you're not careful.

So what we did was devise a new technique that makes cake mixing a snap in the food processor. First of all, combine sugar, butter, eggs, and milk in the food processor bowl all at once. Process, using the steel blade, until the mixture is thoroughly mixed. Next, open the processor top and spoon the dry ingredients on top of the liquids. Replace the processor top and pulse just until the dry ingredients are barely incorporated—no more than five or six on-off pulses. Finish the process by opening the lid and folding in any unmixed ingredients that are clinging to the sides of the processor bowl using a rubber spatula. That's all there is to it. Now you can make a cake on your busiest days.

The other feature of cake baking we note is that you'll get the best results if you use soft-wheat cake flour instead of unbleached all-purpose flour. Cake flour has the least gluten and will give you the tenderest crumb.

We also adore the food processor for flourless cakes, or near-flourless ones. Using the food processor, you can reduce nuts to a fine grind that stands in the place of flour in cakes such as the Queen of Sheba. We discovered that if we combine the food processor for making the almonds into flour, and the microwave oven for melting the chocolates called for in this recipe, we can make a Quick Queen of Sheba that tastes great and looks great and is very little trouble to make.

You will note some half-time cakes don't even need frosting. There are those days when enough is enough.

TIPS FOR BETTER FOOD PROCESSOR CAKES

CHOOSING THE RIGHT PANS

Success in cake baking depends not only on the right ingredients, the right procedure, and the right oven time and temperature, it also depends on choosing the right pan.

We've suggested the ideal pan for each cake recipe given. However, if you'd like to use a differently shaped pan, be sure the pan capacity is the same. If you put cake batter in a pan that's too small, it will run over as it rises in the hot oven. If you put batter into a pan that's too big, it won't achieve the shape that you expect.

To measure pan capacity, pour water to the brim of the pan called for in the recipe. Then pour water into the pan you'd like to substitute. If the pans hold the same amount of water, you can safely substitute.

Remember, loaf cakes are supposed to rise well above the rim of the pan. Round layer cakes ideally will rise and create an even, barely raised top so that you can stack and frost the layers.

GETTING YOUR CAKE INTO AND OUT OF THE PAN

If you have trouble getting cakes out of the pan, remember that you must generously spritz the cake pan—even a so-called nonstick pan—with cooking spray, then evenly coat the pan with flour or—for chocolate cakes—cocoa. Knock out any excess powder before pouring the cake in. Exceptions are angel food or chiffon cakes, which must be placed in a dry, clean pan.

Cool a cake in the pan on a rack for about 10 minutes before attempting to remove it from the pan. The cake will shrink away from the sides slightly. Run a spatula around the edge, cover the cake with another cake rack that you have spritzed with cooking spray, then turn it over. If you want the cake right side up, you can then place a rack on the bottom of the cake and flip it over again.

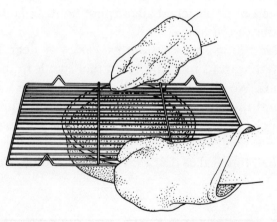

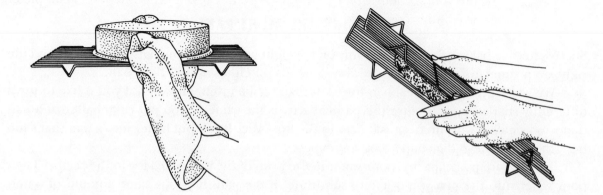

Parchment paper will help you avoid leaving chunks of cake in the pan. Spritz a baking pan with cooking spray, then measure and cut a piece of parchment paper to fit the bottom of the pan. Smooth it into the pan. Now coat the paper with cooking spray and flour. When you remove the cake from the pan, the paper will come with it. Carefully peel the paper away from the hot cake, taking particular care at the edge of the cake, where chunks of cake always want to stick to the paper.

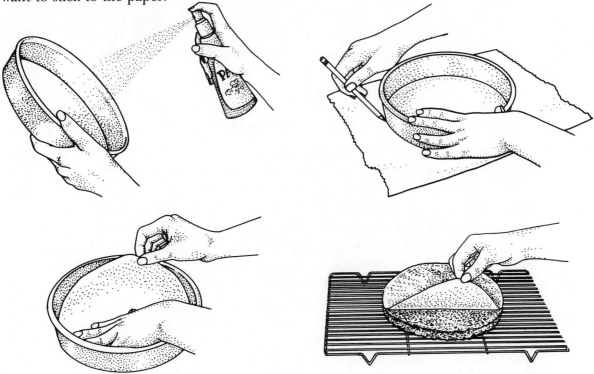

If you have forgotten to take a cake out of the pan until it's cold, pop it back into a hot oven for a couple of minutes to warm it before attempting to remove it from the baking pan.

To prevent the volcano look in a finished cake, remember to cool the layers completely before frosting. Any butter-cream-type frosting will melt and run off a warm cake.

ADDING FRUITS AND NUTS TO CAKE BATTER

Before processor chopping, toss in flour any oily or sticky fruit or nut, such as walnuts, Brazil nuts, dates, or dried apricots. This prevents them from clumping onto the steel blade and making nut butter or fruit blobs. Fruits and nuts that are flour coated, then chopped, will remain suspended in the cake batter and won't sink to the bottom.

Drier nuts like almonds or hazelnuts can be ground in the food processor using the steel blade, then used as a flour in cake recipes. Pulse the machine so as not to release too many nut oils while you pulverize the nut meats.

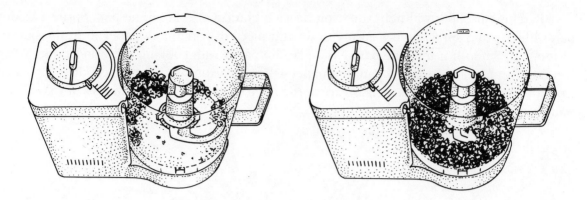

AVOIDING BAKING DISASTERS

- Always preheat the oven for at least 10 minutes. Prepare the pans before you start mixing the ingredients. Allow yourself enough time to get the job done.
- Cream will—in a hot kitchen—sometimes refuse to whip. We recommend chilling the processor bowl and blade before starting on a hot day. And never add sugar or flavoring too soon or too fast. We recommend whipping the cream to soft peaks, then adding sugar a spoonful at a time through the feed tube. Stop the machine the minute the cream seems to firm up, and take a look. No more than 20 seconds or so.

  If cream just won't whip, transfer it to another bowl, place the bowl in a larger bowl filled with ice water, and beat it slowly with a wire whisk. If the cream separates and butter begins to form, start over with new cream. You can always clump the butter together and use it for ad-lib pancakes.
- Egg whites will not stiffen if there is even one drop of oil in the bowl or on the beaters. This means not one drop of egg yolk can be included. Make sure your processor bowl and blade are squeaky clean. Break eggs into an intermediary bowl, one at a time, then pour the separated egg white into the processor bowl. If a yolk breaks, pour the whole broken egg in with the yolks. You can use these to make custard or fertilize the houseplants.

  Warm egg whites beat up higher than cold ones. Once you've separated the eggs, heat the whites 2 seconds per egg in the microwave set at 100% (high) just to room temperature.
- Cakes will be dry if your oven isn't properly calibrated and they are cooked at too high a temperature. An oven thermometer can correct this. A shot of rum, brandy, or fruit syrup can salvage the over-baked dry cake.
- Cakes will be heavy if they're overprocessed or if the ingredients aren't carefully measured. Dip and level the flour, never pack it in the measuring cup, and pulse the processor to avoid overmixing. About all you can do with a heavy cake is crumble it up, toss it with fruit, and make up a name for it.

Busy Day Cake

Makes one 7 × 11 × 1½-inch cake to serve 6
10 minutes to prepare
40 minutes to bake
7 × 11 × 1½-inch glass baking dish

Our grandmothers made wonderful Busy Day Cake using nothing but a big brown bowl and a wooden spoon. You can make the same cake in the food processor if you're careful not to overdo the mixing. Too much mixing and gluten in the batter makes the texture of the cake something like a Florida sponge. Terrific for washing your car, not so great to eat. No food processor? Haul out the bowl. It's still good.

It makes you wonder why they ever invented cake mixes. Why use a box cake when you can make a good scratch cake in 10 minutes?

½ cup (1 stick) butter or margarine
2 cups unbleached all-purpose flour
¼ teaspoon salt
1 tablespoon plus 1 teaspoon baking powder
1 light grating (¼ teaspoon) nutmeg
3 large eggs
1⅓ cups sugar
½ cup milk
Zest and juice (⅛ cup) of ½ lemon
1 tablespoon vanilla extract

1. Preheat the oven to 375° F. Spritz a 7 × 11 × 1½-inch glass baking dish with cooking spray, dust with flour, and set aside. Place the butter or margarine in a 2-cup glass measure and microwave on 100% (high) for 1 minute or until melted. Set aside.

2. Place the flour, salt, baking powder, and nutmeg in the processor bowl with the steel blade and pulse twice to mix. Remove flour mixture to a piece of waxed paper.

3. Turn the processor on and crack the eggs through the feed tube. With the motor running, add the sugar. Process for 30 seconds. Pour the hot melted butter through the feed tube and continue to process for 30 seconds more.

4. Open the lid to the processor and scrape down the sides of the container. Add half the flour mixture, half the milk, the
(continued)

Busy Day Chocolate Frosting

Who could eat any of those frostings out of a can after they've tried this 3-minute frosting? It can easily be doubled for a 2-layer cake.

2 ounces (2 squares) unsweetened chocolate
¼ cup (½ stick) unsalted butter, softened
1 large egg yolk
1 teaspoon vanilla extract
Pinch of salt
2¼ cups confectioners' sugar
2 tablespoons half-and-half or milk

1. Place the chocolate in a small microwavable bowl and microwave on 100% (high) for 2 minutes, or until melted.

2. Meanwhile, fit the processor bowl with the steel blade. Add the butter, egg yolk, vanilla, salt, sugar, half-and-half or milk, and melted chocolate. Process for 15 seconds, or until all the ingredients are well combined and the mixture is smooth. If the frosting seems too stiff, add a little extra half-and-half. Chill the frosting to harden it if it seems too soft.

lemon zest and juice, and the vanilla. Close the lid and pulse 5 times. Open the lid and add the remaining flour mixture and milk. Scrape down the sides of the container. Close and pulse 3 times. Open and scrape down the sides, doing any final mixing with a rubber spatula.

5. Pour the batter into the prepared pan and bake in a preheated oven for 40 minutes. Cool in the pan on a rack for 10 minutes, then turn out of the pan to the rack to cool.

Fudge-Chip Pudding Pie

For Fudge-Chip Pudding Pie, the recipe can be baked in a prebaked 10-inch pastry shell. The pastry will become soggy if it sits, so be sure to eat it as soon as it is cool enough. Garnish the top with whipped cream and chocolate shavings or curls (see page 202).

*F*UDGE-CHIP PUDDING CAKE

Serves 6 to 8
20 minutes to prepare
35 to 40 minutes to bake
9-inch square glass baking pan

We love the ease of putting together a pudding cake. No pan to grease, no egg whites to beat, no icing to make. The pudding forms in the pan. This chocolate version is rich as Midas and can serve 8 people after a big meal. For a mocha version, brew your favorite coffee and substitute it for the water.

¼ cup (½ stick) unsalted butter
1½ teaspoons vanilla extract
¼ cup milk
¼ cup whipping cream
1 cup unbleached all-purpose flour
2 teaspoons baking powder
1 cup granulated sugar, divided
¼ teaspoon salt
7 tablespoons (½ cup minus 1 tablespoon) unsweetened cocoa, divided
6 ounces (1 cup) large or medium semisweet chocolate chips
1 cup chopped walnuts
¾ cup packed dark brown sugar
1¾ cups hot tap water or strong hot brewed coffee
Vanilla ice cream

1. Preheat the oven to 350° F. In a medium microwavable mixing bowl, add the butter and microwave on 100% (high) for 45 seconds, or until completely melted. Add the vanilla, milk, and cream. Stir to mix.

2. Sift into the butter mixture the flour, baking powder, ¾ cup of the sugar, the salt, and 3 tablespoons of the cocoa. Stir to thoroughly mix and add the chocolate chips and walnuts. Mix well. Spread the mixture into an ungreased 9-inch square glass baking pan.

3. In a small bowl, combine the brown sugar, the remaining ¼ cup sugar and 4 tablespoons cocoa (the mixture will have small lumps), and sprinkle over the batter. Pour the hot water or coffee over it. Bake on the middle rack of the preheated oven until the top of the cake is set and bottom mixture is bubbly, about 35 to 40 minutes. Serve warm with vanilla ice cream.

*T*HE QUICK QUEEN OF SHEBA

Serves 6 to 8
25 minutes to prepare
25 minutes to bake
8-inch round cake pan

Julia Child first introduced us to this French-style single-layer dark-as-death chocolate-almond cake, so creamy in the middle it melts in the mouth like a Godiva chocolate. The classic recipe came into the American kitchen long before the food processor or microwave had arrived to foreshorten the work.

Now this once-laborious task is over in less than an hour; cake's on and with little more than a processor bowl to wash. Serve the cake warm to get the ultimate chocolate experience. To finish the cake, you can simply dust the top with confectioners' sugar, or you can lavish it with a thin layer of Chocolate Butter Cream. If you like a little gilt, it's easy to make Chocolate Shards using the microwave. What more do you need? How about a thimble of port and an espresso, please?

(continued)

Espresso Powder

So you don't drink espresso at all, but you like the flavor in baked goods. Buy a jar of instant espresso crystals and put it on the shelf. Then when a recipe calls for espresso, dissolve the crystals according to manufacturer's directions and add to the recipe, measure-for-measure, the same way as if you were using brewed coffee and go forth.

Chocolate Butter Cream

Makes frosting for 1 small layer
5 minutes to prepare
Small microwavable dish

2 ounces (2 squares) bittersweet chocolate or ⅓ cup chocolate chips
1 tablespoon espresso or dark rum
2 tablespoons butter, cut into bits

1. Combine the chocolate and espresso or rum in a small microwavable dish and melt them uncovered in the microwave at 100% (high) for a minute.

2. Meanwhile prepare an ice-water bath by placing ice cubes and a little water in a medium widemouthed bowl.

3. Remove the chocolate mixture from the microwave and stir until it's smooth, using a fork or wooden skewer. Add the butter bits and beat until the butter is thoroughly incorporated. About midway through this beating, lower the bowl into the ice-water bath and continue beating until mixture becomes firm enough to spread on the thoroughly cooled cake.

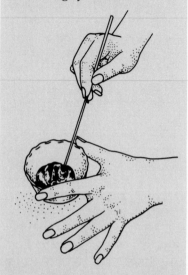

½ cup plus 2 tablespoons unsalted butter, softened, divided
2 tablespoons unsweetened Dutch-process cocoa
3 ounces (¾ bar) German's sweet chocolate
1 ounce (1 square) unsweetened chocolate
2 tablespoons espresso coffee or dark rum
3 large eggs, separated
1 tablespoon fresh lemon juice or white wine vinegar
Pinch of salt
¼ teaspoon cream of tartar
½ cup plus 2 tablespoons granulated sugar, divided
⅓ cup blanched almonds (see sidebar, page 22)
¼ teaspoon almond extract
½ cup cake flour
Confectioners' sugar or Chocolate Butter Cream (see sidebar) and Chocolate Shards (see sidebar, opposite)

1. Preheat the oven to 325° F. Place the baking rack in the lower third of the oven. Prepare one 8-inch round cake pan by coating the inside and bottom with 2 tablespoons of the softened butter, then dusting thoroughly with the cocoa. Turn the pan upside down and knock out the excess cocoa.

2. Combine the chocolates with the espresso or rum in a microwavable dish. Microwave uncovered at 100% (high) for 1 minute and 10 seconds. Leave the chocolate in the microwave until you're ready to incorporate it into the batter.

3. Meanwhile, whip the egg whites until foamy in the processor using the steel blade or beater attachment (see pages 19–20). Add the lemon juice or white wine vinegar through the feed tube with the motor running, then sprinkle the egg whites with the salt and cream of tartar and continue beating until very soft peaks form. Now sprinkle 2 tablespoons of the sugar and beat for another minute or so, until shiny sticky peaks stand. Use a rubber spatula to scoop the beaten egg whites into a medium mixing bowl, and set aside.

4. Wipe out the work bowl and dry it thoroughly. Fit the processor with the steel blade. Add the almonds and pulse to pulverize until they're dry and powdery. Don't overdo it or you'll release the oil and they'll begin to clump up. Now add the almond extract and pulse to mix. Dust the pulverized almonds with the cake flour and pulse to mix thoroughly. Remove the almond flour to waxed paper and set it aside.

5. Wipe out the processor bowl, fit it with the steel blade, and add the remaining ½ cup butter, cut into 4 or 5 pieces. Pulse to distribute it over the bowl, then, with the motor running, pour the remaining ½ cup sugar in through the feed tube, then the egg yolks, one at a time, and process until the mixture is fluffy and soft.

6. Remove the chocolate from the microwave and stir it with a fork or wooden skewer until the mixture is smooth and the espresso or rum is thoroughly incorporated into the warm, soft chocolate. Combine it with the egg yolk mixture in the processor and pulse to mix thoroughly.

7. By thirds, alternately sprinkle almond flour and chocolate mixture onto the stiffly beaten egg whites. Quickly fold with a slotted spoon after each addition, just until the mixture is smooth. Use a light hand here. Do not overmix. Every stroke deflates the batter.

8. Turn the batter into the prepared cake pan, stroking the batter up the sides of the pan, then pop it into the preheated oven. Bake for 25 minutes, until just done. The cake should be soft and jiggly in the center, but a skewer plunged into the cake a couple of inches from the side should come out clean. Do not overcook.

9. Cool the cake in the pan on a rack for 10 minutes, run a spatula around the edge, then flip it over, unmold, and let it cool completely on the rack before finishing. The simplest finish is a dusting of confectioners' sugar tapped on through a strainer. For a more elaborate finish, smooth on Chocolate Butter Cream and maybe some Chocolate Shards.

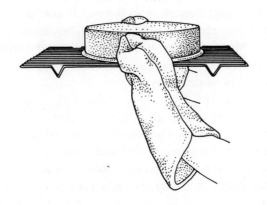

Chocolate Shards

For a really fancy finish, make quick Chocolate Shards and arrange them over the iced cake, then give a final dusting of unsweetened Dutch-process cocoa. Using the microwave is just too easy. If you have a piece of marble to cool the chocolate on, this recipe is, well, a piece of cake.

3 ounces (3 squares) bittersweet, sweet, or milk chocolate or ½ cup chocolate or white chocolate chips
1 tablespoon unsweetened Dutch-process cocoa

1. Place the chocolate in a microwavable dish and melt it in the microwave set at 100% (high) for 1 minute and 10 seconds. Remove the chocolate from the microwave. Use a skewer or chopsticks to mix until the chocolate is shiny and smooth.

2. Spread the melted chocolate onto a piece of waxed paper in a layer no thicker than ¹⁄₁₆ inch (about like a magnolia leaf). Chill it in the refrigerator, or if you have a piece of marble in your kitchen, just leave it there.

3. If you wish, before the chocolate becomes brittle, you can cut it into shapes using a cookie cutter or sharp knife. Otherwise, let it harden completely, then break it into irregular pieces.

4. Arrange the shards on top of the frosted cake, flipping them so the shiny bottom faces upward and the dull side is down, using two skewers, chopsticks, or knives to handle the chocolate so you'll leave no fingerprints. Dust with a fine layer of cocoa knocked through a fine-meshed sieve.

Makes frosting for 2-layer 9-inch cake
4-cup glass measure

In 1932, Baker's chocolate offered this easy frosting. If they'd had a microwave, it would have been even easier. Use it on Grandmother Garrison's or other everyday cakes.

4 ounces (4 squares) unsweetened chocolate
1 14-ounce can sweetened condensed milk
1 tablespoon water

1. Place the chocolate in a 4-cup glass measure and micro-melt it in the microwave at 100% (high) for 2½ to 3 minutes. When it's melted, stir until smooth with a chopstick.
2. Stir in the sweetened condensed milk. Microwave at 100% (high) until thick, about 2 minutes, stirring every 30 seconds. Stir in the water. Cool the frosting before icing the cake.

GRANDMOTHER GARRISON'S CHOCOLATE FLAT CAKES

Serves 8
10 minutes to prepare
15 minutes to bake
Two 9-inch round cake pans

Back in Kentucky, Grandmother Garrison used to hand out wedges of walnut-covered flat cakes to all the neighbor kids. Made in cocoa-dusted cake pans, these quarter-inch-thick flat cakes studded with chopped walnuts make a fine dessert when you're short on time and want something that doesn't even require a plate and fork.

2 tablespoons unsweetened cocoa
2 ounces semisweet chocolate chips or squares
1 cup sugar
½ cup (1 stick) unsalted butter
½ cup unbleached all-purpose flour
2 large eggs
½ teaspoon vanilla extract
½ cup chopped walnuts or other nuts
   Instant Chocolate-Fudge Frosting (see sidebar)

1. Preheat the oven to 350° F. Coat two 9-inch round cake pans with cooking spray. Dust the pans lightly with cocoa, knocking out any excess. Alternately, coat the pans with cooking spray, cut parchment paper to fit the bottom, then coat the paper with cooking spray, and dust with cocoa.
2. Combine the chocolate, sugar, and butter in a 2-cup glass measure. Microwave at 100% (high) for 1 minute to melt the chocolate. Stir and repeat at 30-second intervals until you have a smooth mixture.
3. In a medium bowl combine flour, eggs, and vanilla. Whisk to mix, then pour in the chocolate mixture, using a rubber spatula to get all the chocolate out. Whisk to combine. Pour into the prepared pans. Sprinkle the tops with chopped nuts and bake in the preheated oven for 15 minutes.
4. Cool the cakes in the pans on a rack for 10 minutes, then cut into wedges and lift out onto the rack to continue cooling. Store in a tin. Frost with Instant Chocolate-Fudge Frosting if desired.

BERRIES OR CHERRIES YOGURT CAKE

Serves 6 to 8
15 minutes to prepare
1 hour and 10 minutes to bake
9- or 10-inch springform or cheesecake pan

Blueberries or sweet dark cherries bursting through a cream-colored crust make this a dazzling dessert for company. Purple Bing and just blushing Queen Anne cherries work well, along with the large Oregon blueberries. For the Fourth of July, we mixed the two for a red, white, and blue dessert. Fresh fruit works best; however, frozen fruit, thawed and drained, can be used.

½ cup (1 stick) unsalted butter, softened
1 4-ounce package cream cheese, room temperature
1 cup sugar, divided
1 large egg
1½ cups unbleached all-purpose flour
1½ teaspoons baking powder
4 cups (1 quart) fresh blueberries, picked over, or frozen blueberries, thawed, or fresh sweet cherries, or frozen sweet
  cherries, thawed, or a combination of the two
2 cups (16 ounces) vanilla-flavored nonfat yogurt
2 tablespoons cornstarch
1 teaspoon vanilla extract
2 large egg yolks

1. Preheat the oven to 350° F. Butter a 9- or 10-inch spring-form or cheesecake pan. In a large mixing bowl combine the soft butter, cream cheese, ½ cup of the sugar, egg, flour, and baking powder. Mix well with a wooden spoon. Turn into the prepared pan. Sprinkle the top evenly with fruit.

2. Rinse out the mixing bowl and add to it the yogurt, cornstarch, the remaining ½ cup sugar, vanilla, and egg yolks. Whisk thoroughly and pour the mixture over the fruit. Bake the cake on the middle rack of the preheated oven for 1 hour and 10 minutes. The crust will be light brown around the edges, and the middle will not be quite set. It will set as it cools. Remove the cake from the oven to a rack to cool. When the cake is completely cool, remove the sides of the pan. The cake can be served at room temperature or chilled.

How to Soften Refrigerated and Frozen Stick Butters and Cream Cheese in the Microwave

To soften refrigerated ¼-pound stick butter in the microwave, place one stick of cold butter in the microwave on a saucer. Microwave on 20% (low) for 10 seconds (20 seconds for frozen butter). Turn the butter over and microwave on 20% (low) for an additional 5 seconds (20 seconds for frozen butter). Gently squeeze; the butter should just give a little. Let it stand for 5 minutes on the saucer, and the butter will be perfect room temperature.

To soften cream cheese in the microwave, place a cold, unwrapped 8-ounce brick of cream cheese on a saucer. Microwave on 100% (high) for 10 seconds. Turn the cream cheese over and microwave on 100% (high) for an additional 5 seconds. Frozen and thawed cream cheese tends to crumble; therefore, we don't recommend freezing it.

CROOKNECK SPICE CAKE

Makes one 12-inch tube cake
15 minutes to prepare
1 hour and 30 minutes to bake
12-inch tube pan

Zucchini cakes you've made, but did you ever try one with a golden crookneck squash? A rich, dark, spicy loaf cake flecked with shards of almonds and yellow squash, this moist cake takes a long time to cook, but not long to mix up using a food processor. You can, by the way, substitute green zucchini for the yellow squash if that's what your garden gives. If you'd like, substitute ½ cup currants for half the nuts. This makes a cake that's a good keeper and ideal for picnics because it's sturdy.

¼ cup unsweetened cocoa
1 pound (2 large) crookneck yellow squash
1 cup (4 ounces) almonds
2 large eggs
2 cups sugar
½ cup vegetable oil
½ cup (1 stick) unsalted butter, melted
1 teaspoon vanilla extract
3 cups unbleached all-purpose flour
1 teaspoon salt
1 teaspoon baking soda
½ teaspoon baking powder
1 teaspoon ground cinnamon

1. Preheat the oven to 350° F. Coat a 12-inch tube pan with cooking spray, then dust thoroughly with the cocoa, knocking out any excess. Set aside.

2. Fit the food processor bowl with the shredder and shred the squash. Remove the squash to a colander and drain. Squeeze the excess liquid out by hand. Transfer the squash to a large mixing bowl. Replace the shredder disk with the steel blade and pulse to coarsely chop the almonds. Remove the nuts to the squash and stir to mix with a wooden spoon.

3. Still using the steel blade, and with the motor running, break the eggs into the processor bowl, then pour in the sugar and mix thoroughly. Add the oil and melted butter through

the feed tube and continue to process. Add the vanilla and mix. Pour this mixture over the squash and stir by hand to mix.

4. In the processor bowl combine the flour, salt, soda, baking powder, and cinnamon. Pulse to aerate. Dump this mixture over the squash mixture and use a wooden spoon to stir. It will be thick, but it should begin to thin as you stir.

5. Turn the mixture into the prepared pan and pop it into the preheated oven. Bake for 1 hour and 30 minutes, until a wooden pick inserted into the middle comes out clean and dry.

6. Cool the cake in the pan for 15 minutes. Then cover it with a rack and turn it over. Lift the pan off. Now place a second rack on the cake and flip it over again so that you cool the cake right side up. Let it stand until it's cool. Slice the cake with a serrated bread knife for best results. Wrap the cake in foil. It keeps well.

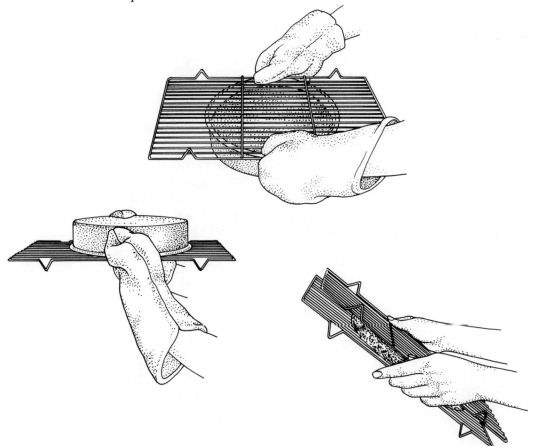

LUSCIOUS LEMON SPONGE CAKE WITH LEMON-BUTTERMILK CURD

Serves 6
10 minutes to prepare
1 hour and 10 minutes to bake
8½ × 3½-inch glass loaf pan

A light sponge cake covering a tart lemon-buttermilk curd could never have been this easy before the invention of the food processor.

¼ cup (½ stick) unsalted butter
　Zest and juice (about ½ cup) of 2 lemons, divided
1 cup granulated sugar
¼ cup unbleached all-purpose flour
3 large eggs
1½ cups buttermilk
　Confectioners' sugar
　Fresh raspberries or blackberries or good-quality prepared
　　berry sauce, for garnish
　Framboise or Chambord (optional)

1. Preheat the oven to 350° F. Lightly coat an 8½ × 3½-inch glass loaf pan with cooking spray.

2. Remove the metal blade from the processor bowl and add the butter. Place the processor bowl in the microwave and microwave at 100% (high) for about 40 seconds, or until the butter is completely melted and hot. Meanwhile, with a zester, remove the lemon zest from 1 lemon.

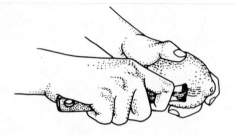

3. Remove the processor bowl from the microwave and place it back on the base. Replace the steel blade and add the lemon zest. Process the butter and zest for 1 minute.

4. Halve both lemons and squeeze until you have ½ cup of juice. Strain the juice into the butter, then add the sugar, flour, eggs, and buttermilk to the processor bowl. Process the ingredients for 3 minutes. Pour the batter into the prepared pan. Place the pan into a larger pan and pour hot tap water into the larger pan until it comes halfway up the sides of the smaller pan.

Getting the Most from Your Lemon

To remove more juice from a cold lemon, pierce the lemon several times with the tip of a sharp knife or stab it with a fork and then microwave at 100% (high) for 30 seconds before squeezing. The warm lemon will give more juice.

5. Place the pans on the middle rack of the preheated oven and bake for 1 hour and 10 minutes, or until the sponge cake is lightly golden around the edges and springs back when touched. Remove the cake from the oven and the water bath and allow it to cool on a rack for 15 minutes. The lemon-buttermilk curd will be forming on the bottom during this time. Spoon the cake and curd into pretty serving bowls and dust the cake with confectioners' sugar and garnish with fresh berries or a good-quality berry sauce if fresh berries are not in season. You may want to toss a tablespoon or two of your favorite liqueur, such as Framboise or Chambord onto the berries. This cake is best served warm the same day as made.

HARRIET AND DAVID'S POUND CAKE

Makes two 3 × 5 × 8-inch loaf cakes or one 10-inch tube cake
20 minutes to prepare
1 hour and 15 minutes to 1 hour and 25 minutes to bake
Two 3 × 5 × 8-inch loaf pans or one 10-inch tube pan

Diana's grandmother Harriet and brother David make this pound cake together every year at Christmas. David, the cook who loves kitchen gadgets, showed Granny how to do it in a food processor, and they've been baking cakes to share with family and friends ever since. Share it with someone in your family this Christmas.

2¾ cups unbleached all-purpose flour
¼ teaspoon baking soda
3 cups sugar
   Zest of 2 lemons, grated
1 cup (2 sticks) unsalted butter, softened
6 large eggs
1 tablespoon fresh lemon juice
½ teaspoon lemon extract
1 cup sour cream
1 teaspoon vanilla extract
   Instant California Frosting (optional; see sidebar)

1. Preheat the oven to 325° F. Grease and flour two 3 × 5 × 8-inch loaf pans or one 10-inch tube pan. Fit the processor bowl with the steel blade. Combine the flour and baking soda; pulse to mix. Turn the flour mixture out onto a piece of waxed paper, and set aside.

2. Combine the sugar and lemon zest in the processor bowl. Process to mince the zest, about 15 seconds. Add the butter and eggs to the sugar mixture. Process for 1 minute, until the mixture looks creamy, scraping down the sides of the processor bowl occasionally with a rubber spatula if needed. Add the lemon juice, lemon extract, sour cream, and vanilla. Process the mixture for 15 seconds.

3. Remove the lid of the processor bowl and sprinkle the butter batter with the flour mixture. Process for 1 minute to mix well, occasionally stopping to scrape down the sides of the processor bowl. Do not overmix. Pour the batter into the prepared pan(s). Bake for 1 hour and 15 minutes to 1 hour and 25 minutes, until a cake tester inserted in the middle of the cake comes out with a dry crumb. Cool in the pan(s) on a wire rack for 20 minutes before removing from the pan(s). Finish cooling on a wire rack. If a soft outer crust is desired, after the cake has been turned out of the pan and allowed to cool for 30 minutes, place the cake in a plastic bag to finish cooling, and the result will be a nice soft crust and crumb throughout.

Instant California Frosting

Makes frosting for 2-layer 9-inch cake

The orange juice people at Sunkist were telling people how to make this instant icing in 1928. They only needed a food processor and a lemon zester to make it instant joy. Garnish the finished cake with shards of citrus zest. If they sell citrus leaves in your grocery store, use those to finish the cake, then top with thin lemon or lime slices you twist into S shapes.

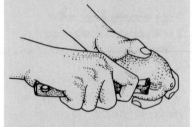

4½ cups confectioners' sugar
3 tablespoons fresh orange juice
1½ tablespoons fresh lemon juice
Zest of ½ orange
Zest of ½ lemon

Add the sugar to the food processor bowl fitted with the steel blade. Pulse to aerate, then with the motor running add the citrus juices through the feed tube. Process until smooth. Then add the citrus zest through the feed tube and pulse to mix.

Processor Whipped Cream

Makes 2½ cups

Even though little air is incorporated into processor whipped cream, it holds its shape better than conventionally whipped cream. This makes it ideal for use in cake-top decorations. It can be used in a pastry bag, or it can be used to top shortcakes well before dinner. Hold the cakes in the refrigerator until serving time, and you'll have perfect snowcapped mountaintops of whipped cream.

2 cups whipping cream, chilled
3 to 4 tablespoons confectioners' sugar

Fit the processor bowl with the steel blade. Process the cream until thickened. Add the sugar gradually, 1 tablespoon at a time, through the feed tube, and process until stiff. Serve, or refrigerate until serving time.

MAMA'S SUNRIVER STRAWBERRY SHORTCAKE

Serves 8
15 minutes to prepare
25 to 30 minutes to bake
9-inch round cake pan

When we were children, virtually everything was made from scratch, from school clothes to shortcakes. Diana can still remember the first time the small hockey puck–looking shortcakes showed up in the grocery store. Her mother tried them once, and only once. "Too dry," Mama said, and went back to her favorite scratch recipe. And why not? It's almost as fast as opening the cellophane package and tastes much better. Mother cut in the shortening by hand, like making a biscuit; we've used the food processor. Sometimes new is better.

2 cups unbleached all-purpose flour
½ cup sugar
1 tablespoon baking powder
½ teaspoon salt
½ cup vegetable shortening
¾ cup milk
2 large eggs
Strawberry Filling (recipe follows)
Sweetened whipped cream, for garnish

1. Preheat the oven to 375° F and coat a 9-inch round cake pan with cooking spray. Add the flour, sugar, baking powder, salt, and shortening to the food processor bowl fitted with the steel blade. Pulse 3 or 4 times to cut the shortening into the flour mixture until the particles are fine.

2. Measure the milk into a 2-cup glass measure, add the eggs, and beat lightly with a fork to break up the eggs. Add the liquid mixture to the dry ingredients through the feed tube and pulse 3 or 4 times, until all dry particles are moistened.

3. Spread the dough into the prepared pan and bake on the middle rack for 25 to 30 minutes, until golden brown. Remove the cake from the pan to a rack to cool. Cut the shortcake into 8 wedges, split, fill with Strawberry Filling, and garnish with whipped cream.

STRAWBERRY FILLING

8 cups fresh ripe strawberries, hulled, divided
½ to ⅔ cup sugar, depending on the strawberries' sweetness
Whipped cream, for garnish

1. Choose 8 perfect strawberries for garnish and set them aside. Place 4 cups of the berries and the sugar in the bowl of the food processor and pulse several times to chop coarsely, then let them sit for 5 minutes or so to allow them to yield some of their juice.

2. Meanwhile, slice the remaining 4 cups of berries and place them in a medium mixing bowl. Pour the processed berries over the berry slices and mix thoroughly. Taste for sweetness, adding more sugar if necessary. On each dessert plate, ladle ⅔ cup of the strawberry filling in the middle and on top of the shortcake wedge, then garnish with whipped cream and the reserved strawberries.

*New-fangled, non-stick finishes
are nothing new. Our grandmothers, who mainly cooked with cast
iron, took care of their pots so that
they were more stick-free than any
new-age finish.*

*To keep your cast iron in good
condition, wash with tap water
only, then dry by placing on the
stove over high heat until all the
water has evaporated. Next,
quickly remove the cast iron from
the heat, wipe with a paper towel,
and add a swipe of plain vegetable
oil just to condition. Think of it as
comparable to putting night cream
on your face before you go to bed. A
little oil will keep both you and
your cast iron looking your best.*

APRICOT UPSIDE-DOWN CAKE

*Makes one 10-inch cake to serve 6
10 minutes to prepare
30 minutes to bake
10-inch iron skillet*

*Bake this American-classic cake in a black cast-iron skillet for the best
results. Pioneer women knew the brown sugar and butter caramelized
best in iron. What they didn't know was that the process is quick and
easy if you use a food processor to whip the egg whites. Used canned
apricots, pineapple rings, fresh apples, pears, plums, or Bing cherries.
Make an artful display of the fruit nestled in its brown-sugar-and-
butter bed, dapple with nuts if you've got 'em, pour the batter over,
bake, then flip the golden cake onto a footed platter. It's dessert in 40
minutes.*

3 tablespoons unsalted butter
3 large eggs, separated
**1 tablespoon fresh lemon juice or white wine
    vinegar**
1 cup granulated sugar
¼ cup buttermilk
1 cup cake flour
½ teaspoon salt
1½ teaspoons baking powder
½ teaspoon baking soda
1 cup packed brown sugar
**1 cup drained apricot halves, pineapple rings, or other fruit, cut
    into ½-inch-thick pieces**
1 cup drained, pitted, and halved sweet cherries (optional)
½ cup pecan halves (optional)

1. Preheat the oven to 350° F. Place the butter in a 10-inch
cast-iron or iron-clad skillet and put it in the oven to preheat.

2. Meanwhile, place the egg whites in the food processor
fitted with the steel blade (see pages 19–20). Process until the
egg whites are foamy, then add the lemon juice or white wine
vinegar through the feed tube, and continue processing until
the whites hold a soft peak. Set aside.

3. While the whites are whipping, in a large mixing bowl, combine the egg yolks with the sugar and stir with a wooden spoon to mix. Stir in the buttermilk and mix thoroughly.

4. Sprinkle the flour, salt, baking powder, and baking soda over the egg yolk–sugar mixture and stir to mix thoroughly. Fold in the beaten egg whites.

5. Remove the hot buttered skillet from the oven, pour the brown sugar into it, and smooth it. Arrange the fruit artfully, with the cut side up, on the bottom of the skillet. Tuck pecan halves in between the pieces of fruit, if desired. Pour the batter over, smooth the top with the back of the wooden spoon, then bake in the preheated oven for 30 minutes, until a toothpick inserted comes out clean.

6. Remove the cake from the oven. Loosen the edges with a sharp knife, then place a serving plate on top of the skillet, and flip it over to place the cake upside down on the plate. Scrape up all that good caramel that clings to the skillet and pour it over the cake.

AUNT MILLIE'S MERINGUE TORTE WITH RASPBERRIES AND COCONUT

Makes one 9-inch torte
25 minutes to prepare
30 minutes to bake
4 hours chilling time
Three 9-inch round cake pans

Meringue tortes have always been crowd pleasers for country folks. Just one more way to use up all of those eggs fresh from the henhouse. Try it the next time you need something extra special.

5 large eggs, separated
1 tablespoon fresh lemon juice or white wine vinegar
¾ teaspoon salt, divided
1½ cups sugar, divided
1¼ cups sweetened shredded coconut
1 cup (2 sticks) unsalted butter or margarine
2 teaspoons vanilla extract
2 tablespoons milk
½ teaspoon baking powder
2 cups unbleached all-purpose flour
1½ cups raspberry jam
2 cups sour cream
Fresh raspberries or unsweetened frozen raspberries, thawed, for garnish

1. Preheat the oven to 350° F. Coat the bottoms of three 9-inch round cake pans with cooking spray. Fit the food processor with the steel blade (see pages 19–20). Add the egg whites. Process until foamy, about 8 seconds. With the machine running, pour the lemon juice or white wine vinegar through the feed tube and process until the whites are stiff, about 1 minute. With the machine still running, gradually add ¼ teaspoon of the salt and 1 cup of the sugar a spoonful at a time through the feed tube. Process until the whites are stiff and hold their shape, about 1 minute. Transfer the egg whites to a medium bowl. Fold in the coconut, using a rubber spatula. Set aside.

2. In the food processor fitted with the steel blade, combine the egg yolks, the remaining ½ cup of sugar, the butter or margarine, vanilla, and milk. Process for 1 minute.

3. In a small bowl, stir to blend the remaining ½ teaspoon of salt, the baking powder, and flour. Spoon the dry ingredients over the batter in the processor bowl and pulse to mix thoroughly, about 3 or 4 pulses. The batter will be stiff. Spread the batter evenly onto the bottoms of the prepared pans.

4. Gently spread ½ cup of the raspberry jam on top of the batter in each pan, leaving a 1-inch margin around the edge. Spread the meringue-coconut mixture over the jam. Bake on the middle rack of the preheated oven for 30 minutes, until the edges are lightly browned.

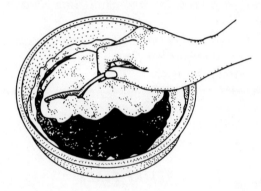

5. Remove the pans to a rack to cool. Cool the cakes in the pans completely on 2 racks and then carefully remove the cakes from the pans onto the racks. Place 1 layer on a serving platter right side up and spread with ⅔ cup of the sour cream. Repeat, using all the layers and sour cream. Chill the torte for at least 4 hours or overnight. Serve chilled, garnished with fresh or frozen raspberries, if you like. This torte may be made up to 1 day ahead of serving time.

PECAN CAKE WITH PRALINE GLAZE

Serves 8
20 minutes to prepare
40 minutes to bake
9-inch springform pan

Pecan Cake with Praline Glaze is the perfect picnic or potluck cake. It travels well, and there's no messy icing to worry about. Make it early in the day so flavors have time to mellow.

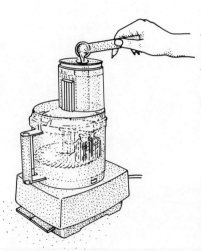

7 large eggs, separated
1 tablespoon fresh lemon juice or white wine vinegar
1 cup sugar, divided
3 cups pecan halves, divided
½ cup unbleached all-purpose flour
1 teaspoon baking powder
¼ teaspoon salt
1 teaspoon vanilla extract
⅓ cup (5 ⅓ tablespoons) unsalted butter, melted
    Pecan halves, for garnish

PRALINE GLAZE

½ cup sugar
2 tablespoons unbleached all-purpose flour
¼ cup (½ stick) unsalted butter
⅓ cup whipping cream

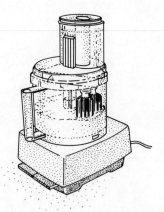

1. Preheat the oven to 350° F. Coat the bottom of a 9-inch springform pan with cooking spray.

2. To warm the egg whites, place in a processor bowl and microwave on 100% (high), about 2 to 3 seconds. Refit the bowl on the processor base (see pages 19–20). Cover and process until foamy, about 8 seconds. With the machine running, pour the lemon juice or white wine vinegar through the feed tube and process until the whites are stiff, about 1 minute. With the machine still running, gradually add ¼ cup of the sugar to the egg whites through the feed tube. Process for 1 minute. Transfer the egg whites to a small bowl. Set aside.

3. Rinse and dry the processor bowl and blade. Fit the bowl with the steel blade. Add 2¼ cups of the pecan halves to the processor bowl. Process until the pecans are finely ground and very light. Transfer them to a large bowl. Add the ½ cup of flour, baking powder, and salt. Stir to blend. Set aside. Add the remaining ¾ cup pecan halves to the processor bowl and pulse until chopped. Remove to a small bowl and set aside to use later for the glaze.

4. In the processor bowl fitted with the steel blade, combine the egg yolks, ¾ cup of the sugar, vanilla, and melted butter. Process for 1 minute. Sprinkle the pecan-flour mixture evenly over the butter mixture and pulse 4 or 5 times, just until combined. The batter will be stiff. Spoon the batter into the large bowl that the pecan-flour mixture was in. Fold in the egg whites.

5. Pour the batter into the prepared pan. Bake on the middle rack of the preheated oven for 40 minutes, until the middle springs back when lightly touched. Cool in the pan on a wire rack.

6. Place the broiler rack 6-inches from the heat source. Preheat the broiler.

7. For the glaze, mix the ½ cup sugar and 2 tablespoons flour in a 1-quart microwavable bowl. Add the ¼ cup butter and the whipping cream. Microwave on 100% (high) for 1 minute, until the butter is melted. Stir to mix well. Microwave on 100% (high) for 2 minutes. Stir in the ¾ cup chopped pecans (the mixture will be thick, but that's OK).

8. Remove the cake from the pan by running a knife or spatula around the outer edge and removing the sides of the pan. Slide the knife or spatula between the cake and the pan bottom. Place the cake and pan bottom on a broiler-proof serving dish; slide the pan bottom out. Spread the nut mixture on top of the cake. Broil 6-inches away from the heat source until the topping bubbles, about 1 minute. Garnish with pecan halves and let the cake cool. This cake is best served the same day it's made.

Reheating Cakes

Cakes with a high fat content reheat well in the microwave. Place the piece of cake or whole cake on a microwavable dish. Microwave uncovered on 70% (medium) to prevent drying out. A slice of cake will take about 40 to 50 seconds, and a whole cake will take 3 to 4 minutes.

2
FAST PIES AND TARTS

An everyday mainstay when women stayed home all day and wanted an easy, satisfying dessert, the pie has—in the past 20 or so years—pretty much gone out of vogue with half-time cooks who simply haven't the time to bake one.

We found some remarkable shortcuts that have put pies back on our everyday menus. First of all is the prepared piecrust. Found in the refrigerator case of the supermarket, this well-made crust simply requires arrangement in the pie pan, filling, and baking. You can also shape it into a tart pan if you'd rather have a thin, intense tart instead of a pie.

We've also had good luck with frozen prepared crusts, used in the same way. And, of course, we sometimes make our own crusts a week or so before a big holiday dinner. Freeze them right in the pie pan and store them in a Ziploc bag until a few hours before you plan to bake.

But our real love is a homemade crust made in the food processor. Piecrust is at its flakiest when it's handled the least, and the food processor allows you to control the process. Ten seconds to work fat into the flour. Twenty seconds to drizzle in the water, and you're ready to roll.

In most cases, we skip the chilling step you see in traditional piecrust recipes. The few times that the crust seems to benefit from chilling, we simply form it into a disk shape, wrap it in plastic wrap, and place it in the freezer or refrigerator a few moments while we're making the filling.

But generally speaking, we don't have time to chill or rest piecrust. If anything, we're the ones who take our rest by eliminating steps in the half-time kitchen. When making pie, we just food processor mix and roll. It's that simple.

ROLLING OUT PIECRUST

Linda has a plastic pie sheet that Tupperware sells, now only by special order. Thanks, Tupperware. This is a great product. Roll a piecrust out on this plastic sheet, put your hand under the sheet, and drape the crust over the rolling pin, and you can have it in the pan with nary a hitch.

We also like to roll pie and tart crusts on our marble countertops, on a finished-wood top, and on Formica or other smooth countertops. Simply wipe the counter with a clean, wet dishcloth, then sprinkle it lightly with flour. Smooth the flour evenly with your hand, and now you have a nonstick surface for rolling pastry. Lightly dust flour onto the rolling pin and your hand, and you're ready to go.

Begin rolling the crust in the center of the dough and roll outward, using light, sure strokes. Roll away and toward your body, then right and left. Run your hand over the dough, then roll out any rough spots or hills.

If the dough cracks around the edges, wet your hands with cold water and smash the crack together with your fingertips, then roll it smooth.

Just as you've read in every pie book you ever saw, don't reroll piecrust. Handle it lightly and deftly, and you're sure to get a good flaky piecrust.

For best results use a heavy, 6-pound or so rolling pin at least 19-inches long. We like ball-bearing handles on our pins or those long French pins with no handles at all, which are simply rolled using the palms of both hands.

Making piecrust takes practice, but it's a skill the half-time cook can master after some trial runs. Just don't get scared off by complicated directions, demands for pastry cloths and pin socks, or other arcane instructions. Remember that pie making, like many other kitchen tasks, began when kitchens were far less automated than they are now. You have a food processor. You have a good rolling pin. You're ready to roll. And if all else fails, buy the dang thing. The commercial piecrusts are quite acceptable.

PREBAKING PIECRUST

For single-pastry pies, Diana prebakes her bottom piecrust in the microwave to ensure a pastry that is dry and cooked. This is a good idea for any single-pastry pie that is baked in a glass pie pan and will be filled and finished in the conventional oven (such as pumpkin or pecan).

To prebake in the microwave, lay a sheet of waxed paper or parchment paper across the pastry-lined glass pie pan. Fill the pie pan with microwavable pie weights or dried beans. Microwave on 100% (high) for 3 minutes. Remove the paper and beans. Allow the pastry to cool for 5 minutes. Fill and bake in the conventional oven as called for in the recipe. This prebaking will ensure a crisp, dry bottom crust.

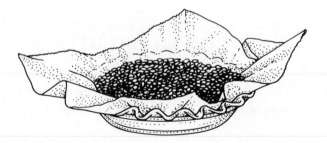

Gas ovens are wonderful pastry ovens. To ensure a crisp and brown bottom crust on any type of pie in a gas oven, place the pie directly on the preheated oven floor for the first 10 minutes of baking time. After 10 minutes, carefully remove the pie and place it on a rack in the middle of the oven and continue baking until done.

Electric ovens have a coil on the bottom as a heat source, so it is impossible to place the pie on the floor of these ovens. We suggest placing a rack in the lower third of the oven and baking the pie there for 15 minutes. Carefully remove the pie from the lower third and place it on a rack in the middle of the oven to continue baking.

For frozen fruit pies it helps if you start out with an oven temperature that is high, such as 425° F, for 10 minutes and then turn down the heat to the temperature called for in the recipe and continue baking until the crust is nice and brown and the filling is bubbling.

FOOD PROCESSOR PIECRUST MADE SIMPLE

Streamlined and easy as pie, crust made in the food processor can be a foolproof craft. The only thing you have to worry about is how much ice water to add. Because flour is hygroscopic (absorbs water from the air), it may carry more moisture in certain conditions: hot, humid weather, during the rainy season. Then you may need to drizzle in less water before the dough forms a ball that rides the blade around. Conversely, in dry climates, or in hot, centrally heated houses, flour can be dry as house dust, in which case you may need to add a few drops more water. The idea is to create—quickly—a soft, friable dough that you can squeeze into a ball before rolling.

The main trick to learn when making piecrust in the food processor is not to *overdo* it. An overworked piecrust will be tough as shoe leather. One that's been lightly handled will be flaky and melt in your mouth. Actually, this is the main advantage to making pie dough in the food processor. You have greater control than when you make the dough by hand. All you have to do is count. Ten seconds to work the fat into the flour. Twenty seconds to make a dough ball. In half a minute you're ready to roll.

We've given you recipes for piecrusts made with butter, shortening, lard, and vegetable oil. Each crust tastes a little different from the others. You decide which one you like. All crusts can be interchanged according to your personal tastes. We've suggested the ones we like, but you decide what pleases you.

Don't worry if your efforts at making crusts don't look as gorgeous as the ones in the ladies' magazines. Linda said to herself the other day, rolling out yet another crust: There are some things I'd never do in public and making piecrust is one of them. No matter how many times I make it, it still looks ragged on the edges. Oh, well. It's flavor that counts. Remember that.

FILLINGS

As for pie fillings, we find that the microwave is a good friend to cornstarch. Any pudding or custard filling that's thickened with cornstarch is better when made in the microwave. Look in our pudding and custard chapter for other ideas. Fill a cookie crumb crust with a microwave custard, and you've made a quick and satisfying pie.

We live in the fruit-growing paradise of Oregon so we're always hunting for new and old ideas for pies and tarts that use fruits and berries, singly and in combination. We hope you'll soon become as happy making fruit and berry pies as we are.

Storing Pastry

Unbaked dough or pastry shells can be stored in the refrigerator, covered in plastic wrap, for a day, or frozen, well wrapped, for up to a month. The dough thaws on the counter quickly. Baked shells can be well wrapped, placed in a non-crushable container, and held in the freezer for a month. Remove from the freezer and thaw on the counter 15 minutes, then fill with ice cream or fully cooked filling.

BASIC BUTTER CRUST (PATE BRISEE)

Makes one 9-inch piecrust or one 10-inch tart crust
10 minutes to prepare
10 to 12 minutes to bake
9- or 10-inch pie or tart pan

The flavor of baked butter surpasses all. For the crust made famous by the French, use their ingredients and a half-time method for a fast, foolproof, heavenly, flaky crust. Feel free to double the recipe for a 2-crust pie. This crust is a breeze to make in a small-capacity processor.

1 cup unbleached all-purpose flour
½ teaspoon salt
½ teaspoon sugar (optional)
6 tablespoons (¾ stick) unsalted butter, cold
2 to 3 tablespoons ice water

1. Place the oven rack in the center of the oven and preheat to 425° F. Combine the flour, salt, and sugar, if desired, in the food processor bowl fitted with the steel blade. Pulse to mix. Cut the cold butter into 6 pieces and place them around the top of the flour mixture. Pulse 10 times to create a mixture that resembles coarse meal.

2. With the processor motor running, drizzle in the ice water, a tablespoon at a time, until the dough forms a loose ball that leaves the sides of the bowl and begins to ride the blade, no more than 20 seconds.

3. Dust your hands lightly with flour, then remove the ball of dough from the processor bowl and squeeze it into a tight ball, and then flatten into a disk.

4. To roll, place the dough disk either between sheets of flour-dusted waxed paper or on a lightly floured board. Using light, sure strokes, roll the disk into an ⅛-inch-thick 12-inch circle that will fit into the 9-inch pie pan or 10-inch tart pan.

5. Drape the piecrust over the rolling pin to lift it, then move it over the pie or tart pan and loosely place it in the pan. Try not to stretch the dough. Turn the extra edge under or, using a sharp knife, cut off the excess crust around the top edge. Crimp or flute the edges for pie. For a tart, simply roll the rolling pin across the top to cut off excess pastry.

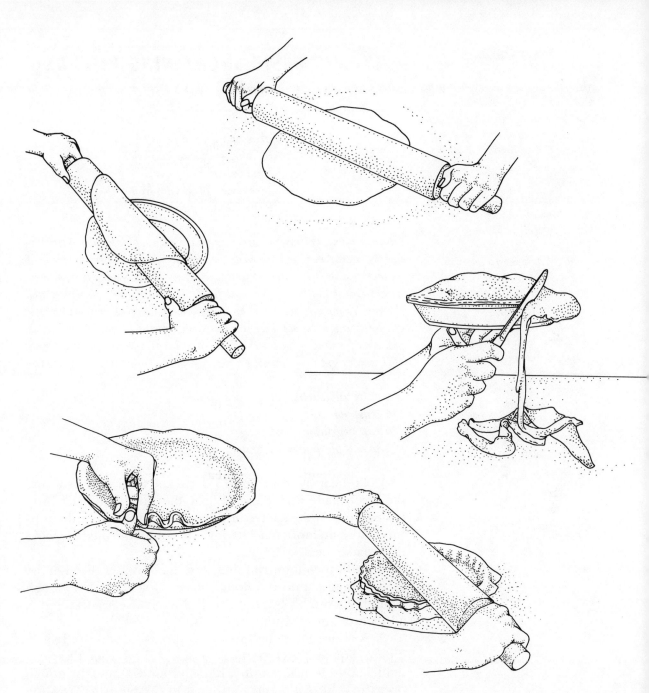

6. For a prebaked crust, prick the bottom and sides of the pastry with a fork, then bake in the preheated oven for 10 to 12 minutes, until beginning to brown. If you want the crust for a custard pie, bake it only 5 minutes, then fill it and continue baking as directed in your recipe.

About 3 cups of fruit sweetened to taste with sugar and sprinkled with flour make an ample pie filling. Use fruits alone or in combination. Cut or chop the fruit into bite-sized pieces. Dapple the top of the fruit with butter, season with the appropriate spices, and you've got an all-American pie.

Fruit combos we like:

- Rhubarb and strawberry or raspberry
- Pineapple and banana
- Apple and blackberry
- Orange and cranberry
- Coconut and lemon
- Queen Anne and Bing cherries
- Pears and crystallized ginger
- Peach and lemon zest
- Apricot with lime zest
- Figs and peaches

MOM'S BASIC SHORTENING PIECRUST MADE EASY

Makes one 2-crust pastry
10 minutes to prepare
12 minutes to bake blind
1 hour to bake filled with fruit
9- to 10-inch pie pan

OK. Admit it. Unless you grew up in a really sophisticated American family, most American piecrusts were made by our mothers and grandmothers using Crisco or—if you were lucky—lard. Today, we hunt for a shortening that's half animal fat (a.k.a. lard) and half vegetable shortening for piecrusts and biscuits. We like the flaky crust this kind of shortening gives us. Feel free to cut this recipe in half for a 1-crust pie. And for that apple pie that's as American as Mom and all the rest of it, you've got to begin with a piecrust made with shortening or lard.

2¼ cups unbleached all-purpose flour
½ teaspoon salt
¾ cup vegetable shortening
4 to 6 tablespoons ice water

1. Preheat the oven to 375° F. In the food processor, use the steel blade and pulse to mix the flour and salt. Drop tablespoons of the shortening evenly over the top of the mixture. Pulse no more than 10 times, just until the mixture looks like coarse meal.

2. With the motor running, add the ice water through the feed tube just until the dough masses together. The dough should be crumbly but not dry. If the mixture seems too dry, add a little more water, then pulse.

3. Remove the dough from the processor and divide it in 2 parts. Squeeze each part into a disk and roll each disk on a lightly floured surface into a 12-inch round. Drape the dough over the rolling pin and transfer it to the pie pan. Press the bottom and sides down carefully.

4. Fill the crust with fruit fillings, cover with the second layer, then squeeze the top and bottom crusts together, and finish by crimping or fluting. Bake until brown and bubbly in preheated oven, about 1 hour.

SHORTCUT PROCESSOR CRUST

Makes one 9-inch crust to serve 8

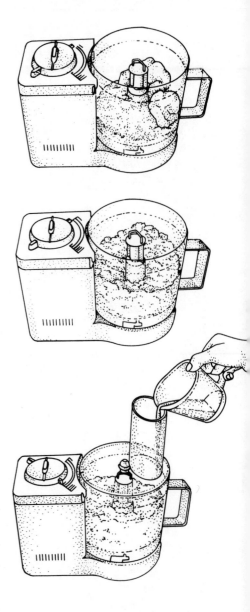

We agree with Julia Child. A food processor is worth the investment cost even if the only thing you use it for is to make pastry or piecrust. A double crust for a 9-inch pie literally can be made in 10 seconds or less. Another plus for this recipe is that it does not need a long chilling time before it can be rolled because the mixture of butter and shortening makes the dough more tender and supple.

1¾ cups unbleached all-purpose flour or pastry flour
  1 teaspoon salt
¾ cup (1½ sticks) butter, cut into 6 equal pieces
  2 tablespoons vegetable shortening, chilled
½ cup ice water

1. Fit the processor bowl with the steel blade. Add the flour and salt and pulse to blend. Add the butter and shortening and process for 5 seconds, until the fats are incorporated into the flour and are the size of small peas.

2. Turn on the machine and pour the water through the feed tube, holding back 2 tablespoons or so to see if they are needed. When the dough begins to mass around the blade, the pastry is done. Turn off the machine. This process should take no more than 6 to 8 seconds. Carefully remove the dough from the machine and flatten it into a disk shape. Wrap with plastic and chill for 20 minutes. The pastry is now ready to be rolled and shaped on a well-floured surface.

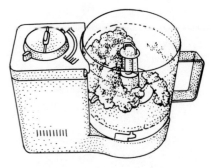

BASIC MICROWAVE PASTRY

Makes one 9-inch crust
10 minutes to prepare
6 to 7 minutes to bake in the microwave
9-inch glass pie pan

If your oven is occupied, and you still need to get a cooked piecrust ready, bake it in the microwave. Granted, the crust won't brown, but it will taste cooked, and, once it's covered up with filling, no one will see that it's as pale as Camille on her deathbed.

1 cup unbleached all-purpose flour
½ teaspoon salt
⅓ cup plus 1 tablespoon vegetable shortening
2 to 4 tablespoons ice water

1. In the food processor fitted with the steel blade combine the flour and salt. Pulse to mix. Drop the shortening over the flour mixture in tablespoon-sized chunks, then pulse to mix it to a texture like coarse meal, no more than 10 pulses.

2. With the motor running, drizzle in the ice water and process until the mixture forms a ball, no more than 20 seconds.

3. Squeeze the dough into a tight ball, then flatten into a disk, and then roll it into a 12-inch round on a lightly floured surface. Drape the dough over the rolling pin, then transfer it to a 9-inch glass pie pan. Press the dough down into the pan. Flute or crimp the edges. Prick the bottom and sides of the crust with a fork.

4. Place the piecrust into the microwave. Microwave at 100% (high) for 6 to 7 minutes, until the pastry is opaque and the bottom is dry. (If you want a browned look, run the crust under the broiler of your oven for about 30 seconds, until it's lightly browned.)

*F*AST AND FLAKY NO-ROLL SHORT CRUST

Makes one 11-inch tart shell to serve 6 to 8
15 minutes to prepare
20 to 25 minutes to bake
11-inch tart pan

We wanted a basic crust that would be delicate yet able to stand on its own; fast, so it must come out of a food processor; quick to form, so it could be pressed into the pan. This recipe fits the bill and as a bonus it adds only 2 teaspoons of fat per serving to a recipe.

1¼ **cups unbleached all-purpose flour**
½ **teaspoon salt**
1 **large egg yolk**
½ **teaspoon vanilla extract**
⅓ **cup (5⅓ tablespoons) unsalted butter, cold**
3 **to 4 tablespoons ice water**

1. Preheat the oven to 350° F. Fit the food processor with the steel blade and add the flour, salt, egg yolk, and vanilla. Pulse 3 or 4 times to blend. Rapidly cut the butter into tablespoon-sized pieces and drop them into the machine. Process for 5 to 10 seconds, until the butter bits are dispersed throughout the flour.

2. Stop the machine and add 3 tablespoons of cold water. Process for 5 to 10 seconds, just until the dough has begun to mass around the blade. If the dough does not mass around the blade in 10 seconds, with the machine running, slowly dribble the remaining tablespoon of water through the feed tube until it does. Carefully remove the dough from the machine to a lightly floured surface and form into a 5- to 6-inch-diameter disk.

3. If the dough seems a little sticky after it is removed from the machine, dust it lightly with a little extra flour. If the pastry seems dry, sprinkle on a few drops of water and knead in by hand.

4. The dough is now ready to be pressed into the tart pan. Coat the bottom of an 11-inch tart pan with cooking spray.

(continued)

Variations on Short Crust

Lemon or Orange Short Crust

Prepare Fast and Flaky No-Roll Short Crust, except add 1 teaspoon of finely minced lemon peel or orange peel to the flour in the processor bowl and substitute lemon juice or orange juice for the water.

Brown Sugar–Cinnamon Short Crust

Prepare Fast and Flaky No-Roll Short Crust, adding ¼ cup brown sugar, substituting milk for the water, and adding ½ teaspoon ground cinnamon to the flour in the processor bowl.

With your fingers, press the dough from the middle of the pan to the edges on the bottom and up the sides of the pan. Generously pierce the bottom and the crease of the dough along the edge of the pan with the tines of a fork. Bake on the middle rack of the preheated oven for 20 to 25 minutes, until lightly browned. Remove the crust to a rack to cool. When cool, remove the crust from the pan.

Crumb Crusts

Crumb crusts are a natural for microwave custard and pudding fillings. Here's where to put your best banana cream pie or your crème anglaise dappled with pistachio nuts. Any pie filling that doesn't require oven baking is a natural for a crumb crust.

COOKIE CRUMBLE CRUST

Makes one 9-inch piecrust
5 minutes to prepare
20 minutes to chill
9-inch pie pan and 8-inch pie pan

Nothing is easier than whizzing up crumbs in the food processor, drizzling them with butter, and pressing them into a pie pan. Choose a 9-inch pan to hold the crumbs, mash the crumbs with the bottom of an 8-inch pan that you've spritzed with cooking spray to shape the crust, and the shell is formed in a flash.

Besides graham crackers, you can also use vanilla wafers, Oreos (scrape out the white filling and discard) or other dark chocolate wafers, or your favorite shortbread-type cookies.

30 graham cracker squares or equal amount cookies to make 1½ cups crumbs
½ cup (1 stick) unsalted butter
2 tablespoons sugar or to taste

1. Break the crackers or cookies into pieces and process with the steel blade until you have about 1½ cups crumbs.
2. Microwave the butter in a microwavable dish at 100% (high) to melt, about 30 seconds.
3. Dump the crackers or cookies into a 9-inch pie pan. Drizzle the melted butter over all, and sprinkle on the sugar. Stir with a fork to moisten the crumbs. Then spritz the outside bottom of an 8-inch pie pan with cooking spray and press this over the crumbs to form the pie shell. Remove the 8-inch pan, and smooth any rough places with your hands. Chill the crust for 20 minutes or until you're ready to fill it.

Bride's Crust Revisited

Makes three 9- or 10-inch piecrusts
10 minutes to prepare
Three 9- or 10-inch pie pans

In the early 1950s every young bride had a copy of a recipe for "Bride's Crust" tucked safely away inside her cedar chest. Bride's Crust is so simple to make and roll, we see why it was the piecrust of choice for the novice baker as well as the experienced.

Bride's Crust can be rolled on a lightly floured surface as soon as it is removed from the processor. We use pie weights to weight the crust when we bake it empty. Dried beans can be used for this purpose also. The crust can be baked without using weights if you pierce the sides and bottom with the tines of a fork. This method may allow liquid fillings to leak through, however, and sometimes the pierced crusts crack as they cool.

The original recipe for Bride's Crust contained all lard. Lard assures the tenderest and flakiest crust possible. We added butter for the taste and kept some of the lard for the flakiness. Bride's Crust is especially compatible with mincemeat, apples, and dried fruits. We freeze an extra crust or two to use later when we're in a time crunch. Just thaw the extra crust on the countertop for 30 minutes, or until pliable, and roll, fill, and bake. If you have an extra supply of pie pans, you can roll the extra crust, fit it to the pan, wrap it, and freeze it in the pan. Don't worry if any small pieces chip off of the lip of the pastry; just wet them and press the chipped pieces back in their place.

2½ cups unbleached all-purpose flour
1 teaspoon salt
½ cup (1 stick) unsalted butter, cold
½ cup lard, chilled
½ cup or more ice water

1. Using the steel blade, pulse to mix the flour and salt in the processor bowl. Cut the butter and lard into tablespoon-sized pieces and add to the flour mixture. Pulse on and off just until the mixture has crumbs the size of small peas.

2. With the motor running, add the water through the feed tube just until the dough masses together. The dough should be crumbly but not dry. If the mixture will not mass

(continued)

In 1492, when apples were the most cultivated fruit in Europe, Spanish missionaries and explorers, including Columbus, brought them to America. Colonists selected seeds from the best European varieties and planted orchards. By 1741, apples from New England were being exported to the West Indies in the empty holds of slave ships.

together and seems too crumbly, add more ice water, 1 tablespoon at a time.

3. Remove the dough from the processor and divide into thirds. Each third will make one piecrust. The crusts may be frozen at this point for up to three months or refrigerated for up to three days. Roll each crust to a thickness of ⅛-inch and place in the pie pan. Trim and flute edges. The crust is now ready to be filled and baked or may be baked "blind" or empty.

4. To completely bake the piecrust, preheat the oven to 400° F.

5. Line the piecrust with a sheet of aluminum foil. Fill with the pie weights or dried beans. Bake until the edge of the crust looks opaque and feels set to the touch, about 10 minutes. Remove from the oven and discard the foil and weights from the crust.

6. Pierce the bottoms and sides with the tines of a fork. Return the crust to the oven. Check the crust several times during the remaining baking period and pierce again if the crust begins to puff up. Bake for an additional 15 minutes or until golden brown.

FAST FRENCH APPLE TARTS

Four 6-inch tarts to serve 4
15 minutes to prepare
25 minutes to bake
10 minutes to cool
Nonstick baking sheet

Tarts this fast and delicious are now our family favorites. The advantage here is to use frozen puff pastry available in 1-pound boxes in the frozen-food section of the supermarket. Each box contains 2 half-pound sheets. Two types are available, one made with vegetable shortening and one made with butter. The butter pastry is about twice the price of the shortening pastry; however, it tastes better and raises somewhat higher when placed into the preheated hot oven.

We usually pop the tarts into the oven just as we are sitting down to dinner. Then they are finished when we are and are ready to eat once the table is cleared and the coffee is ready. Serve them on your prettiest dessert plates and enjoy!

½ pound (1 sheet) frozen puff pastry, thawed
2 Granny Smith or other tart cooking apples
2 tablespoons packed light brown sugar
2 tablespoons granulated sugar
½ teaspoon ground cinnamon
⅛ teaspoon freshly grated nutmeg
1 tablespoon golden raisins (optional)
2 tablespoons unsalted butter, cold, cut into bits
4 tablespoons apricot jam
Vanilla ice cream

1. Preheat the oven to 400° F. On a lightly floured surface roll out the puff pastry to ¼ inch thick. Cut out four 6-inch rounds and transfer them to a nonstick baking sheet. A standard baking sheet lightly greased or sprayed with cooking spray or lined with parchment paper will do nicely.

2. Peel, core, and halve the apples lengthwise. Slice the apples thinly and arrange half an apple on each pastry round, overlapping the slices slightly. In a small bowl, combine the sugars, cinnamon, and nutmeg. Add the raisins if you wish. Sprinkle the mixture evenly over the tarts and tuck the raisins under the apple slices if they are used (this is to prevent them from browning and burning before the tarts are done). Sprinkle the tarts with the bits of butter and bake on the middle rack of the preheated oven for 25 minutes, or until the pastry is golden brown. Remove to a rack to cool.

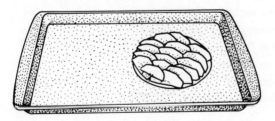

3. When the tarts are cooked, microwave the jam at 100% (high) for 45 seconds and using a pastry brush, brush the tops lightly with the liquid jam, avoiding the clumps of solid apricot. Return the solids to the jam jar. Serve the tarts warm with the vanilla ice cream.

TRIPLE-CRUST APPLE PIE WITH CINNAMON-CIDER SAUCE

Makes one 9-inch pie to serve 8
20 minutes to prepare
50 minutes to bake
9-inch glass pie pan

Don't panic. Yes, that's right, triple crust, but you only make one, and that in the food processor. Six Granny Smiths smothered with a traditional Dutch crumb crust and covered again with a crisp pastry crust, and if that's not enough, gild the lily with cinnamon-cider sauce made in 3½ minutes in the microwave.

1 teaspoon unbleached all-purpose flour
2 9-inch unbaked piecrusts, 1 <u>double</u> recipe of Basic Butter Crust (see page 56) or store-bought

CRUMB CRUST

¼ cup granulated sugar
¼ cup packed light brown sugar
¾ cup unbleached all-purpose flour
⅓ cup (5⅓ tablespoons) unsalted butter, softened

APPLE FILLING

6 Granny Smith or other tart cooking apples
¼ cup firmly packed light brown sugar
½ cup granulated sugar
1 tablespoon fresh lemon juice
¼ teaspoon freshly grated nutmeg
½ teaspoon ground cinnamon
¼ teaspoon salt
3 tablespoons unbleached all-purpose flour

CINNAMON-CIDER SAUCE

1 tablespoon cornstarch
½ cup granulated sugar
⅛ teaspoon ground cinnamon
⅛ teaspoon freshly grated nutmeg

*1 cup apple juice (Granny Smith apple juice commercially made
is wonderful if it is available in your area) or apple cider*
1 tablespoon fresh lemon juice
2 tablespoons unsalted butter, cut into bits

1. Remove 1 rack from the oven and place the other oven rack in the lower third of the oven. Preheat to 475° F. Sprinkle the bottom of a 9-inch glass pie pan with the flour. Carefully open and lay one of the prepared crusts in the pie pan, gently patting it into the bottom and side of the pan. Set aside.

2. For the crumb crust, in the bowl of a food processor fitted with the steel blade, combine the ¼ cup sugar, ¼ cup light brown sugar, and ¾ cup flour. Pulse several times to combine. Add the ⅓ cup butter cut into tablespoon-sized pieces and process with on-off turns until the mixture forms crumbs the size of small peas. Remove from the processor bowl and set aside.

3. For the apple filling, replace the processor bowl on the base and add the slicing blade. Peel and core the apples. Slice them in the food processor. Measure out 5½ cups sliced apples (do not use more than this amount or the pie will not thicken). Place the apples in a large mixing bowl and toss them with the sugars, lemon juice, nutmeg, cinnamon, salt, and flour.

4. Pile the apples into the pie pan and press down lightly. Cover with the crumb topping (the pie will look very tall, but that's OK). Cover the crumb crust with the remaining prepared piecrust. Trim and crimp the edges. Make four 1-inch slits in the top crust to allow steam to escape.

5. Bake for 10 minutes on the bottom rack of the preheated oven. After 10 minutes, carefully remove the pie from the oven and place the second rack back in the middle of the oven. Reduce the oven temperature to 375° F and place the pie back in the oven on the middle rack. Bake for an additional 40 minutes, until the juices bubble and the crust is nicely browned. Remove to a rack to cool.

6. Meanwhile, prepare the cinnamon-cider sauce. Combine the cornstarch, sugar, cinnamon, and nutmeg in a 4-cup glass measure. Whisk in the apple juice or cider and lemon juice. Microwave at 100% (high) until it starts to boil, about 2½ minutes. Boil for 1 minute. Remove from the microwave and whisk in butter bits. Serve warm over the pie.

The Right Apple

Looking for great cooking apples? Try some of these alone or combine varieties in your favorite apple dishes.

Stayman-Winesap
Cortland
Jonathan
Rhode Island Greening
McIntosh
Macoun
York Imperial
Northern Spy
Newtown Pippin
Yellow Transparent

The following apples are considered all-purpose apples and may also be used for cooking: Rome Beauty, Baldwin, Wealthy, and Gravenstein.

SHORTCUT TARTE TATIN

Makes one 9-inch pie
20 minutes to prepare
35 minutes to bake
9-inch metal pie pan

One of France's best fruit desserts, the tarte tatin *made by the tradi-tional method demands almost constant attention for about a half hour plus 20 minutes or so in the oven, then a cooling period of 20 more minutes before you can serve the delectable dessert.*

Borrowing a restaurant technique for caramelizing sugar that cuts the time for that step down to about 1 minute, making quick work of the fruit preparation by simply coring fruits with the skins on, then using a prepared piecrust, you can be eating the tatin *in the time it takes to do the* first *customary step.*

Use the fruits of your choice. Apples are the traditional favorite. Here in the Rogue Valley, we adore pear tatins. You can use bananas, kiwis, peaches, apricots, plums, nectarines, even persimmons. If you're feeling adventuresome, combine 2 fruits. Peaches and blueberries work quite well.

But whatever fruit you choose, layer it neatly over the caramelized sugar so that when you turn the pan upside down, after baking, the single-crust tart will feed the eyes first.

¾ cup sugar, divided
¼ cup (½ stick) unsalted butter
8 medium cooking apples or pears (about 3 cups fruit slices)
1 9-inch unbaked piecrust, homemade or store-bought
Cream

1. Preheat the oven to 375° F. Place ½ cup of the sugar in a 9-inch metal pie pan. Using tongs, place the pan directly over a burner set at medium and heat until the sugar begins to melt and turn golden. Lift the pan off the heat source with the tongs and shake it so that the sugar won't burn but will caramelize evenly. When the mixture is golden brown, re-move the pan from the heat source.

2. Dot the surface with chips of butter and stir. Wash and core the fruit. Cut the fruit in halves or other good-sized, attractive-looking chunks or slices. Arrange the fruit, skin side down, over the caramelized sugar and butter. Continue layering the fruit until it is even with the top of the pan. Sprinkle the remaining ¼ cup of sugar over the top.

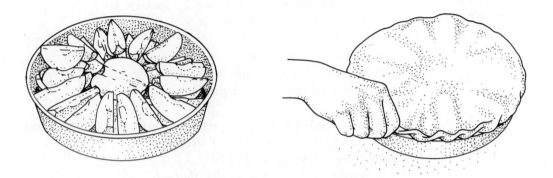

3. Place the prepared piecrust over the top of the fruit. Press the dough against the pie pan to seal the edges, then make a zigzag fluted edge, using your fingers.

4. Bake the tart in the preheated oven until the crust is a light golden brown, about 35 minutes. Remove to a rack to cool for about 5 minutes before inverting on a serving plate.

5. To serve, loosen the crust from the edge of the pie pan with a sharp knife. Place a flat serving dish or platter over the tart, then quickly invert the dish. Serve immediately. Pool a little cream on dessert dishes and serve the pie wedges in the cream, scooping up the golden caramel and drizzling it over the top of the fruit.

Fresh blueberries are available June through August in most areas of the United States. We freeze or dehydrate them to use in the winter. Look for large berries that are dark blue, plump, and wrinkle free. Discard any green berries or berries with mold. Dried blueberries have a concentrated blueberry flavor and are delicious when mixed in with frozen berries in your favorite muffin recipe.

BRAMBLEBERRY PIE WITH BRIDE'S CRUST

Makes one 9-inch pie to serve 6 to 8
15 minutes to prepare
55 minutes to 1 hour and 5 minutes to bake
9-inch pie pan

Be sure to try this one. When the berries are in season in June and July, we serve it once a week. Frozen berries work equally well in the off-season. You and your guests will eat it up.

1 9-inch unbaked piecrust, ⅓ recipe (1 crust) of Bride's Crust Revisited (see page 63), or store-bought
1 large egg white, lightly beaten
4 cups fresh or frozen blueberries, thawed
⅔ cup sugar
4 tablespoons unbleached all-purpose flour
¼ teaspoon ground cinnamon
¼ teaspoon ground nutmeg
1 tablespoon fresh lemon juice
2 tablespoons unsalted butter, cut into bits

1. Preheat the oven to 425° F. Lay the prepared piecrust or the Bride's Crust rolled ⅛-inch thick into a 9-inch pie pan. Trim and flute the edges. Brush the bottom of the piecrust with 2 tablespoons of the lightly beaten egg white. Discard the remaining egg white or use it to glaze the twisted crust strips in step 2 if they are being used.

2. In a large bowl toss the blueberries, sugar, flour, cinnamon, nutmeg, and lemon juice. Transfer the mixture to the piecrust. Dot with the butter. Reroll any remaining scraps if using Bride's Crust. Cut them into ½-inch-wide strips and twist each strip several times. Starting in the center, place the twisted strips spoke fashion on the top of the pie. Glaze the strips with the remaining egg white.

3. Bake the pie on the middle rack of the preheated oven for 25 minutes. Reduce the heat to 350° F and bake for an additional 30 to 40 minutes, until the center bubbles and the crust is brown. If the rim of the pie browns too quickly, cover

it with aluminum foil strips and continue to bake. Cool to room temperature and serve.

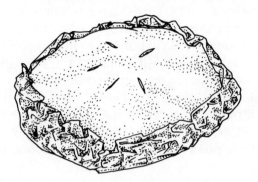

ALOHA PIE: CHOCOLATE, PINEAPPLE, AND MACADAMIA NUTS IN A BUTTER CRUST

Makes one 9-inch pie
30 minutes to prepare
1 hour to chill
9-inch pie pan

PUDDING

1⅓ cups sugar
½ cup unbleached all-purpose flour
½ teaspoon salt
3 cups half-and-half
3 large egg yolks, slightly beaten
2 tablespoons unsalted butter
1 tablespoon vanilla extract
1 8-ounce can (1 cup) crushed pineapple, drained
3 ounces (3 squares) unsweetened chocolate
¾ cup macadamia nuts, divided

1 recipe Basic Butter Crust (see page 56), baked
⅓ cup sweetened shredded coconut
   Whipped cream (optional)

(continued)

1. For the pudding, in a 2-quart microwavable bowl combine the sugar, flour, salt, and half-and-half. Whisk to mix thoroughly. Microwave at 100% (high) for 4 minutes, whisk, then microwave at 100% (high) for 3 minutes. Whisk. Pour a small amount of the hot pudding into the beaten egg yolks, whisking thoroughly, then pour the mixture back into the pudding, whisking again. Microwave at 100% (high) an additional minute. Whisk in the butter and vanilla.

2. Divide the pudding into 2 equal parts. Fold the drained pineapple into one part. Micro-melt the chocolate in a microwavable bowl at 100% (high) for 2 minutes, until melted, then blend the melted chocolate into the second part of the pudding.

3. Sprinkle half the macadamia nuts onto the baked pie shell. Spoon ⅔ of the chocolate pudding over the nuts. Spoon all the pineapple pudding over the chocolate. Sprinkle with the coconut. Drizzle the remaining chocolate pudding over the yellow pineapple layer, making a 2-colored top. Arrange the remaining macadamia nuts over the top. Refrigerate at least an hour before serving. Top each wedge with a dollop of whipped cream if you wish.

Swiss Tart with Fresh Fruit of the Season

Makes one 12-inch tart
20 minutes to prepare
20 minutes to bake
12-inch tart pan with a removable bottom

If pastry making is your nemesis, do try this one. It's too easy and so delicious. A cheesy short paste topped with coconut, then finished with fruit of the season, it's gorgeous. Try blood oranges and kiwi. Grapefruit and pomegranate seeds. Strawberries and bananas. Red-flame-grapes and honeydew melon. What fruits do you like together?

½ cup (1 stick) unsalted butter
¼ cup sugar
¼ teaspoon salt
3 ounces (1 cup) shredded Swiss cheese
1¼ cups unbleached all-purpose flour
2 tablespoons half-and-half
1 cup sweetened shredded coconut
2 cups fruit of the season
⅓ cup apple jelly or orange marmalade
½ teaspoon spirits of your choice: brandy, crème de cassis, bourbon, rum (optional)

1. Preheat the oven to 375° F. Fit the processor bowl with the steel blade, then combine the butter, sugar, and salt. Pulse to mix. Now add the shredded cheese, flour, and half-and-half. Process to make a ball (about 20 seconds). Dump the mixture into a 12-inch tart pan with a removable bottom. Spread and pat the mixture over the bottom and up the sides, creating a slight lip around the edge.

2. Bake the tart shell in the preheated oven for 5 minutes. Remove it from the oven and sprinkle it evenly with the coconut. Return it to the oven and continue baking for 15 minutes, until the crust is lightly browned. Cool the crust in the pan on a rack.

3. While the crust is baking, prepare the fruits. Peel, seed, and cut the fruits into attractive, thin slices. Once the crust is baked, arrange the fruits artfully on the top. If you're using strawberries, don't slice them at all, just hull them and set the bottoms down onto the crust in rows alternating with kiwi or banana slices, for example. Leave berries whole.

4. Place apple jelly or orange marmalade in a 2-cup glass measure and microwave at 100% (high) for about 30 seconds, until bubbly. Stir in the spirits, if desired, then drizzle the glaze over the fruit.

5. Serve the tart the same day it's made, at room temperature or chilled. A dollop of whipped cream is always a welcome addition.

STRAWBERRY GLAZE PIE

Makes one 9-inch pie to serve 6 to 8
20 minutes to prepare
25 minutes to bake
1 hour to chill
9-inch pie pan

A dessert they will praise—an open-faced pie filled with shiny, red strawberries. This beauty tastes as good as it looks.

> 5 pints ripe strawberries, hulled
> 1 cup granulated sugar
> 3 tablespoons cornstarch
> ½ cup water
> 1 tablespoon unsalted butter
> 1 9-inch unbaked piecrust, ⅓ recipe (1 crust) Bride's Crust Revisited (see page 63), or store-bought
> 1 cup whipping cream, chilled
> 2 tablespoons confectioners' sugar

1. Fit the processor with the steel blade and process enough berries for 1 cup of puree (about 1 pint). In a microwavable bowl, combine the sugar and cornstarch and stir to blend. Add the puree and water.

2. Microwave the mixture at 70% (medium) for 9 minutes, stirring well with a wooden spoon after every 3 minutes. The mixture will be thick and translucent. Add the butter and stir until it's melted. Cool.

3. Pile the remaining strawberries in the baked piecrust and spoon the cooled glaze over all. Chill for at least 1 hour.

4. Fit the processor bowl with the steel blade. Process the cream until thickened. Add the sugar gradually, 1 tablespoon at a time, through the feed tube, and process until stiff. Refrigerate until serving time. Top the pie with the whipped cream just before serving. This pie is best eaten the day it's made.

PEAR-COCONUT PIE

Makes one 9-inch pie to serve 8
25 minutes to prepare
55 minutes to 1 hour to bake
9-inch pie pan

Don't you love sweet and tart flavors together? Use field pears, winter Comice pears, or substitute tart green apples, and you'll discover a dessert that hits all the bases. It's sweet, tart, crunchy, and satisfying. Use a prepared piecrust, and this 1-crust pie becomes too easy.

> Zest and juice of ½ lemon (about ¼ cup)
> 3 medium pears, peeled, cored, and sliced
> 1 9-inch piecrust unbaked, homemade or store-bought
> ⅔ cup sugar, divided
> 2 tablespoons butter
> Ground cinnamon
> 2 cups sweetened shredded coconut
> ½ cup half-and-half
> 1 large egg
> 1 teaspoon vanilla extract

1. Preheat the oven to 425° F. Place the lemon zest and juice in a medium bowl. Toss the pear slices into the bowl, turning to coat the surfaces with lemon juice. Pour the fruit, juice, and zest into the prepared piecrust. Sprinkle ⅓ cup of the sugar over the fruit, dot with the butter, and dust with cinnamon.

2. Place the pie in the lower third of the preheated oven and bake until the crust is golden, about 25 minutes.

3. Meanwhile, combine the coconut, half-and-half, egg, remaining ⅓ cup of sugar, and vanilla. Stir to mix.

4. Remove the pie from the oven and pour the coconut mixture over it, evenly covering the pears. Tent the edges of the piecrust with foil to prevent burning, lower the oven temperature to 325° F, and replace the pie in the oven.

5. Bake the pie until the coconut custard is cooked through and toasted evenly on the top, about 30 to 35 minutes. Remove to a rack to cool.

Picking Perfect Pears

You can't judge a pear by its color. Only Bartletts turn yellow. Winter pears such as Bosc, Anjou, Comice, and Seckel most likely won't be ripe when you first buy them. Leave them in your warm kitchen for a few days and they'll ripen—but they won't look much different. To determine ripeness, give a little squeeze up near the stem end with your thumb. If the pear yields to the gentle pressure, you have a ripe pear. Now, cut into it and you'll find it sweet, tender, and dripping with juice.

If you'd like to speed up the ripening process, place the pears in a bowl, preferably with a ripe apple, cover and leave them in your warm kitchen. Then when they're ripe, refrigerate until you're ready to use.

If you wish to delay ripening, store pears in the refrigerator. Most varieties except Bartlett will keep for weeks in the refrigerator.

COMICE PEAR–MINCEMEAT TART

Serves 8
30 minutes to prepare
45 minutes to bake
9-inch tart pan

A tart is simply an open-faced pie, usually cooked in a fluted, straight-sided tart pan instead of a traditional pie pan. With intense flavors, such as this pear-mincemeat flavor, a small serving will do—a thin wedge of tart is ideal. You can also make individual tarts if you have twice the time and patience. Just 3 or 4 bites to the serving, they're lovely for special occasions. The tart is delicious served with vanilla ice cream or a dollop of unsweetened whipped cream. Sometimes we put a few drops of brandy in the cream.

   1 recipe Basic Butter Crust (see page 56), unbaked
   2 large Comice pears
½ teaspoon cornstarch
   Zest and juice (about ¼ cup) of ½ lemon
   1 9-ounce package condensed mincemeat, crumbled
   1 cup apple juice
   1 teaspoon sugar

1. Preheat the oven to 375° F. Gather the dough of the butter crust in your hands and form it into a soft ball, then flatten into a disk, and wrap the dough in plastic and refrigerate it for 15 minutes.

2. While the dough is chilling, make the filling. Core, then coarsely chop 1 pear in the food processor, using the metal blade and pulsing 4 or 5 times. Add the cornstarch and lemon zest and juice and stir to mix.

3. Combine the prepared mincemeat and apple juice in a microwavable dish and raise to a boil in the microwave set on 100% (high), about 3 minutes. Stir, then boil 30 seconds more. Remove from the microwave and combine with the chopped pear and set aside.

4. To make the tart, remove the chilled dough from the refrigerator, and roll it between sheets of plastic wrap or waxed paper into a 10-inch circle. Place the circle in the freezer for a few moments until the paper peels off readily.

5. Fit the dough into a 9-inch tart pan, prick the dough with a fork, and parbake the tart shell until lightly browned, about 18 to 20 minutes.

6. Spoon the pear-mincemeat mixture into the tart shell. Now core and peel the remaining pear. Cut the pear in half lengthwise, cutting the stem in half if possible. Slice each half into about 6 thin slices, leaving the pear attached at the stem end so you can fan each pear half out over the top of the tart. Sprinkle with the sugar.

7. Place the tart in the preheated oven and turn the oven down to 350° F. Bake for 25 minutes. Cool on a rack.

Anjou, *available from October to May, are lovely egg-shaped light green or yellow-green pears that are sometimes more difficult to ripen than others. These are best when eaten fresh, but are also wonderful in crisps, pandowdies, and pies.*

Bartletts, *available from August to December, are both yellow and red and shaped like a bell, and terrific for eating fresh or used as a garnish on top of a cake or focaccia. Bartletts are frequently canned. In France they are called "Williams."*

Bosc, *available from September to May, these dusky brown pears with long tapered necks are so gorgeous you may be tempted to use them for decoration. They are also ideal cooking pears, whether baked, broiled, or poached. Their flesh is tender, buttery, and aromatic.*

Comice, *available from October to March, have been made famous by mail-order houses such as Harry & David and Pinnacle. They are greenish chubby pears that when ripened are so good and tender you could eat them with a spoon—which is what many people do. They also can be used in baking because they are super sweet and peary tasting.*

Seckels, *available from August to January, are little bite-sized green pears with a red blush. As they ripen the red and green colors intensify. The flesh is a warm light ivory color. These are best eaten fresh.*

If some of your pie pans are old
family friends handed down from
aunts, grandmothers, and mothers and show the full life they've
led with nicks and scars, you can
dress them up by setting the pie
inside a lined basket made beautiful with fabric, a doily, or a colorful napkin. Present the pie as a
gift, and the lucky person who re-
ceives the pie also gets a basket to
keep after the pie is just a memory.
But tell them you want your mama's pie pan back.

Tuck fresh flowers of the season
in around the edge of the basket, or
if the pie is fruit, add the same
whole fruit to the basket for a
mouth-watering garnish.

COCONUT-CUSTARD CREAM PIE

Makes one 9-inch pie to serve 6 to 8
10 minutes to prepare
40 to 50 minutes to bake
2 hours to chill
9-inch deep-dish pie pan

A pie that forms its own crust while it bakes makes this recipe especially
speedy. To make a piña colada version, garnish the pie with additional sweetened whipped cream and pineapple slices. Sprinkle with 1
tablespoon or so of Jamaican rum.

½ cup unbleached all-purpose flour
¾ cup sugar
1 cup milk
1 cup whipping cream
4 large eggs
¼ cup (½ stick) unsalted butter, melted
1 tablespoon vanilla extract
¼ teaspoon salt
2 cups lightly packed, sweetened shredded coconut

1. Preheat the oven to 350° F. In the bowl of the food
processor fitted with the steel blade, process the flour, sugar,
milk, whipping cream, eggs, butter, vanilla, and salt for 10
seconds. Pour the mixture into a lightly greased 9-inch deep-
dish pie pan. Let it sit for 5 minutes.

2. Sprinkle the top of the pie with the coconut and push
it down into the liquid with the back of a spoon. Bake on the
middle rack of the preheated oven for 40 to 50 minutes, until
the middle is set and the coconut is lightly browned. Remove
to a rack to cool to room temperature and then refrigerate
until well chilled, about 2 hours. This pie is best served the
same day as made.

TASTE-OF-TEXAS BEST PECAN PIE

Makes one 9-inch pie to serve 8
15 minutes to prepare
50 minutes to bake
9-inch pie pan

You'd be surprised how many recipes float through the South for pecan pie. Everyone is sure theirs is the best. Even though Texas bakers began cooking this pie filling on a wood stove, I'm sure they'll applaud the use of the microwave to melt the sugar and make a perfect beginning for that divine opalescent custard that floats a colony of crunchy pecans.

¾ cup sugar
½ teaspoon salt
1 cup dark corn syrup
1 cup (2 sticks) unsalted butter
1 teaspoon vanilla extract
3 large eggs
1¼ cups coarsely chopped pecans
1 9-inch unbaked piecrust, homemade or store-bought

1. Preheat the oven to 325° F. Place the sugar, salt, corn syrup, and butter in a 2-quart microwavable bowl and stir to mix. Microwave, uncovered, at 100% (high) for 2½ minutes. Remove from the microwave and stir to mix and complete the melting of both the butter and the sugar granules.

2. Add the vanilla and eggs to the hot syrup and whisk briskly with a balloon whisk until the mixture is foamy. Stir in the pecans, then pour into the prepared piecrust.

3. Bake the pie in the preheated oven until a knife inserted into the filling comes out clean, about 50 minutes. Cool on a rack.

PEANUT BUTTER PIE

Makes one 9-inch pie
20 minutes to prepare
1 hour to chill
9-inch pie pan

Dredged up from Mama's flour-spotted recipe box, this pie is easy to make and sure to please.

FILLING

1 cup confectioners' sugar
½ cup creamy peanut butter
1 9-inch piecrust, baked, homemade or store-bought
2 cups half-and-half
⅔ cup granulated sugar
3 tablespoons cornstarch
⅛ teaspoon salt
3 egg yolks
¼ teaspoon vanilla extract
1 cup whipping cream

1. Combine the confectioners' sugar and peanut butter in the food processor bowl fitted with the steel blade and process until the mixture resembles coarse meal. Spread ⅔ of this mixture over the baked piecrust and set aside. Reserve the last third to top the pie.

2. Combine the half-and-half with the sugar, cornstarch, and salt in a microwavable bowl. Heat this cream custard in the microwave at 100% (high) for 4 minutes. Whisk with a balloon whisk.

3. Whisk a little hot cream custard into the egg yolks, then pour all this mixture into the hot cream custard and return to the microwave and heat at 100% (high) for an additional 2 minutes, until the mixture is thick. Whisk, then whisk in the vanilla.

4. Pour the cooked custard over the peanut butter mixture, cover, and refrigerate until serving time, at least 1 hour.

5. Just before serving, beat the whipping cream to soft peaks in the food processor (see page 17), then spread it over the chilled pie. Sprinkle the reserved peanut butter crumbles over the top and serve.

BUTTERMILK CHESS PIE

Makes one 9-inch pie
10 minutes to prepare
45 to 50 minutes to bake
9-inch pie pan

Tangy Buttermilk Chess Pie is divine with fresh blueberries or straw-berries on top. Make a glaze by heating some clear apple jelly and brushing it over the ripe fruit. Heaven.

½ cup (1 stick) unsalted butter
2 cups sugar
3 tablespoons unbleached all-purpose flour
3 large eggs
1 teaspoon vanilla extract
¼ teaspoon almond extract
1 cup buttermilk
1 9-inch piecrust unbaked, homemade or store-bought
  Dash freshly grated nutmeg

1. Preheat the oven to 425° F. In the processor bowl fitted with the steel blade, cream the butter, sugar, and flour until the mixture resembles coarse meal (count to 10). Add the eggs, one at a time, through the feed tube with the motor running. Add the vanilla, almond extract, and buttermilk.

2. Pour the filling into the prepared crust, sprinkle the top with nutmeg, and bake in the preheated oven for 10 minutes, then reduce the heat to 350° F and continue cooking 35 to 40 minutes, just until the custard sets. (It shouldn't tremble.) Cool on a rack.

❖   ❖

Although the story is apocryphal, it has the ring of truth to it that the origin of chess pie was some fine old gentleman of the South who was heard to exclaim, "Mama, git me some of that pie out the chess for supper." To which Mama replied, "One chess pie, comin' up."

Buying Lemons

Buy lemons that are large, shiny, bright yellow, heavy, and unwrinkled. If the lemons are dull and light, they have lost some of their juice and are beginning to spoil. Lemons are in season and cheapest from December through March.

For herbs that have the same fresh, clean scent, try lemon balm and lemon mint. Lemon balm goes well with jellies, jams, and fruit and can be grown indoors or out. Lemon mint in iced tea, salads, and salad dressings adds a lemon flavor and citrusy scent.

LAUREN'S PUCKERY LEMON MERINGUE PIE

Makes one 9-inch pie to serve 6 to 8
20 minutes to prepare
2 hours to cool
9-inch pie pan

Good cooks usually start at an early age, in this case 10 years old. Lauren loves lemons and has cooked her way through the entire section of lemon recipes in her grandmother's old cookbook. Mom helped her update this recipe by using the microwave and a prepared piecrust.

Be sure to stir only with a wooden spoon or plastic spoon because the acid combined with the heat can corrode a metal whisk or spoon just enough to give the filling a metallic taste.

1½ cups sugar, divided
⅓ cup cornstarch
   Pinch of salt
2 cups water
   Zest of 1 lemon, minced
¼ cup (½ stick) unsalted butter
4 large eggs, separated
½ cup plus 2 teaspoons fresh lemon juice (juice of 2 or 3 lemons)
1 prepared 9-inch piecrust or your favorite crust, baked and cooled

1. In a 2-quart microwavable mixing bowl, combine 1 cup of the sugar, cornstarch, and salt. Mix well. Blend in the water and lemon zest. Microwave at 100% (high) for 6 minutes, stirring with a wooden spoon after every 3 minutes. Add the butter and stir until melted.

2. In a small mixing bowl, lightly stir together the egg yolks and ½ cup lemon juice. Pour about ½ cup of the hot mixture into the egg yolks and lemon juice. Stir well with a wooden or plastic spoon. Pour the egg yolk mixture back into the hot mixture and stir well.

3. Microwave on 100% (high) for 4 minutes, stirring with a wooden spoon after every 2 minutes. Cool for 5 minutes and then pour into the baked piecrust.

4. Preheat the oven to 400° F. Meanwhile, warm the egg whites (see page 18). Place the egg whites in the bowl of the food processor fitted with a plastic or steel blade (see pages 19–20). Process for 10 seconds, add the remaining 2 teaspoons lemon juice, and process until the foam just begins to hold a shape and the egg whites are still dull. Gradually add the remaining ½ cup sugar a tablespoon at a time through the feed tube and process just until the egg whites will hold a peak when lifted with a spoon. Do not overprocess the egg whites, or the meringue will not spread easily over the pie. Pile the meringue evenly on the pie and spread to the edge, touching the crust. Bake on the middle rack of the preheated oven for 4 to 6 minutes, until the meringue is golden brown. Cool completely, about 2 hours. Serve at room temperature.

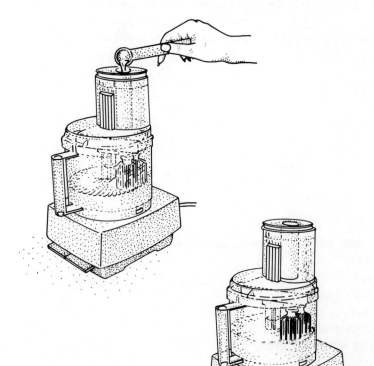

Raspberry Coulis

You can also make individual tarts using this filling; you'll get at least 10 tarts from this recipe. If you wish to make a 4-star dessert from this recipe, finish it with a raspberry-red puree, what the French call coulis. *Ladle a generous tablespoon of* coulis *onto a dessert plate, then top with a slice of lime tart. If you make individual tarts, top each tart with a dessert spoon of Raspberry Coulis and a jot of whipped cream.*

1 pint fresh raspberries
1 tablespoon sugar
1 tablespoon light corn syrup

1. *Combine the raspberries, sugar, and corn syrup in the food processor fitted with the steel blade. Puree until smooth.*

2. *Pour the puree through a strainer to remove the seeds, then store for up to 2 weeks, refrigerated, in a clean, covered jar.*

ORANGE-LIME TART

Makes one 12-inch tart to serve 8 to 10
20 minutes to prepare
12 minutes to bake
1 hour to chill
12-inch tart pan with removable bottom

Begin with a prepared piecrust, except slide it into a 12-inch tart pan instead of a pie pan. Heat the citrus in the microwave before you squeeze so that you'll get every last drop of that good juice, and you're on your way to an Orange-Lime Tart that's rich and delicious. Both sweet and puckery sour, this buttercup-yellow tart is smooth as slipper satin.

To garnish this and other citrus desserts, use the back side of a lemon zester to scrape off green snakes of lime peel. Roll this peel in granulated sugar, then decorate the top of the tart. Easy and gorgeous.

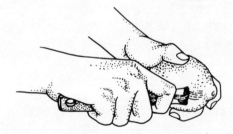

1 9-inch unbaked piecrust, homemade or store-bought
4 limes
2 oranges
¾ cup sugar
¼ cup (½ stick) unsalted butter
2 tablespoons cornstarch
½ cup whipping cream
2 large eggs
6 large egg yolks
  Lime and/or orange zest, cut in strips and rolled in sugar, for garnish
  Whipped cream, for garnish

1. Preheat the oven to 425° F. Place the prepared piecrust in a 12-inch tart tin with a removable bottom. Press the dough carefully into the corners and up the sides. Press the dough against the sharp rippled edge to cut off the excess. Prick the dough thoroughly using the tines of a fork, then bake in the preheated oven until it's golden brown all over, about 12 minutes.

2. Meanwhile, make the filling. First, before juicing them, microwave the limes and oranges a minute at 100% (high) until they're warm to the touch. Then squeeze the fruit to make about ¾ cup lime juice and about ½ cup orange juice. Add water if necessary to get the correct volume.

3. Combine the lime and orange juices with the sugar and butter in a microwavable dish and microwave at 100% (high) for 3 minutes.

4. While that's heating, stir the cornstarch into the whipping cream and mix thoroughly. Then add the eggs and egg yolks to the cream. Whisk with a balloon whisk to mix thoroughly.

5. Whisk the egg-cream mixture into the hot citrus juice, then return the mixture to the microwave. Microwave for 2 minutes at 100% (high), then remove and whisk thoroughly with the balloon whisk. Microwave an additional 1 minute at 70% (medium-high). Whisk thoroughly. The mixture should be thick and smooth.

6. Pour the tart filling into the browned crust. Garnish with lime or orange zest. Chill at least 1 hour. Top each wedge with a dollop of whipped cream before serving.

Years before vanilla was discovered, brandy and cognac were used to flavor cakes. Not only do they help preserve the cake and add their own spirited taste, they have a leavening power that makes the product lighter.

Pure vanilla extract is sublime and very easy to make. Ounce for ounce it's cheaper than commercially prepared "pure" vanilla extract.

To make 5 ounces of vanilla, you will need 2 vanilla beans, ½ cup plus 2 tablespoons of 190-proof grain alcohol, and an airtight, sterile glass container. Slit the vanilla beans lengthwise to expose the hundreds of black seeds. Then cut the beans crosswise into 1-inch pieces. Add the beans and the alcohol to the container and seal. Shake the bottle every other day for 2 to 3 weeks. The vanilla beans may be used again for 2 or 3 more batches; after that toss the beans and start over with fresh ones. Store at room temperature for up to 6 months.

PASTRY CREAM

Makes 1½ cups
5 minutes to prepare
1 hour to several days to chill
2-quart microwavable bowl

Use this cream to fill pies and tarts. Scented with the finest vanilla extract, it makes a splendid base for a variety of fresh fruits and berries that you might want to showcase on top: strawberries, olallieberries, blackberries, raspberries, kiwis, peaches, mangoes, papayas—any berries or fruits that taste divine picked fresh, sliced artfully or stood on their heads, and served soon.

Squeeze the juice of an orange into the cream, add some zest, and you've made a base for an orange cream pie. Spoon the orange cream filling into a baked nut crust, then top with sliced oranges, overlapped and fanned over the top. Tangerines? Same thing. Blood oranges? That red-tinged juice stirred into pastry cream, then spooned into a sweet butter crust and topped with overlapping paper-thin slices of blood oranges, makes a dessert that takes your breath away.

For the simplest pie of all, bake the piecrust of your choice empty, then spoon in pastry cream and top with whipped cream, unsweetened but nipped with brandy or bourbon.

3 large egg yolks
1 cup milk or half-and-half
⅓ cup sugar
    Pinch of salt
¼ cup cornstarch
1½ teaspoons vanilla extract, rum, or kirsch
1 tablespoon unsalted butter

1. In a 2-quart microwavable bowl place the egg yolks, and whisk until ropy and well blended. Add the milk or half-and-half and whisk again until the mixture is foamy, about 30 seconds.

2. Combine the sugar, salt, and cornstarch. Stir to mix thoroughly with a fork, then dump the dry ingredients into the egg mixture. Whisk to mix thoroughly.

3. Microwave at 100% (high) for 1½ minutes. Remove from the microwave and whisk thoroughly, until the mixture is perfectly smooth. Microwave again at 100% (high) for 1 more minute. Remove from the microwave and whisk thoroughly. Whisk in the vanilla or other flavoring and the butter. If the cream seems too thick, add a few drops of milk or half-and-half to thin.

4. Cover with plastic wrap that you fit carefully onto the top of the cream so that it won't form a skin, and refrigerate until you're ready to assemble the pie.

5. Always spoon this cream into a *baked* pie shell. Top with berries or fruit if desired. It's also good with whipped cream.

Coconut Swirls

To make fresh coconut swirls, crack open and drain a fresh coconut. Pry out a large piece of coconut meat. Run a potato peeler along the edge of the coconut to make swirls.

POOLSIDE RUM PIE

Makes one 10-inch pie to serve 8
30 minutes to prepare
1 hour and 30 minutes to chill
10-inch pie pan

Warm tropical breezes, palm leaves waving, warm sugar sand. Whoa! Where are the plane tickets? Meanwhile, for a taste of the Caribbean, wrap pineapple, coconut, and rum all in one glorious bite. Just pull out the turtle pool for the kids, dunk your feet, sit back, and enjoy.

COCONUT CRUST

¼ cup (½ stick) unsalted butter or margarine
¼ cup granulated sugar
2 tablespoons unbleached all-purpose flour
⅔ cup finely chopped macadamia nuts, walnuts, or pecans
1 7-ounce package (2½ cups, lightly packed) sweetened shredded coconut

FILLING

2 tablespoons (2 envelopes) unflavored gelatin
½ cup granulated sugar
2 large egg yolks
½ cup milk
1 8-ounce can (1 cup) crushed pineapple
2 cups (16 ounces) vanilla- or pineapple-flavored yogurt
⅓ cup rum
½ teaspoon coconut extract
1½ cups whipping cream, chilled
3 tablespoons confectioners' sugar
Fresh pineapple wedges (optional)
Fresh Coconut Swirls (optional; see sidebar)

1. Preheat the oven to 350° F. For the coconut crust, in a 1-cup microwavable measure melt the butter or margarine in the microwave on 100% (high) for 1 minute. Remove and stir to melt any unmelted bits. In a large bowl, stir together the sugar, flour, nuts, and coconut. With a fork, stir in the butter or margarine until blended. Press the coconut crust onto the

bottom and sides of a 10-inch pie pan. Bake for 12 to 15 minutes, until the edges are nicely browned. Cool on a wire rack. Meanwhile, make the filling.

2. For the filling, in a large 2-quart microwavable bowl, mix the gelatin and sugar. Blend in the egg yolks and milk. Microwave at 50% (medium-low) for 2 minutes. Stir and microwave at 50% (medium-low) for an additional 90 seconds, until the mixture thickens. Whisk in the pineapple, yogurt, rum, and coconut extract. Place the bowl in a clean sink or a large bowl filled with ice water. Chill until the mixture is the consistency of mayonnaise, about 10 minutes.

3. Meanwhile, pour the whipping cream into the food processor bowl fitted with the steel blade. Process until the cream thickens; continue processing, and gradually add the confectioners' sugar through the feed tube until the cream is stiff. Refrigerate until ready to use.

4. When the pineapple-rum mixture is the proper consistency, fold in ⅔ of the whipped cream. Pour the filling into the cooled coconut crust and garnish the top decoratively with the remaining whipped cream. Place the pie in the freezer for 15 minutes. Remove and finish chilling in the refrigerator, about 1 hour or until the pie is set. Garnish with fresh pineapple wedges and fresh coconut swirls if desired.

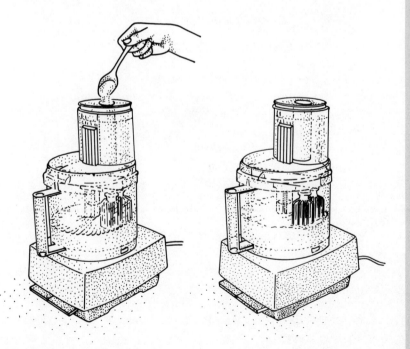

How to Pick a Ripe Pineapple

There are several tests for a ripe pineapple. First, look at the pineapples. See if you can find one that's a deep green with some yellowing near the base. Pick that one up and take a deep whiff. It should smell aromatic, the way you remember pineapple. If there is no aroma, it may be immature. If it smells fermented, it's overripe.

Next pluck a leaf from the center of the pineapple. It should come out with little resistance. If the leaf clings tenaciously to the pineapple, it's probably immature.

Finally, squeeze the pineapple. It should be firm, with no soft spots.

Pineapples should be picked when they are ripe and not green. They won't ripen any more after being cut. Store the pineapple upside down to distribute the sugar throughout the meat and at room temperature if you plan on using it within a couple of days; otherwise, refrigerate the pineapple, and it will keep for 5 to 7 days.

3 CHOCOLATE

CHOCOLATE BASICS

e love chocolate so much, this book threatened to turn into *Chocolate in Half the Time.* Because of chocolate's ability to provide almost instant joy, we keep it on hand, in many forms, for impromptu half-time desserts.

And once we discovered you can melt chocolate in the microwave with greater ease and more certainty than with any of the conventional methods, we knew we were well on our way to terrific half-time chocolate desserts.

There is some confusion over what's what in the chocolate department—and can you substitute one type for the other? The answer to that question is a qualified but resounding *yes* (see the conversion chart that follows), but first to clear up some of the confusion.

Chocolate is a complex product of the cocoa bean, which is roasted much as coffee beans are roasted, then processed in various ways. First, roasted beans are ground into a thick paste that's basically unsweetened chocolate. This paste contains both chocolate liqueur (solids) and cocoa butter. Remove some of the cocoa butter, dry the paste, and you have *cocoa.* Add sugar to the paste in varying amounts, and you get anything from bittersweet dark chocolate to sweet chocolate.

Cocoa comes in many forms. For baking, always make sure you're using *unsweetened* cocoa. The stuff with the sugar in it is just for making the drink, cocoa. Dutch-process cocoa is processed with alkali and is darker but less bitter than regular cocoa. It is definitely our preference. If you can't find it in your supermarket, it's available by mail or at fine confectioneries. You may interchange regular unsweetened cocoa for Dutch-process cocoa in a recipe, measure for measure.

Unsweetened chocolate has no sugar at all and can be used in baking in combination with other sweeteners. Sold in squares or bars, it's usually a best buy if you're price shopping.

Bittersweet chocolate is the darkest, barely sweetened chocolate on the market, sold in bars, squares, and chips. There's a lot of difference in taste and quality from brand to brand. Sometimes the best-tasting and the smoothest chocolate is sold in the candy section, not in the baking section. We find it works, measure for measure, in any chocolate recipe we have.

Semisweet chocolate is a dark, sweetened chocolate product that's sold in chips from mini and maxi and in 1-ounce squares. In our experience, these are interchangeable, measure for measure, even though there are slight variations from brand to brand and type to type. This does mean, however, that if you're using a recipe that calls for 4 ounces of chocolate, you must weigh the chocolate chips to get an equivalent measure. Or, even simpler, remember that

> 3 ounces chocolate chips = ½ cup
> 6 ounces chocolate chips = 1 cup

German's sweet chocolate, by the way, doesn't come from Germany. It was invented by a fellow named German who worked in a Pennsylvania chocolate factory. Made from sugar, chocolate, cocoa butter, and lecithin (to smooth it), this is chocolate so edible, you have to hide it from the family if you plan to have enough to cook with. It's sold in 4-ounce bars.

The famous German chocolate cake was invented in Oklahoma and Texas during the fifties and became the trendy cake to serve at backyard barbecues, wienie roasts, and fund-raising bake sales. We still do adore it.

Milk chocolate is a sweet chocolate with added powdered milk. This is another chocolate so temptingly edible, you may have to hide it in the pantry. This chocolate is sold in bars and as chips from mini to maxi.

White chocolate has no chocolate liqueur (solids), but instead is made up of cocoa butter, sugar, and powdered milk. By law in the United States, without chocolate liqueur a product cannot be labeled "chocolate." This product varies in quality markedly from brand to brand. Be sure that what you buy is not imitation white chocolate. Read the fine print on the label. The real item is made only from cocoa butter, sugar, and powdered milk. The fake stuff is made from palm oil or shortening. The fake stuff tastes like shortening looks and coats the inside of your mouth when you put it on your tongue to melt. Ick. Frequently, the best source for authentic white chocolate is a confectionery, where it is sold in bulk and sometimes called bark. Most supermarkets carry a product by Guittard which is a hybrid of sugar, partially hydrogenated palm kernel oil and cocoa butter, nonfat milk, cream, whey, lecithin emulsifiers, and real vanilla. This is certainly a serviceable alternative.

Coating chocolate, or couverture, is chocolate with the highest cocoa-butter content, suitable for coating truffles and other candies. Buy it by mail order or in fine confectioneries as bittersweet chocolate, milk chocolate, or white chocolate.

BRANDS OF FINE CHOCOLATE

Aside from the chocolate brands you'll find at the supermarket—Hershey's, Nestle, Guittard, Ghiradelli, and Baker's—all of which are suitable for the recipes in this book, you can order by mail or find in confectioneries these extraordinary, excellent brands:

Droste (Dutch)
Lindt (Swiss)
Tobler (Swiss and French)
Ghiradelli (American), types other than those in the supermarket
Guittard (American), ditto
Van Leer American Chocolate (American)

STORING CHOCOLATE

Light and heat are detrimental to the quality of chocolate, so store it in a cool, dark place. A whitish "bloom" can develop on the surface of chocolate from too-fast changes in heat and humidity. For dessert recipes, the white blush makes no difference. The dark chocolates keep for ages, but milk and white chocolates should be used within a year of purchase.

CHOPPING AND GRATING CHOCOLATE

If your kitchen is hot, place the food processor bowl and blade in the freezer for 10 minutes before you begin. Then you can chop chocolate bars in the food processor easily. Cut the chocolate into chunks, using a sharp knife, then place it in the food processor bowl fitted with the steel blade. Pulse to chop the chocolate, just until it reduces to small pieces.

You can grate chocolate in the food processor using the grating disk. Again, on a hot day, chill the bowl and disk. Dump the grated chocolate onto waxed paper. Remember, it will melt in your hand.

MAIL-ORDER SOURCES FOR CHOCOLATE PRODUCTS

Maison E. H. Glass, Inc.
111 E. 58th St.
New York, NY 10022
(800) 822–5564
(212) 755–3316

Maid of Scandinavia
3244 Raleigh Ave.
Minneapolis, MN 55416
(800) 328–6722
(612) 927–7996

Williams-Sonoma
Mail-Order Department
P.O. Box 7456
San Francisco, CA 94120–7456
(open 24 hours)
(800) 541–2233
fax (415) 421–5153

CHOCOLATE CONVERSION CHART

Unsweetened chocolate squares, 1 ounce	= 3 tablespoons cocoa + 1 tablespoon shortening
Unsweetened liquid baking chocolate, 1 ounce	= 3 tablespoons cocoa + 1 tablespoon vegetable oil
Semisweet chocolate chips, ¼ cup	= 1-ounce square unsweetened chocolate + 4 teaspoons sugar
Semisweet chocolate square, 1 ounce	= ½ ounce unsweetened chocolate + 1 tablespoon sugar
Semisweet chocolate chips or squares, 6 ounces	= 6 tablespoons cocoa + 7 tablespoons sugar + ¼ cup shortening
Semisweet chocolate chips 3 ounces 6 ounces	 = ½ cup volume measure = 1 cup volume measure

MICRO-MELTING CHOCOLATE

Chocolate is heat sensitive and if overheated will "seize," as the French say, meaning it will go past the runny state and become turgid as mud pies, never to liquefy properly again. Grainy, overheated chocolate cannot be saved. Throw it out.

In the past, melting chocolate required stints over hot (120° F) water, stirring, with great care taken not to overdo it.

But here's a task so made-to-order for the microwave that, once you try it, you'll never do any other way. Use a small microwavable container. A Pyrex custard cup is ideal for 1 or 2 squares. Always begin by microwaving the chocolate, *uncovered,* at 100% (high) for the minimum time called for in the recipe. You'll notice that it still holds its shape. But give it a stir, and it will dissolve like young love into that first good kiss.

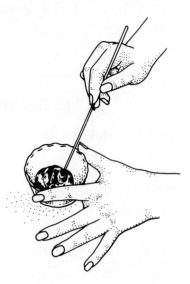

If the chocolate isn't quite melted, microwave it again, in 15-second intervals, at 100% (high), stirring after each time period, until the chocolate is thoroughly melted. For stirring, we like to use a single wooden skewer. It keeps the chocolate in the bowl, not on the utensil. Scoop the runny chocolate into the recipe using a rubber spatula, and you won't waste any at all. There may be enough for one good lick, but none clinging to wire whisks, wooden spoons, or other large utensils.

Melt chocolate chips after measuring the chocolate by *weight or volume* and matching it to the type listed below.

Semisweet or milk chocolate chips should be microwaved at 100% (high) for a minimum time of:

> 1 cup (6 ounces) for 30 seconds
> 2 cups (12 ounces) for 1 minute

Stir both with a wooden skewer or fork and heat for an additional 30 seconds. Stir until smooth.

We frequently use chips for melting, even though they weren't designed for that. They make instant icing on a cake or brownies—all you do is sprinkle the chips of your choice on a hot cake, let it stand a moment, then spread the melted chocolate evenly over the cake.

White chocolate chips can be difficult to manage. Microwave them at 50% (defrost) for a minimum time of:

> 1 minute for 2 cups (12 ounces)

Stir thoroughly. Microwave at 30-second increments, stirring, until the mixture is smooth and evenly melted.

Unsweetened chocolate microwave at 100% (high) for a minimum time of:

1 minute for 2 squares	2 minutes for 6 squares
1½ minutes for 4 squares	2½ minutes for 8 squares

Microwave an additional 15 seconds, stir, and continue until the chocolate is melted. Don't overdo it!

Semisweet chocolate microwave at 100% (high) for a minimum time of:

2-ounce bar, for 1½ minutes

4 ounces for 2½ minutes

8 ounces for 3 minutes

Sweet (German's) chocolate microwave at 100% (high) for a minimum time of:

4-ounce bar, broken in 2 pieces, for 1½ minutes

Then stir and microwave an additional 30 seconds if needed.

CHOCOLATE HOT LINES

If you have problems with chocolate, or wish more information or additional recipes, the major chocolate companies maintain consumer hot lines. Call them up weekdays. They're there to serve. Look on the back of the package for additional 800 numbers.

Ghiradelli (800) 488–0078, 8:30 A.M.–4:30 P.M. (Pacific time)

Nestle's (800) NESTLES, 9:00 A.M.–5:00 P.M. (Eastern time)

CHOCOLATE DRIZZLE DREAMS

We've been reading instructions lately from experts advising shoppers how to save money at the grocery store. On everybody's list it says ''Don't buy prepared foods'' and ''Leave the kids at home.''

Swimming always upstream, we say take the kids with you but give them something specific to hunt for and the promise that when you get home you'll make something wonderful. Say something with chocolate, perhaps?

The word ''chocolate'' will usually get compliance from anybody. Grab a container of ice cream, get the cocoa to make your own chocolate syrup, and you're on your way to 2—count 'em—2 chocolate sauces that will make the children happy.

Plain chocolate syrup is a staple in most homes where children reside. Why don't you and your kids make it together? You'll save money. You'll begin teaching your kids to cook. You'll have on hand the beginnings for chocolate milk, ice-cream topping, even a swirl to top fresh fruit.

Transform that syrup into Hot Fudge Sauce with our easy recipe that follows, and you've stepped into the category of sublime. And all for about 25% of what it costs to buy the stuff already prepared. Made in half the time in the microwave, it is simply irresistible.

HOMEMADE CHOCOLATE SYRUP

Makes 2 cups syrup
3 minutes to prepare
Sterile pint jar

7 tablespoons unsweetened cocoa
1 cup sugar
¾ cup evaporated milk
¼ cup (½ stick) unsalted butter
⅛ teaspoon salt
½ teaspoon vanilla extract

Combine in a 1-quart microwavable dish the cocoa, sugar, and evaporated milk. Whisk together with a balloon whisk. Cook in the microwave at 100% (high) for 1 minute. Remove from the microwave, and stir in the butter and salt. Replace in the microwave and cook at 100% (high) for 1 minute and 30 seconds more. Remove from the microwave and stir in the vanilla. Whisk thoroughly. Pour into a sterile jar, cover, and refrigerate for up to 2 months.

HOT FUDGE SAUCE

Makes 2 cups
4 minutes to prepare
Sterile pint jar

This is the sauce that cracks when you spoon it over ice cream, making a shell so delicious that it will transport you to wherever it is that good chocolate takes you when you want to be taken.

½ cup homemade (see above) or store-bought chocolate syrup
½ cup (1 stick) butter
1 cup confectioners' sugar

1. Combine the chocolate syrup and butter in a 1-quart microwavable dish. Heat in the microwave oven at 100% (high) for 1 minute.

2. Remove from the microwave and beat with a wire whisk to combine. Then whisk in the confectioners' sugar and replace in the microwave.

3. Heat for 2 minutes at 100% (high), whisk again, then pour into a sterile glass pint jar.

4. Store, covered, in the refrigerator. To reheat, remove the metal lid from the jar and reheat in the microwave until bubbly, about 30 seconds at 100% (high).

ANN'S EASY CHOCOLATE POTS-DE-CREME

Serves 4
5 minutes to prepare
1 hour to chill
4 pots-de-crème dishes or glass custard cups

Ann serves these mainline chocolate desserts in miniature soufflé dishes. No more than ¼ cup per serving—since it's as rich as the center of a fine truffle, it's just enough.

1 4-ounce bar German's sweet chocolate
1 tablespoon sugar
½ cup whipping cream
2 large egg yolks
½ teaspoon vanilla extract

1. Break the chocolate into 2 pieces and place it in a microwavable bowl. Heat, uncovered, at 100% (high) for 1½ to 2 minutes. Remove from the microwave and stir until the chocolate is completely melted.

2. While the chocolate is melting, whisk together the sugar, whipping cream, and egg yolks. Stir this mixture into the melted chocolate, mixing thoroughly.

3. Cook the pudding, uncovered, for 1 minute at 100% (high). Remove from the microwave and stir in the vanilla. Divide the pudding among the serving dishes. Cover and refrigerate for about 1 hour or until serving time.

Make a banana split using the traditional ingredients. Start with 3 scoops of ice cream—vanilla, chocolate, and strawberry. Bracket the ice cream with a banana cut in two, lengthwise, then top with this Hot Fudge Sauce and butterscotch sauce, and don't forget the whipped cream on top. A maraschino cherry, chopped peanuts, and sugar sprinkles will surely gild this lily.

You can make an instant sundae pie by beginning with a graham cracker crust, filling it with best-quality vanilla ice cream, drizzling fudge sauce over that, then heaping the top with fresh sliced strawberries.

Make a grown-up's split by bracketing 3 flavors of frozen yogurt with a split banana, then drizzling Hot Fudge Sauce over the top, and finishing with a dollop of crème fraîche and a sweet fresh Bing or Queen Anne cherry.

INTENSE ESPRESSO-CHOCOLATE CAKE

Makes 1 ten-inch cake to serve 8
20 minutes to prepare
1 hour to bake
10-inch springform pan

If you have an espresso machine, you can make a heavenly espresso-chocolate cake and use all your kitchen toys at once. The cake is deep, rich, and complex. Serve it plain or topped with whipped cream or Chocolate Butter Cream. For heaven on earth, pave the frosted cake with fresh raspberries.

1½ cups cake flour
½ teaspoon baking powder
½ teaspoon baking soda
4½ ounces (¾ cup) semisweet chocolate chips or bars
1 cup (2 sticks) unsalted butter
1¾ cups dark brown sugar
3 large eggs
1 tablespoon vanilla extract
¼ cup very strong espresso or brewed black coffee
¾ cup buttermilk
    Confectioners' sugar, whipped cream,
        or Chocolate Butter Cream (see sidebar, page 34)

1. Preheat the oven to 350° F. Butter the bottom of a 10-inch round springform pan. Cut and fit a piece of parchment paper to the bottom of the pan. Butter and flour the paper and sides of the pan. Set aside.

2. Add the flour, baking powder, and baking soda to the food processor bowl fitted with the steel blade. Pulse to aerate. Remove the mixture to a piece of waxed paper.

3. Melt the chocolate in a glass measure in the microwave, uncovered, set at 100% (high) for 1 minute, until the chocolate melts when stirred with a skewer or chopstick. Set aside.

4. In the food processor bowl fitted with the steel blade, process the butter for 2 minutes, then add the brown sugar through the feed tube and continue to process for a minute. Now break the eggs, one at a time, through the feed tube and continue processing until thoroughly mixed. Finally, add the

vanilla and melted chocolate through the feed tube and process to mix thoroughly.

5. Mix the espresso or coffee with the buttermilk, then add the coffee-buttermilk mixture by thirds, alternating with the flour mixture, through the feed tube, pulsing to mix no more than 4 or 5 pulses each time. Do not overprocess. Stir the mixture together, finally, using a rubber spatula, then spoon it into the prepared cake pan.

6. Bake in the preheated oven until the cake springs back at a touch, about 1 hour. Cool in the pan on a rack for about 10 minutes, then remove the springform and continue to cool. When the cake is room temperature, flip it over onto a second rack, then lift off the bottom and peel off the parchment. Holding the cake between the racks, flip it over again, so that the right side will be up for finishing. You may leave it plain, dust it with confectioners' sugar, or frost with whipped cream or Chocolate Butter Cream.

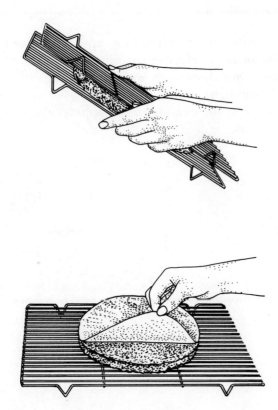

OK. Admit it. Hot, runny choco-late sauce would make your run-ning shoes edible. But here are some other less drastic items you could chocolate coat before you eat them.

    Chunks of French bread
    Pieces of plain cake
    Big strawberries with stems
    Apple and orange wedges
    Bing or Queen Anne cherries
    Kiwi coins

    Add a scoop of vanilla ice cream to a footed dish, thin slices of store-bought pound cake, blow up the balloons, and pass out the bells and whistles. It's somebody's birthday and it didn't take but 5 minutes to get ready. Instant fes-tivities. Like those times you forgot it was somebody's birthday until it was almost too late to be forgiven.

CHOCOLATE FONDUE

Makes 2 cups
5 minutes to prepare
4-cup glass measure

Here's a quick party that satisfies children from the age of 2 to 102. Hot fondue with cold foods to dip into it makes simple ingredients festive. If you don't have a fondue pot, serve the fondue in a chafing dish with a candle under it. Barring that, serve the fondue in an ordinary bowl, then reheat periodically in the microwave. If you don't have fondue forks, pick up a package of wooden skewers. They work fine.

  1 tablespoon unsalted butter
16 ounces semisweet chocolate chips or squares
30 large marshmallows
1½ cups half-and-half

    Combine the butter, chocolate, and marshmallows in a 4-cup glass measure. Heat in the microwave at 100% (high) for 1 minute. Stir thoroughly with a rubber spatula, then stir in the half-and-half, mixing thoroughly. Microwave at 100% (high) for 1 minute. Transfer to an appropriate serving dish and serve warm.

$\mathcal{P}$EANUT BUTTER–CHOCOLATE CUPS

Makes 30 candy cups
15 minutes to prepare
45 minutes to chill in refrigerator
30 minutes to chill in freezer
13 × 9-inch baking pan

These chocolate cups are like a candy bar. Diana keeps this recipe in her hip pocket for last-minute school functions. When a hysterical child informs you at 7:00 A.M. that treats are needed today for her class at school, these can be in the backpack by 8:15.

1 cup creamy peanut butter
2 cups graham cracker crumbs
2 cups confectioners' sugar
6 tablespoons (¾ stick) unsalted butter
12 ounces (2 cups) semisweet chocolate chips

1. Mix the peanut butter, cracker crumbs, and confectioners' sugar in a large mixing bowl. In the microwave on 100% (high) heat the butter for 1 minute, until thoroughly melted. Add the butter to the mixing bowl and combine thoroughly. Press into the bottom of a 13 × 9-inch baking pan.

2. Place the chocolate chips in a microwavable container and microwave on 100% (high) for 2 minutes. Remove the chips from the microwave and stir until completely melted. Spread the melted chocolate over the peanut butter base. Refrigerate for at least 45 minutes to allow the chocolate to harden, or place in the freezer for 30 minutes (these also taste great frozen).

3. To serve, cut out circles using a round 1½-inch canapé or biscuit cutter, or cut into bars. Refrigerate, covered loosely with plastic wrap. The leftover scrap pieces can go into a plastic bag and be refrigerated for a later snack.

Storing Chocolate Bars, Candies, and Cups

The best way to store chocolate bars, candies, and confections is in a cool place in an airtight non-plastic container between layers of waxed paper. Any container made out of tin, paper, or glass allows the chocolate to breathe.

KATHERINE'S FAUX TRUFFLES

Makes 24 medium truffles
15 minutes to prepare and to chill
4-cup glass measure and cookie sheet

Nothing this easy could be real. All it takes is a microwave, a willingness to get your hands into chocolate, and a desire to lick your fingers. Voilà! Truffles in no time flat.

No need for a special chocolate thermometer. No need for a marble board. No need for anything but a craving for chocolate.

8 ounces (1⅓ cups) semisweet chocolate chips
1 cup (2 sticks) unsalted butter
1 tablespoon cognac or liqueur of your choice
 Raisins (optional)
 Hazelnuts (optional)
 Unsweetened, Dutch-process cocoa
 Ground cinnamon

1. Combine the chocolate and butter in a 4-cup measure, then microwave at 30% (medium-low) for 1 minute, until the chocolate and butter soften. Stir with a wooden skewer or fork. Then stir in the cognac or other liqueur to taste, and continue stirring until the mixture is completely smooth.

2. Refrigerate until the mixture can be handled, about 10 minutes. Meanwhile, lay out raisins if you wish to roll them into the truffles, or finely chop the hazelnuts if you wish to roll the truffles in nuts. Mix the cocoa with a whiff of cinnamon to coat the truffles.

3. When you're ready to form the truffles, tear off a sheet of waxed paper and place it on a cookie sheet. Lay out the additional ingredients, and the cocoa mixture in which to roll the truffles. Butter your hands, then spoon a heaping tablespoon of chocolate mixture into your left hand. Roll the truffles between your hands, making a rough globe. Roll raisins or nuts into the truffle if you wish, then roll the globe in cocoa mixture and additional chopped nuts if desired. Place the truffles onto the waxed paper. Once you've rolled them all, place the truffles in the refrigerator to chill. Later, pack into tins and store, covered, in the refrigerator.

*T*OAD 'N A HOLE CHOCOLATE CAKE

Makes one 10-inch tubecake to serve 10
15 minutes to prepare
1 hour to bake
10-inch tube pan

Diana's mother, a born baker, gave us enough material for a whole chapter using chocolate syrup. This recipe makes a rather big cake, good for large gatherings or enough to feed 3 teenage boys for at least 2 days.

The crumb is fine, and the cake is breathtaking when sliced because the chocolate tunnel is completely surrounded by golden cake.

1 cup (2 sticks) unsalted butter
3 large eggs
2 cups sugar
2 teaspoons vanilla extract
1 cup whole milk
3 cups unbleached all-purpose flour
2 teaspoons baking powder
½ teaspoon salt
¼ teaspoon baking soda
¾ cup chocolate syrup, homemade (see page 96) or store-bought

1. Preheat the oven to 350° F. Coat a 10-inch tube pan with cooking spray. In the food processor fitted with the steel blade, combine the butter, eggs, sugar, vanilla, and milk. Process until light and fluffy, about 30 seconds.

2. In a small bowl, combine the flour, baking powder, and salt. Mix to blend. Spoon the dry ingredients over the batter in the processor and pulse 3 or 4 times just to combine. Pour ⅔ of the batter into the prepared pan.

3. Thoroughly mix the baking soda and chocolate syrup into the remaining third of batter. Spoon the chocolate batter over the vanilla batter already in the pan. Bake on the middle rack of the preheated oven for 1 hour, until a cake tester inserted in the center comes out clean. Remove the cake to a wire rack to cool for 20 minutes and then carefully remove the sides of the cake pan while holding on to the middle cone of the pan. Let the cake cool completely before removing from the bottom and cone of the pan.

Chocolate Leaves

Chocolate leaves are impressive to look at and easy to make. Choose clean and dry nontoxic leaves, such as lemon or rose leaves. On 100% (high), microwave 2 ounces (2 squares) semisweet chocolate for about 90 seconds or ½ cup semisweet chocolate chips for about 1 minute. Stir to melt any remaining bits. Brush the melted chocolate evenly on the underside of the leaves. Wipe off any chocolate that drips onto the side or front of the leaves. Refrigerate for 10 minutes, until set. Apply a second layer of chocolate over the first. Refrigerate until set. Working quickly and carefully, use a pair of clean tweezers to peel the chocolate leaf away from the real leaf. The tweezers will keep the chocolate from melting in your hands. Store the leaves in the refrigerator or freezer in a crushproof container until ready to use. Keep chocolate garnishes in the refrigerator and handle with tongs or forks.

Nut crusts give pies a toasty, nutty underpinning. You can make them with a variety of nuts: hazelnuts, almonds, pecans, macadamia nuts, or walnuts all work well.

Toast nuts before chopping or grinding for the most enhanced flavor. Spread the nuts over a baking sheet and toast in a 400°F oven or toaster oven. Mix around or shake them every couple of minutes, keeping a close eye on them. They can burn. Most nuts should be toasted in about 5 minutes. Cool before you proceed with chopping or grinding.

Both chopping and grinding can be done easily in the food processor, using 2 to 3 pulses for chopping and 5 to 6 pulses for grinding. Over processing will release nut oil and result in grease balls. Pulse and look. Pulse and look.

CHOCOLATE SILK PIE IN A WALNUT-BUTTER CRUMB CRUST

Makes one 9-inch pie to serve 8
20 minutes to prepare
25 minutes to bake
1 hour to chill
13 × 9-inch baking dish
9-inch pie pan

Once you've made this piecrust, you'll want to try different fillings in it. In fact, it's so good, you can eat it plain. Or maybe with vanilla-ice-cream filling. Just try it once. The aroma alone is enough to knock you out. Walnuts, brown sugar, and butter baked together. Need we say more?

And the filling is aptly named. Process the chocolate, butter, and eggs into the sugar until every granule of sugar is dissolved, and it will produce a texture so silky you may want to hold it in your mouth forever. Almost too good to swallow. But not quite.

WALNUT-BUTTER CRUMB CRUST

¼ cup dark brown sugar
1 cup unbleached all-purpose flour
½ cup (1 stick) unsalted butter
1 cup chopped walnuts

CHOCOLATE SILK FILLING

¾ cup (1½ sticks) unsalted butter
1 cup granulated sugar
4 ounces (⅔ cup) bittersweet chocolate chips
1½ teaspoons vanilla extract
3 large eggs
Sweetened whipped cream topping

1. Preheat the oven to 375° F. For the crust, combine the brown sugar, flour, butter, and walnuts in the food processor bowl fitted with the steel blade and process until the mixture resembles coarse meal.

2. Dump the mixture into a 13 × 9-inch baking dish and bake for 15 minutes. Remove it from the oven and stir it with a fork. Now pour the partially cooked mixture into a 9-inch pie pan and press it with the back of a fork into a piecrust shape. Place the crust back in the oven and cook until light brown, about 10 minutes. Remove the crust from the oven and cool on a rack.

3. For the filling, cream the butter and sugar in the processor fitted with the steel blade until fluffy, about 20 seconds.

4. Meanwhile, melt the chocolate in a microwavable dish by microwaving at 100% (high) for about 1½ minutes. Stir to mix thoroughly.

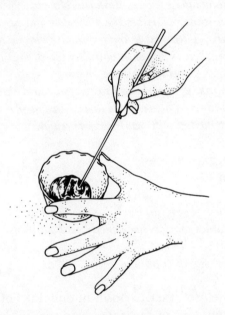

5. Add the melted chocolate to the sugar and butter along with the vanilla. Add 2 eggs, then process for 5 minutes. Break the remaining egg through the feed tube. Now process until every sugar granule has dissolved. (You can tell by rubbing a bit of filling between your finger and thumb. The filling should be silky smooth.)

6. Scrape the filling into the cooled crust. Freeze 1 hour. You may serve the pie either frozen or about half-thawed. If you wish to gild the lily, top with a dollop of whipped cream scented with cognac, brandy, or bourbon.

MAIDA HEATTER'S CHOCOLATE BIRTHDAY CAKE

Makes one 2-layer frosted cake
20 minutes to prepare
30 to 35 minutes to bake
Two 9 × 2-inch round cake pans

Maida's choice for her own birthday cake is kind of a chocolate soufflé, layered and finished with flavored whipped cream.

Our adaptation of these 2 thin, dark chocolate layers can be quickly made at your convenience—either the day before you need it or a week before—and frozen. Then just before serving, the layers are filled and frosted. Maida fills the layers with plain whipped cream, then covers the cake with coffee-chocolate whipped cream.

This flourless cake is so rich and tasty, you could skip frosting all together, put a little jam between the layers, say raspberry or apricot, then simply dust the top with confectioners' sugar.

6 extra-large eggs, separated
¼ teaspoon salt
2 tablespoons fresh lemon juice
¾ cup granulated sugar, divided
¼ cup plus 1 tablespoon unsweetened cocoa, divided
  Jam or whipped cream
  Confectioners' sugar (optional)

1. Adjust the oven rack to position one-third of the way up from the bottom, and preheat the oven to 375° F. Spritz two 9 × 2-inch round layer-cake pans with cooking spray. Cut two 9-inch rounds of waxed or parchment paper and fit them into the bottom of the pans. Generously spritz with cooking spray or butter the bottom and sides, then evenly dust the pans with cocoa. Invert the pans and gently knock out any excess cocoa.

2. Place the egg whites in the food processor bowl fitted with the plastic or steel blade or the whisk attachment, add the salt, and process until the whites increase in volume and barely hold a soft shape (see pages 19–20). Add 2 tablespoons lemon juice, then reduce the speed to moderate (if adjustable) while gradually adding half the sugar, spoonful by spoonful. Increase the speed to high again and continue to

beat until the whites hold a definite shape. Remove the beaten egg whites to another bowl and set aside.

3. In the processor bowl now place the egg yolks. Process for 2 minutes, until they're a light lemon color. Add the remaining half of the sugar, a spoon at a time, through the feed tube, then continue processing until the mixture is thick and forms a wide ribbon.

4. Lift the lid and sprinkle the cocoa evenly over the top, then replace the lid and process just until the cocoa is completely incorporated.

5. In several small additions, using a slotted spoon or rubber spatula, fold half the beaten egg whites into the chocolate mixture. Then fold the chocolate mixture into the remaining whites. Don't overhandle.

6. Turn half the mixture into each of the prepared pans. Gently smooth each layer. Bake in the preheated oven for 30 to 35 minutes, until the layers spring back when lightly pressed with a fingertip and the cake is beginning to come away from the sides of the pans.

7. Remove the cake from the oven. You'll notice that even though it is high and handsome, like a soufflé, it will almost immediately begin to deflate. Not to worry. That's what it's supposed to do. With a small sharp knife, carefully cut around the edge of the pans to release the cake layers from the sides. Cover each layer with a rack, invert the pan and rack, then remove the pan. Carefully peel off the paper lining, cover the layer with another rack, and invert again to let the layers cool right side up.

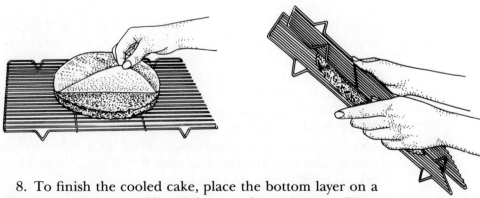

8. To finish the cooled cake, place the bottom layer on a white paper doily, then fill with jam or whipped cream. Place the second layer atop the first and either dust with confectioners' sugar or frost with additional whipped cream.

*H*OT *FUDGE SUNDAE CAKE*

Serves 12
20 minutes to prepare
40 minutes to bake
9 × 9 × 2-inch glass baking dish

This is too easy to believe and will fill the kitchen with the aroma of chocolate before you get it out of the refrigerator.

Buy a pint of Häagen-Dazs vanilla, top this cake—hot—with cold ice cream, top the ice cream with a maraschino cherry, and you'll see there is some merit in getting the cart before the proverbial horse.

  1 cup unbleached all-purpose flour
⅔ cup granulated sugar
¼ cup plus 2 tablespoons unsweetened cocoa, divided
  2 teaspoons baking powder
¼ teaspoon salt
½ cup whipping cream
  2 tablespoons butter, melted
  1 teaspoon vanilla extract
½ cup pecan halves
  3 ounces (½ cup) semisweet chocolate chips
  1 cup dark brown sugar
1¾ cups strong hot brewed coffee or hot tap water
    Vanilla ice cream
    Maraschino cherries

1. Preheat the oven to 350° F. In an ungreased 9 × 9 × 2-inch ovenproof glass baking dish, stir together the flour, granulated sugar, 2 tablespoons of the cocoa, baking powder, and salt. Pour in the cream, melted butter, and vanilla, then stir with a fork until smooth.

2. Stir in the nuts and chocolate chips and spread the batter evenly in the pan. Sprinkle with the remaining ¼ cup cocoa and the cup of brown sugar. Pour hot coffee or water over all. Bake in the preheated oven for 40 minutes, until the cake is bubbling in places and the top looks glazed.

3. Remove the baked cake from the oven and let it stand on a rack for 15 minutes. Now spoon it into dessert dishes and top with vanilla ice cream. Be sure to scrape up that good, hot, runny chocolate sauce onto the ice cream. Top with a maraschino cherry and serve.

KAKI'S QUICK CHOCOLATE DROPS

Makes 36 little cookies
5 minutes to prepare
7 minutes to bake
One 7 × 12-inch baking sheet

When Christmas rolls around and people drop by to visit, Kaki drops everything and makes these pure chocolate bites in 12 minutes flat. Pack in decorated tins for gifts.

1 14-ounce can sweetened condensed milk
6 ounces (1 cup) semisweet chocolate chips
¼ cup (½ stick) butter
1 cup unbleached all-purpose flour
1 teaspoon vanilla extract

1. Preheat the oven to 350° F. Spray a 7 × 12-inch baking sheet with cooking spray and set aside.

2. In a microwavable bowl combine the milk, chocolate chips, and butter. Heat in the microwave set at 100% (high) power for 2 minutes. Remove from the microwave and whisk together using a balloon whisk.

3. Dump in the flour and vanilla and whisk to mix thoroughly. Drop by the teaspoon onto the prepared baking sheet. Each cookie should be no bigger than a bite. Bake in the preheated oven for exactly 7 minutes.

4. Remove the cookies to a rack to cool.

Sweetened Condensed Milk

Nothing is more convenient to have on hand for baking than canned milk. Take care when choosing a canned milk product to pick the exact milk called for in the recipe. Kaki's recipe calls for sweetened condensed milk, which is made of evaporated milk, sweetened by additional sugar, and then canned. A rich, creamy color, it's as thick as molasses.

Other canned milk products include so-called evaporated milk, which is plain milk that's had half its water removed by placing the milk in a vacuum. The milk is then canned and sterilized. You'll note it's a caramel color, about as thick as cream and has a cooked, caramel flavor. You can use it in any recipe that calls for fresh milk by mixing evaporated milk in equal amounts with water and using this evaporated milk–water mixture, measure-for-measure, in place of fresh milk. The finished product will not taste exactly the same, of course, because evaporated milk lends it's caramel taste to the final product.

You cannot, however, interchange evaporated milk with sweetened condensed milk because the added sugar and processing done in sweetened condensed milk changes the flavor and end result in a recipe.

Another canned milk product known as skimmed milk is made with low-fat milk. This product is used in recipes calling for fresh milk, by mixing it half and half with water. You'll get a lowered-fat content, a different tasting end result, but hey. Who knows? Maybe it will taste even better.

DARK CHOCOLATE FUDGIES

Makes 20 cookies
20 minutes to prepare
15 minutes to chill
10 to 12 minutes to bake
Two 16 × 14-inch baking sheets

Devilishly dark, moist, and packed with chocolate and nuts, these cookies originated in a cookie store and are their number-one best-seller. Chocolate chunks or large chocolate chips must be used to keep the cookies from spreading on the cookie sheets. If large chocolate chips are not available in your area, buy chocolate bars and with a large knife chop them into chunks the size of a large peanut.

18 ounces (3 cups) large semisweet chocolate chips or chunks,
    divided
 4 ounces (4 squares) unsweetened chocolate
½ cup (1 stick) unsalted butter
 1 tablespoon vanilla extract
 3 large eggs
⅓ cup packed light brown sugar
 1 cup granulated sugar
⅔ cup unbleached all-purpose flour
¼ teaspoon salt
¼ teaspoon baking soda
1½ cups coarsely chopped pecans

1. Place 1 oven rack in the upper third of the oven and 1 rack in the lower third. Preheat the oven to 350° F. Coat two 16 × 14-inch baking sheets with cooking spray.

2. Place in a large microwavable mixing bowl 1 cup of the semisweet chocolate chips or chunks, the unsweetened chocolate squares, and the butter. Heat the chocolates and butter in the microwave set on 100% (high) for 2 minutes. Meanwhile, in a large mixing bowl, add the vanilla extract, eggs, and sugars. With an electric mixer set at high speed, beat the egg mixture for 5 to 7 minutes, until the mixture forms a pale, thin ribbon when the beaters are lifted.

3. Remove the chocolate mixture from the microwave and stir to melt any remaining bits. At low speed, beat this into the egg mixture. By hand, stir in the flour, salt, and baking soda.

Fold in the remaining 2 cups large semisweet chocolate chips or chunks and the pecans. Cover and chill for 15 minutes.

4. Drop the cookies onto the prepared baking sheets using a 2-ounce ice-cream scoop or by ¼ cupfuls. Leave at least 2 inches between the cookies and do not flatten them.

5. Bake the cookies for 10 to 12 minutes, until they are barely firm when lightly touched and a thin cracked layer shows on the top. If in doubt, it is better to underbake to ensure a moist, fudgy texture. For even baking, halfway into the baking period rotate the baking sheets from top to bottom and front to back. Cool the cookies on the baking sheets for several minutes and then carefully remove them to a rack to cool. These cookies are best eaten the same day as made but will store in an airtight container no more than 2 days.

Cookie Crumb Crusts

Cookie Crumbs can be substituted for graham crackers in recipes that call for the traditional graham cracker crust. Simply process the homemade or store-bought cookies in the food processor until crumbs form. Substitute measure for measure and add a little less fat than called for in the original recipe. Some of our favorite combinations are Oreos for the base of chocolate cheesecakes (they're good sprinkled in the filling also), pecan sandies for the crust in praline cheesecakes, and Lorna Doones with any pie or cheesecake containing fruit or a fruit topping.

Where Are the Ladyfingers?

Ladyfingers may be located in your supermarket in the produce department with shortcake cups and angel food cakes. Look for them near the berries. (See page 200 for a mail-order source.)

CHOCOLATE MIGHTY MOUSSE

Serves 8
20 minutes to prepare
2 hours and 15 minutes to 2 hours and 45 minutes to chill
2-quart clear glass trifle bowl

Here's an easy but impressive-looking dessert for you and your guests. A basic microwave chocolate custard is lightened with egg white, and the whipping cream carries the chocolate flavor throughout and adds smoothness.

If the mousse is eaten before the ladyfingers soften, there is the nice contrast of smooth and crisp. If you allow the ladyfingers to soften, the dessert becomes more like a pudding cake. Either way, it's very simple and worth the effort.

⅔ cup unsweetened cocoa
2 tablespoons (2 envelopes) unflavored gelatin
1¼ cups sugar, divided
2⅓ cups milk
4 large eggs, separated
24 ladyfingers
1 teaspoon fresh lemon juice or white wine vinegar
2 cups whipping cream
Chocolate Curls (optional; see sidebar, page 202)

1. In a microwavable 8-cup measure, mix the cocoa, gelatin, and 1 cup of the sugar. Whisk in the milk and egg yolks. Let stand for 1 minute. Microwave on 70% (medium) for 3 minutes. Whisk until the chocolate is blended and smooth.

2. Cover and chill until the mixture mounds slightly when dropped from a spoon, about 45 minutes. Meanwhile, line the bottom and the sides of a clear glass trifle bowl with the ladyfingers.

3. When the chocolate mixture has chilled to the proper consistency, place the egg whites in the processor bowl fitted with the plastic or steel blade and prepare to beat (see pages 19–20). Process for 10 seconds, until foamy. With the machine running, add the lemon juice or white wine vinegar

through the feed tube. Continue processing for 20 seconds and slowly pour the remaining sugar through the feed tube. Process until the whites are stiff. Fold the egg whites into the chocolate mixture.

4. Rinse the processor bowl and blade. Add the whipping cream and process until the cream is whipped (see page 17). Fold ⅔ of the whipped cream into the chocolate mixture. Pour the mousse into the ladyfinger-lined bowl. Garnish the top with the remaining whipped cream and chocolate curls, if desired. Cover with plastic wrap and refrigerate for 1½ to 2 hours. Serve well chilled.

4
*L*OW-FAT, LOW-CHOLESTEROL DESSERTS IN A HURRY

alf-time cooks often use their spare time in health-improving exercise and conditioning activities instead of cooking. The attitude we hear is that the best way to deal with desserts is to forget the whole fattening idea. We say balderdash. Everybody wants a little sweet comfort from time to time.

But since we find ourselves at that age wherein we not only have to worry about stamina and strength, but also about our cholesterol and fats—and all on a tight schedule—we knew we'd have to come up with some great sweet stuff that wouldn't clog our arteries.

The first great discovery we made was that you can make that grandest of fat-free desserts, an angel food cake, in the food processor. The only alteration in ingredients from classic recipes is that you must add a little lemon juice or white vinegar to the egg whites to further stabilize them. The main difference in technique is that instead of sifting the cake flour three times, we simply aerate it in the food processor bowl along with the sugar. The resulting cake looks a lot like the angel food cakes you buy at the bakery. We know it may not be as high as your grandmother's angel food cake mixed with a wire whisk in a copper bowl, but then again, your grandmother isn't in your house to whip up her old-fashioned cake, either.

Another discovery we made is that you don't have to make a trip to TCBY for great frozen yogurt. You can make it at home. Kids like it as well as ice cream, and if you have an automatic ice-cream maker, it's a cinch to make.

We also discovered a way to make low-fat piecrust so we wouldn't have to do without pie when we had so much good fruit around. This crust is a terrific impostor.

But maybe our best discovery in the low-fat world is a luscious low-fat, no-cholesterol brownie. I mean, isn't it the truth? We may do without fat, we may do without calories, but no way will we do without chocolate. These brownies, plumped with nonfat yogurt and made rich with low-fat cocoa, are a must. We do cheat sometimes and frost them with chocolate chips. It's sort of the same idea as low-fat frozen yogurt smothered in M&M's. Salves the conscience, feeds the sweet tooth.

We also made our share of cakes with less fat than usual. The greatest surprise was the new-age cousin to a pineapple upside-down cake we made using egg whites only. This cake is easy to make and brightly flavored.

Besides the recipes in this chapter, we'd also like to steer you to the fruit and custard chapters. You'll find additional simple desserts in those chapters that are also low in fat and sometimes in calories as well.

If you overprocess the egg whites and they become dry and lumpy instead of smooth and silky, add an extra unbeaten white and fold it in gently just to distribute it evenly throughout. If it seems the volume of your meringue, cake, or pudding will be affected by this extra white, remove 1/3 cup of the beaten egg white before continuing.

SNOW-WHITE ANGEL FOOD CAKE

Makes one 10-inch cake
20 minutes to prepare
50 minutes to bake
10-inch tube pan

We were so thankful to learn that the food processor could whip egg whites. Use the plastic or metal blade or the whisk attachment, which adds more volume when whipping egg whites. Be sure your egg whites are at least 3 days old and bring them to room temperature as soon as you separate them from the yolks. (For more on beating egg whites, see pages 19–20).

1¼ cups sugar, divided
  1 cup cake flour
 ½ teaspoon salt
12 egg whites, separated
  2 tablespoons fresh lemon juice or white wine vinegar
  1 teaspoon vanilla extract

1. Preheat the oven to 350° F. In the food processor bowl fitted with the metal blade, combine ¼ cup of the sugar, flour, and salt. Pulse several times to blend. Pour the dry ingredients out onto a piece of waxed paper. Rinse the processor bowl and dry. Refit with the blade or whisk attachment.

2. Meanwhile, warm the egg whites (see page 18). Add the egg whites to the processor bowl. If your processor has variable speed control, process on low speed until foamy, about 30 seconds. If your food processor only has 1 speed, process the egg whites about 8 seconds, until foamy.

3. Add the lemon juice or white wine vinegar through the feed tube. Use high speed and process until the whites are stiff but not dry, about 1 minute. Add the vanilla through the feed tube along with the remaining 1 cup sugar, 1 tablespoon at a time. Process until the peaks are stiff and glossy and just tip over.

4. Scrape the egg whites into a large bowl. Gently fold the reserved dry ingredients into the egg whites, adding them a third at a time. Pour the batter into an ungreased 10-inch

tube pan. Bake on the middle rack until the cake springs back when lightly touched and turns golden brown, about 50 minutes. Invert the cake pan over a rack and let it cool completely, at least 1½ hours. Run a knife around the side of the pan to loosen the cake and invert the cake onto a cake plate. Cut the angel food cake with a cake breaker or with 2 forks, not with a knife. Store in a plastic bag at room temperature.

Variation: Chocolate Angel Food Cake

Substitute ¼ cup of cocoa for a ¼ of the cake flour.

❖   ❖

Be an Angel and Bring Me That Piece of Cake, Please?

Like sponge cakes, angel food cakes are made without shortening or fat. So for those of you watching your fat grams, feel free to have your cake and eat it too. We like to start with a homemade or store-bought angel food cake and add a scoop of Low-Fat Vanilla Frozen Yogurt (see page 118). And, finally, top with pureed fresh strawberries that have been lightly sweetened for a dieter's version of strawberry shortcake.

FROZEN YOGURT

Makes 1 quart to serve 4
1 hour to freeze
6 hours to chill
Ice-cream freezer

Summer just wouldn't be summer without digging out the old ice-cream maker and cranking your way to a delicious, creamy frozen treat. Here's one place we will gladly give up the fat grams as we are convinced it's hard to tell the difference between ice cream with all those fat calories and a well-balanced frozen yogurt.

LOW-FAT VANILLA FROZEN YOGURT

With only the mellow, sweet taste of vanilla, this will soon become a family favorite.

4 cups (32 ounces) sweetened vanilla-flavored low-fat yogurt
1 teaspoon vanilla extract
2 tablespoons confectioners' sugar

CHOCOLATE SWIRL FROZEN YOGURT

Kids like this healthy alternative to ice cream. Don't forget to swirl the chocolate into the yogurt at the very last minute by hand or it will dissolve into the yogurt and you will lose the swirl.

4 cups (32 ounces) sweetened vanilla-flavored low-fat yogurt
1 teaspoon vanilla extract
3 ounces semisweet chocolate, melted in the microwave and cooled to room temperature

VERY BERRY LOW-FAT FROZEN YOGURT

Berries are our fruit of choice because they have thin skins that break down in most ice-cream machines, and do not turn dark, like bananas. Stone fruits and firm fruits such as peaches and apples tend to freeze and turn to icy rocks.

> **4 cups (32 ounces) sweetened berry-flavored low-fat yogurt, drained of any liquid that may be floating on top**
> **1 cup fresh berries (optional)**
> **1 teaspoon vanilla extract**
> **¼ cup confectioners' sugar or to taste (optional)**

1. Mix the yogurt and other ingredients for each recipe (except the chocolate in Chocolate Swirl Frozen Yogurt) in a 1½-quart mixing bowl. Cover and chill in the refrigerator overnight or at least for 6 hours. Stir to blend. Freeze according to the manufacturer's instructions for your ice-cream freezer.

2. When the paddle stalls and the yogurt is fairly stiff, remove the paddle immediately from the frozen yogurt. (If you're making Chocolate Swirl Frozen Yogurt, gently stir the chocolate into the frozen yogurt just until swirled.) Place the frozen yogurt in the freezer compartment of the freezer. Let it freeze solid for 1 hour. Scoop the yogurt into pretty dessert dishes and serve immediately.

The Color of Raspberries

A bright-red raspberry may be tempting to the eye, but raspberry growers assure us that the sweetest berries are those that have been allowed to ripen on the vine a little longer. The vine-ripened berries will be darker in color, almost a purple-red or magenta color. These berries will begin to appear on the market 2 to 3 weeks after the season starts.

✧   ✧

Blueberries

Fresh blueberries are available June through August in most areas of the United States. We freeze or dehydrate them to use in the winter. Look for large berries that are dark blue, plump, and wrinkle free. Discard any green berries or berries with mold. Dried blueberries have a concentrated blueberry flavor and are delicious when mixed in with frozen berries in your favorite muffin recipe.

A deep-dish apple pie with a crust on the top only is a good choice when you need a pie that will not be served immediately, because the crust will not get soggy. Select a baking dish that is 2 to 3 inches deep and fill with the filling. Place the crust on top and slit several times to allow steam to escape and bake as directed. Watch the last 5 minutes or so, as the crust may brown a little faster, being on top.

LEAN AND LUSCIOUS DEEP-DISH APPLE PIE

Serves 8
20 minutes to prepare
35 minutes to bake
10-inch deep-dish pie pan

In a fruit pie most of the fat is located in the crust and not the filling, so one of the secrets to cutting back on fat in pies is to eliminate one of the crusts. This low-fat piecrust only has 4 grams of fat per serving and no cholesterol at all. Add the topping and you still only have 6 grams of fat per serving.

The food processor is a wonderful tool to use to distribute the fat evenly when using reduced amounts of fat in piecrusts and pastries. We promise you won't feel deprived when you taste this luscious impostor.

LOW-FAT PIECRUST

1 cup unbleached all-purpose flour
2 tablespoons granulated sugar
3 tablespoons vegetable shortening
3 to 4 tablespoons ice water

FILLING

4 large Granny Smith apples, peeled, cored, and cut into 8 wedges each
½ teaspoon ground cinnamon
⅛ teaspoon freshly grated nutmeg
⅓ cup granulated sugar
3 tablespoons unbleached all-purpose flour

TOPPING

3 tablespoons packed brown sugar
¼ cup unbleached all-purpose flour
1½ tablespoons margarine
¼ teaspoon ground cinnamon

1. Preheat the oven to 425° F. For the piecrust, fit the processor bowl with the steel blade, add the flour and sugar. Pulse to mix. Add the shortening and process until the mixture resembles coarse meal. Add 3 tablespoons of the ice water and process. Remove the lid and feel the crust, checking to see if it will hold together when squeezed between your fingers. If not, add 1 tablespoon of water and process. The dough should now hold together when squeezed.

2. Dump the crust onto a well-floured surface. Squeeze the dough together and flatten into a 6-inch disk. Roll the piecrust into a 12-inch circle. Carefully fit the piecrust into a 10-inch deep-dish pie pan. Trim and flute the edges.

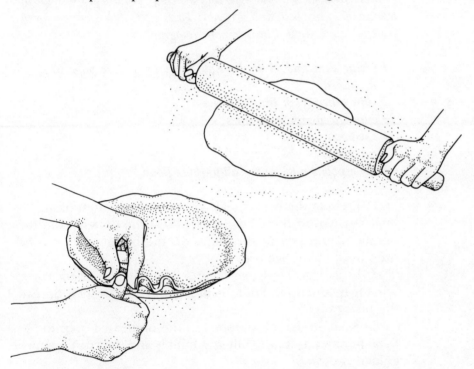

3. For the filling, in a large bowl toss the apples, cinnamon, nutmeg, sugar, and flour. Place in the prepared crust.

4. For the topping, wipe out the processor bowl and process the brown sugar, flour, margarine, and cinnamon until crumbly. Pour the topping over the apples. Bake on the middle rack of the preheated oven for 30 to 35 minutes, until the crust and apples are browned and the apples are tender when pierced with a knife. Serve warm or at room temperature.

NECTARINE–BING CHERRY TART

Serves 6
30 minutes to prepare
40 to 50 minutes to bake
11-inch tart pan

A beauty to behold, this tart will bring rave reviews. Nectarines that are not too ripe are best, and frozen cherries that have been pitted, thawed, and drained may be substituted for the fresh.

Fresh fruit tarts are so light and delicious you'll want to have the leftovers for breakfast, and why not? Tarts offer endless variety for the fruit at hand, limited only by your imagination.

1 recipe Fast and Flaky No-Roll Short Crust (see page 61), unbaked
3 cups pitted fresh Bing cherries
3 cups sliced ripe nectarines
¼ teaspoon salt
⅔ cup sugar
3 tablespoons unbleached all-purpose flour

1. Preheat the oven to 375° F. Coat the bottom of an 11-inch tart pan with cooking spray. Press the dough from the middle of the pan to the edges on the bottom and up the sides of the pan. Set aside.

2. In a large bowl toss together the cherries, nectarines, salt, sugar, and flour. Pour the filling into the tart shell. Spread the filling evenly.

3. Bake on the middle shelf of the preheated oven for 40 to 50 minutes, until the filling is bubbly and the crust is a nice golden brown.

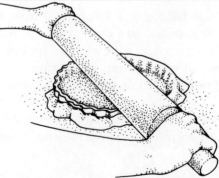

FRESH STRAWBERRY TART

Serves 6 to 8
20 minutes to prepare
20 minutes to bake
11-inch tart pan

We love summer strawberries, and this tart shows them off in their full glory. Each perfect berry sits atop the flaky, easy short crust and is napped with strawberry spread spiked with Grand Marnier. Choose a shallow, fluted tart pan with a removable bottom. Garnish with a few fresh mint leaves for a real grand finale. This tart is best eaten the same day as baked.

1 heaping quart fresh ripe strawberries
1 10-ounce jar all-fruit strawberry spread
⅓ cup Grand Marnier
1 recipe Fast and Flaky No-Roll Short Crust (see page 61), baked
Fresh mint leaves, for garnish (optional)

1. Stem and wash the strawberries and reserve.

2. Fit the food processor with the steel blade and combine the strawberry spread and Grand Marnier. Process for 10 seconds. Pour this glaze into a deep small bowl and set aside.

3. Place the cooled crust on a serving tray. Brush the bottom lightly with some of the glaze. Dip the strawberries into the glaze and place them in the crust stem end down. To serve, garnish with fresh mint leaves, if desired.

Other berries, such as blackberries, blueberries, or raspberries, and fruits such as nectarines, peaches, and plums, will work with this simple crust. You may also use fruit spreads with the same fruit as that in the tart, or try complementary flavors, such as fresh blueberries with peach fruit spread or nectarines with cherry fruit spread; the combinations are endless.

Sometimes nothing but chocolate will do. If you're watching your fat intake, you may want to try substituting cocoa for baking chocolate or chocolate chips in recipes. Naturally low in fat, cocoa can be used in most recipes that call for baking chocolate or chocolate chips that are melted.

Whack away at the fat content by shaving off the amount of shortening you add to the cocoa to approximate the chocolate called for in your favorite recipe. If you want to tinker with a recipe's fat content, cut back from the standard listed on page 93. You're on your own once you start experimenting. We've made things that tasted like sponges when the fat content got too low. We've also had some pleasant surprises. Good luck.

LUSCIOUS LOW-FAT
NO-CHOLESTEROL BROWNIES

Makes 9 squares
10 minutes to prepare
25 to 30 minutes to bake
9-inch square baking pan

If you like the texture of gingerbread and the taste of chocolate, try these low-fat brownies. Made without the chocolate chip icing, they weigh in at a respectable 5.6 grams of fat per serving. Top the brownies with chocolate chips, and you still only get 6.9 grams of unsaturated fat per serving, and no cholesterol at all.

3 large egg whites
1 cup sugar
1 teaspoon vanilla extract
¼ cup vegetable oil
¼ cup (2 ounces) plain nonfat yogurt
¼ teaspoon salt
¼ teaspoon baking powder
⅓ cup unsweetened cocoa
½ cup unbleached all-purpose flour
¼ cup semisweet chocolate chips (optional)

1. Preheat the oven to 375° F. Coat a 9-inch square baking pan with cooking spray.

2. Combine in a food processor bowl fitted with the plastic blade the following ingredients, adding in order and beating after each addition: egg whites, then sugar, vanilla, oil, yogurt, salt, baking powder, and cocoa. Finally, open the top, and sprinkle the flour evenly over the mixture. Hand stir just until the flour is barely mixed in.

3. Pour the mixture into the prepared pan, smoothing the batter evenly. Bake in the preheated oven until the center is cooked, 25 to 30 minutes, until a toothpick inserted in the middle comes out barely moist.

4. Remove the brownies from the oven and, if you wish, sprinkle with chocolate chips. Once the chips have melted, smooth them evenly over the top for the simplest icing you ever made. Cut the brownies into 9 squares and serve warm.

CHOCOLATE RITZ RASPBERRY CHEESECAKE CUPS

Makes 36 to serve 10 to 12
15 minutes to prepare
18 minutes to bake
3 miniature-muffin tins

A bite-sized morsel that tastes oh so rich. Creamy cheesecake flavored with Framboise or Chambord. With such a creamy center and luscious taste you would expect to find them tucked away inside an extremely expensive box of chocolates wrapped in gold. But no. You made them yourself.

8 ounces light process cream cheese product
⅔ cup sugar
½ cup 1% low-fat cottage cheese
2 tablespoons unbleached all-purpose flour
3 tablespoons Framboise or Chambord, raspberry-flavored liqueur
3 tablespoons unsweetened cocoa
½ teaspoon vanilla extract
1 large egg
   Pinch of salt
2 tablespoons semisweet mini–chocolate chips
36 fresh raspberries and fresh mint leaves, for garnish (optional)
   Mint Chocolate Curls (optional; see sidebar)

1. Preheat the oven to 300° F. In the bowl of a food processor fitted with the steel blade, process the cream cheese product, sugar, cottage cheese, flour, liqueur, cocoa, vanilla, egg, and salt until smooth and creamy. Fit 3 miniature-muffin pans with paper liners (batter may be stored, covered, at room temperature if you need to bake these in 2 batches).

2. Carefully pour the batter evenly into the lined pans or pour all of the batter into a large measuring cup with a lip and pour into the liners. Sprinkle each with 4 or 5 mini-chocolate chips. Bake for 18 minutes. Let cool in pans for 10 minutes. Remove and allow to cool to room temperature. Cover and refrigerate for at least 2 hours. Garnish with optional raspberries, mint leaves or Mint Chocolate Curls just before serving.

Mint Chocolate Curls

One of our favorite garnishes for Chocolate Ritz Raspberry Cheesecake Cups, chocolate cakes, cookies, or any dessert where a chocolate-mint flavor is appropriate is the Andes mint chocolate curl. Andes mints are the small rectangular mints in green foil found in restaurants by the cash register. The mint is chocolate with a green mint center. Using a potato peeler, shave curls off the side of the mint. Gently sprinkle the curls on the top of your favorite brownie, chocolate pudding, or any cooled dessert.

Diana's Mocha Moo Shake

Makes 1 cup to serve 1
2-cup container with a tight lid

Chocolate for breakfast or for a snack, nothing could be easier!

- ¼ cup strong cold brewed coffee
- ⅓ cup skim milk
- ⅓ cup water
- 1 tablespoon chocolate syrup, homemade (see page 96) or store-bought

In a 2-cup container with a tight-fitting lid, add the coffee, milk, water, and chocolate syrup. Toss in a few ice cubes and shake until well blended and frothy. Pour into a large iced-tea glass and serve immediately.

CHOCOLATE CUPCAKES WITH COCONUT-CHEESE ICING

Makes 12 muffins to serve 12
15 minutes to prepare
20 minutes to bake
Standard 12-muffin tin

Two flavors from one of our favorite candy bars come together in these moist cupcakes—chocolate and coconut. Sit back with a good book or video and enjoy with a nice cold glass of skim milk.

- ½ cup 1% low-fat cottage cheese
- 3 tablespoons light corn syrup
- 4 tablespoons sweetened shredded coconut
- ¾ teaspoon coconut extract, divided
- ½ cup sugar
- ¼ cup (½ stick) margarine, softened
- 1 large egg
- ⅔ cup skim or low-fat milk
- 1¼ cups unbleached all-purpose flour
- ½ teaspoon baking soda
  Pinch of salt
- 3 tablespoons unsweetened cocoa
- 2 ounces (2 squares) semisweet chocolate, melted or ½ cup semisweet chocolate chips, melted (optional)

1. Preheat the oven to 375° F. In the bowl of the food processor fitted with the steel blade, combine the cottage cheese and corn syrup. Process until smooth. Scrape into a small mixing bowl. Add the coconut and ½ teaspoon of the coconut extract. Set aside.

2. In a clean processor bowl fitted with the steel blade, process the remaining ¼ teaspoon coconut extract, sugar, margarine, egg, and milk until light and fluffy, about 1 minute.

3. In a small bowl, combine the flour, soda, salt, and cocoa. Stir to mix well. Pour the flour mixture over the cottage cheese and coconut mixture in the processor bowl. Pulse 4 or 5 times until all dry ingredients are incorporated.

4. Line 12 muffin cups with paper liners. Divide the chocolate batter evenly among the muffin cups. Top with equal amounts of the coconut mixture. Bake on the middle rack of the preheated oven for 20 minutes. Remove from the pan to a rack to cool. When the cupcakes are room temperature, drizzle them with the melted chocolate, if you wish.

*L*IGHT CARROT CAKE WITH ORANGE–CREAM CHEESE FROSTING

Serves 8 to 10
20 minutes to prepare
35 minutes to bake
13 × 9 × 2-inch baking pan

Packed with carrots and pineapple, this moist cake will soon become a family favorite. We cut down on oil and eggs and eliminated the walnuts from the traditional recipe. However, we kept the cream cheese frosting made with Neufchâtel cheese, which is lower in fat and, to some, the best part anyway.

2¼ cups unbleached all-purpose flour
1 teaspoon ground cinnamon
2 teaspoons baking soda
¼ teaspoon freshly grated nutmeg
¾ teaspoon ground allspice
⅛ teaspoon salt
¾ cup firmly packed light brown sugar
3 tablespoons vegetable oil
2 large eggs
4 large carrots, cleaned and lightly scraped or enough to make 3 cups grated carrot
½ cup raisins
⅔ cup nonfat or low-fat buttermilk
2 teaspoons vanilla extract
1 8-ounce can (1 cup) crushed pineapple, drained

(continued)

Carrot cake is one way to use large carrots that may be sitting in the bottom of your vegetable bin. Before using very large carrots, clean, trim, and taste one. If it's bitter, remove the core, and it will be more tender and less bitter.

Carrots like to be stored in a plastic bag at low humidity levels with their green tops removed. Properly stored carrots should keep for up to 2 weeks.

ORANGE–CREAM CHEESE FROSTING

3 cups confectioners' sugar
4 tablespoons Neufchâtel cheese, room temperature
3 tablespoons fresh orange juice
½ teaspoon minced orange zest
½ teaspoon vanilla extract

1. Coat a 13 × 9 × 2-inch baking pan with cooking spray. Preheat the oven to 350° F. In a small bowl, combine the flour, cinnamon, baking soda, nutmeg, allspice, and salt. Stir to combine and set aside.

2. In a large bowl, whisk together the brown sugar, oil, and eggs.

3. Fit the processor with the grater attachment and grate enough carrots to make 3 cups. Add the carrots, raisins, buttermilk, vanilla, and pineapple to the brown sugar–oil–egg mixture. Stir well. Add the flour mixture and stir just to combine.

4. Pour cake batter into the pan. Bake on the middle rack of the preheated oven for 35 to 40 minutes, until a toothpick inserted comes out clean. Cool completely in the pan on a wire rack. Meanwhile, prepare the frosting.

5. Place in a clean processor bowl the confectioners' sugar, Neufchâtel cheese, orange juice, orange zest, and vanilla. Process until smooth and creamy. Spread on the cooled cake. This cake remains moist for up to a week if stored in an airtight container in the refrigerator.

FAT-FREE GLAZED ORANGE-PINEAPPLE CAKE

Serves 6
15 minutes to prepare
30 minutes to bake
9-inch square baking pan

This is a fat-free cousin to pineapple upside-down cake, only easier and better for you.

1 cup sugar

¼ cup cornstarch

1 cup unbleached all-purpose flour

1½ teaspoons baking powder

½ teaspoon salt

2 large egg whites

⅓ cup skim milk

⅓ cup light corn syrup

⅓ cup fresh orange juice

1 teaspoon orange extract

1 teaspoon grated orange zest or 1 teaspoon dried orange peel

GLAZE AND TOPPING

½ cup fresh orange juice

½ cup sugar

1 8-ounce can (1 cup) pineapple rings, drained

9 maraschino cherries

1. Preheat the oven to 350° F. Coat a 9-inch square baking pan with cooking spray.

2. In a large bowl, combine the sugar, cornstarch, flour, baking powder, and salt. Mix well.

3. In a medium bowl, combine the egg whites, milk, corn syrup, orange juice, orange extract, and orange zest or dried orange peel. Whisk until the egg whites are fully incorporated into the liquids. Add the liquids to the flour mixture and whisk until smooth.

4. Pour the batter into the prepared pan and bake on the middle rack of the preheated oven for 30 minutes, until a tester comes out clean when inserted into the center and the cake starts to pull away from the sides of the pan. Remove the pan to a rack to cool. Preheat the broiler.

5. Meanwhile, in a 2-cup glass measure combine the orange juice and sugar for the glaze. Microwave on 100% (high) for 2 minutes. Stir the orange juice–sugar mixture until the sugar has thoroughly dissolved. Pour the hot juice glaze over the warm cake and lay the pineapple rings on top. Add maraschino cherries in the middle of the pineapple rings. Broil 6 inches from the heat source, until the pineapple is lightly browned. Serve warm with any extra glaze that is not absorbed into the cake spooned on top.

Makes 1¼ cups
5 minutes to prepare
8-cup glass measure

Any berry sauce is delicious over pound cake or ice cream. Here is one of the easiest.

5 cups fresh or thawed frozen blackberries, blueberries, or raspberries
1 teaspoon cornstarch
Pinch of salt
Sugar to taste
2 teaspoons margarine

Press the berries through a sieve into an 8-cup microwavable bowl or glass measure. Pour a little of the juice into a small bowl and whisk the cornstarch into this juice. Add this juice back to the bowl and whisk again. Whisk in the salt and sugar to taste. Microwave on 100% (high) for 2 minutes, until the sauce begins to simmer. Whisk and microwave for an additional minute, until the sauce is thickened and will coat the back of a spoon dipped into it. Remove the sauce from the microwave and whisk in the margarine until melted. Serve warm or at room temperature.

LOW-CHOLESTEROL POUND CAKE

Serves 8
15 minutes to prepare
55 minutes to 1 hour to bake
8½ × 4½ × 4-inch glass loaf pan

If you do watch your cholesterol (and who doesn't?), now you can have your cake and eat it too!

We tested the cake with commercial egg substitute and plain egg whites. Both were delicious, so use whatever you have handy. Enjoy!

½ cup (1 stick) margarine, softened
⅔ cup sugar
½ cup egg substitute or 3 large egg whites
1 cup (8 ounces) low-fat vanilla-flavored yogurt
1 tablespoon vanilla extract
1 teaspoon almond or lemon extract
¼ teaspoon salt
¾ teaspoon baking soda
2½ cups sifted cake flour
Easy Breezy Berry Sauce (optional; see sidebar)

1. Preheat the oven to 350° F. Coat an 8½ × 4½ × 4-inch glass loaf pan with cooking spray.

2. In the food processor bowl fitted with the steel blade, process the margarine, sugar, and egg substitute or egg whites until light and fluffy, about 1 minute. Add the yogurt, vanilla, and almond or lemon extract. Process for 1 minute.

3. Add the salt and baking soda to the sifted cake flour. Stir to combine. Remove the lid from the processor bowl and pour the flour over the top of the batter. Pulse 4 to 6 times to blend the flour into the batter. More than 6 pulses and the cake may become rubbery. With a spoon fold in any flour that remains on top of the batter.

4. Pour the batter into the prepared pan and bake on the middle rack of the preheated oven for 55 to 60 minutes, until lightly browned and a tester comes out clean when inserted into the middle of the cake. Cool in the pan for 10 minutes and then turn out onto a rack to cool completely. Serve plain or with your favorite fruit sauce if desired.

CRATER LAKE CAKE

Makes one 9-inch cake to serve 12
15 minutes to prepare
45 minutes to bake
9-inch cheesecake pan with removable bottom

As mysterious as our own neighborhood lake, and cratered in the middle besides, how could a chocolate cake this rich be both delicious and healthy? No egg yolks, no butterfat, no ugly surprises. Just a luscious, darkly dangerous, fat-free cake.

1 cup (6 large) egg whites
2 teaspoons fresh lemon juice
1¼ cup sugar, divided
1 cup cake flour
¾ cup unsweetened cocoa
1½ teaspoons baking powder
1½ teaspoons baking soda
¼ cup nonfat dry milk
1 cup warm water
2 teaspoons vanilla extract
  Raspberry jam, orange marmalade, confectioners' sugar
  (optional)

1. Preheat the oven to 350° F. With cooking spray coat a 9-inch cheesecake pan that's 3 inches deep and has a removable bottom.

2. In the food processor bowl, fitted with the plastic or steel blade or the whisk attachment, process the egg whites until frothy (sees page 19–20). Add the lemon juice through the feed tube, then ½ cup of the sugar, a tablespoon at a time, processing until stiff, moist peaks form. Remove to a medium bowl and set aside.

3. Combine in the food processor bowl the flour, cocoa, baking powder, baking soda, remaining sugar, and nonfat dry milk. Pulse, then pour in the warm water and vanilla. Process to mix.

4. Use a rubber spatula to fold the egg whites into the chocolate mixture until evenly blended. Pour the batter into the prepared pan and bake in the preheated oven for about

(continued)

Rescuing Egg Whites

If you overprocess the egg whites and they become dry and lumpy instead of smooth and silky, add an extra unbeaten white and fold it in gently just to distribute it evenly throughout. If it seems the volume of your meringue, cake, or pudding will be affected by this extra white, remove ⅓ cup of the beaten egg white before continuing.

45 minutes, until a toothpick inserted into the center comes out clean.

5. Cool the cake in the pan on a rack. The center will sink as it cools. Remove the pan sides. Fill the crater with raspberry jam, orange marmalade, or simply dust the top with confectioners' sugar. Serve the cake on a paper doily on a footed cake stand. Cut into wedges.

MERINGUE TORTE WITH LEMON AND STRAWBERRIES

Serves 6
30 minutes to prepare
1 hour to bake
2 hours to dry in turned-off oven
9½ × 12½-inch baking sheet

A beauty to behold, this torte stars as a centerpiece on a spring table laden with daffodils, tulips, and azaleas. Meringues are the perfect substitute for a high-fat pastry crust when you want to cut back on fat and calories in dessert. Fresh strawberries or fresh blueberries can be interchanged with equally good results.

Although the meringue is in the oven for a total of 3 hours, 2 hours are unattended, with the oven turned off while the meringue dries out.

MERINGUE TORTE

3 large egg whites, separated
2 teaspoons fresh lemon juice or white wine vinegar
⅛ teaspoon salt
½ cup sugar

FILLING

⅔ cup sugar
2 teaspoons cornstarch
1 teaspoon minced lemon zest
⅓ cup water
⅓ cup fresh lemon juice
1 large egg yolk
4 cups fresh strawberries or blueberries
Fresh mint leaves, for garnish (optional)

1. Preheat the oven to 275° F. Meanwhile, warm the egg whites (see page 18). For the meringue torte, fit the processor bowl with the plastic or steel blade. Add the egg whites. Process until foamy, about 8 seconds (see pages 19–20). With the machine running, pour the lemon juice or white wine vinegar through the feed tube and process until the whites are stiff, about 1 minute. With the machine running, add the salt and gradually add the sugar through the feed tube. Process until stiff and the whites hold their shape, about 1 minute.

2. Using an 8-inch round cake pan, trace a circle on a piece of parchment paper. Place the circle on a rectangular baking sheet. Spoon the egg whites onto the paper pattern. Shape the egg whites into a circle and mound up the sides at least 2 inches higher than the center.

3. Bake on the middle rack of the preheated oven for 1 hour. Turn the oven off and let the meringue dry out in the oven for 2 hours. Carefully peel the meringue off the paper and place it on a serving platter.

Browning a Meringue

If you like your meringue to be a little more golden, after the shell has baked for 1 hour, carefully place it on the top rack under the broiler and watch carefully for 1 to 2 minutes until it browns. Place the meringue back on the middle shelf and let it dry in the oven for the remaining 2 hours.

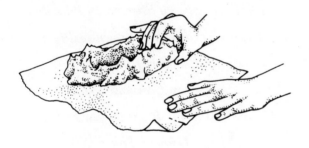

4. Meanwhile, prepare the filling. In a microwavable bowl, combine the sugar, cornstarch, lemon zest, water, and lemon juice. Stir well with a plastic or wooden spoon to combine. Microwave on 70% (medium) for 4 minutes, stirring after every 2 minutes. Place the egg yolk in a small bowl and add a little of the hot mixture to it. Stir well. Add the egg yolk mixture to the lemon filling and stir well. Microwave on 70% (medium) for 2 minutes. The mixture will now be thick. Let it cool to room temperature.

5. Meanwhile, gently wash, hull, and slice the strawberries, if using. When the meringue is cooked and dried and the filling is cool, fold the strawberries or washed, whole blueberries into the lemon filling and pour into the meringue. Garnish with mint leaves if desired and serve immediately.

5
COOKIES, BROWNIES, AND BARS

e better start off this behemoth chapter by telling you what you won't find here. There are no cutout cookies that are eaten up before you can get the flour scraped off the countertop. No hard to make, decorated, and doodad cookies here either.

Instead, you'll find quick, easy, delicious recipes for cookies that are cut into bars, dropped, or baked whole and then sliced.

Brownies, we learned, are a task made to order for the half-time cook. Use the food processor to mix the batter, the microwave oven to melt the chocolate, and the conventional oven to bake so that you get a crisp, brown crust, and you'll have a pan of brownies before you can say Girl Scout. We like brownies so well, we've included more than one version. (See also page 124 for low-fat, low-cholesterol brownies.)

We also love shortbread-based cookies. These are too easy in the food processor. Whiz up the butter with flour and sugar, then dump the batter into a baking pan. Don't press down too hard, or you'll have a shingle instead of a cookie. Just lightly pat the shortbread into the pan, and you'll get that crumbly, sweet, baked butter flavor that makes our mouths water at the very thought.

Here are a couple of shortcuts we've learned in the process. Use waxed paper or parchment paper on the cookie sheets, and you can whisk the sheets onto a rack to cool.

Borrow a technique from Mrs. Fields and use an ice-cream scoop to measure out drop cookie dough. You'll get equal-sized cookies easily.

Another of our favorite tools for half-time cookie baking is the pizza-cutting wheel. A cookie sheet dough or baked cookies can be cut into diamonds or squares quickly and cleanly using this tool.

Lemon Cups

Lemon cups can be used to serve sorbets as a light refresher between courses or after a large meal.

To make lemon cups, choose large lemons. At one end, slice off just enough so that the lemon will stand. Slice the other end deeply enough to extract the juice and pulp with a lemon reamer or juicer. Fill with sorbet and store in the freezer until serving time. Garnish with mint, candied violets, or other edible garnish.

*L*EMON-CURD BUTTER BARS

Serves 6 to 8
15 minutes to prepare
35 to 40 minutes to bake
2 hours to chill
9-inch square glass baking pan

This classic bar cookie has been updated with lemon curd instead of the usual not-so-lemony topping. Lemon curd is usually cooked separately in a double boiler. We've eliminated that step and cook the curd on top of the baking crust. The base and the curd are made in the food processor, leaving little else to wash. Enjoy with an ice-cold glass of milk.

CRUST

1⅓ cups unbleached all-purpose flour
¼ cup granulated sugar
½ cup (1 stick) unsalted butter, cut into 4 pieces

CURD

3 large lemons
1 cup granulated sugar
5 large egg yolks
½ cup (1 stick) unsalted butter
Confectioners' sugar

1. Preheat the oven to 350° F. Lightly coat a 9-inch square glass baking pan with cooking spray. For the crust, in the processor bowl fitted with the steel blade, combine the flour and sugar and pulse to blend. Add the butter and pulse to blend until the butter is finely cut in and almost disappears. Pour the crumbs into the prepared pan and smooth. Don't pat the crumbs down too tightly. Bake on the middle rack of the preheated oven for 15 to 20 minutes, until the edges are just beginning to brown.

2. Meanwhile, for the curd, wipe out the processor bowl with a paper towel and replace the steel blade. Remove the zest from 2 of the lemons with a zester or grater, and combine with the sugar. Process until the lemon peel is finely minced, about 1 minute.

3. Slice the lemons in half and squeeze enough juice to make ½ cup. Add the egg yolks and lemon juice to the sugar mixture and process for 5 seconds. Melt the butter in the microwave on 100% (high) for 1 minute, until thoroughly melted. With the processor running, slowly pour the melted butter through the feed tube. Process for 5 seconds.

4. When the crust's edge is lightly browned, remove it from the oven and pour the lemon-curd mixture over the top. Return to the oven and bake an additional 20 minutes, until the middle is just set (the middle will jiggle a bit when moved). Remove the uncut bars to a rack to cool to room temperature. When the uncut bars have reached room temperature, sift confectioners' sugar on the top. Refrigerate overnight or for at least 2 hours and then cut into bars.

RASPBERRY-HAZELNUT CHOCOLATE BARS

Makes 36 bars
15 minutes to prepare
35 to 40 minutes to bake
13 x 9-inch glass baking pan

A very adult brownie is this bar, moist and rich with just a hint of liqueur. A last-minute dessert, it's easily prepared.

¼ cup (½ stick) unsalted butter
1 ounce (1 square) unsweetened chocolate
2 teaspoons vanilla extract
1 large egg
2 cups sugar, divided
⅓ cup unbleached all-purpose flour
   Pinch of salt
½ cup seedless raspberry all-fruit spread or seedless raspberry jam
2 tablespoons Grand Marnier or Frangelico
2 cups shelled hazelnuts
½ teaspoon salt
6 large egg whites
3 ounces (½ cup) mini-chocolate chips

Chocolate Glaze

Drizzle Raspberry-Hazelnut Chocolate Bars with a rich chocolate glaze if you want to show off.

4 ounces (4 squares) semisweet chocolate or 1 cup semisweet chocolate chips
¼ cup (½ stick) unsalted butter
1 tablespoon light corn syrup

In a microwavable bowl, combine the chocolate, butter, and corn syrup. Microwave uncovered on high (100%) for 3 minutes. Stir to melt any remaining bits. Using the tines of a fork, drizzle the chocolate glaze over the cooled bars.

1. Preheat the oven to 350° F. Coat a 13 × 9-inch glass baking pan with cooking spray. In the bowl of a food processor *without* a blade combine the butter and chocolate. Cover the bowl with waxed paper and microwave on 100% (high) for 90 seconds. Stir to melt any remaining bits.

2. Add the steel blade to the processor bowl and place on the processor base. Add ½ teaspoon of the vanilla, the egg, and ½ cup of the sugar. Process until thoroughly combined, about 30 seconds. Open the lid and sprinkle the flour and pinch of salt on top of the chocolate mixture. Pulse 3 or 4 times, just until the flour is incorporated. Spread into the bottom of the prepared pan and bake on the middle rack of the preheated oven for 10 minutes.

3. Meanwhile, in a small bowl whisk together the raspberry all-fruit spread or jam and liqueur. Set aside.

4. In a clean processor bowl fitted with the steel blade, combine the hazelnuts, ½ teaspoon salt, egg whites, the remaining 1½ teaspoons vanilla, and the remaining 1½ cups sugar. Process until the hazelnuts are finely ground, about 1 minute.

5. Cool the brownie layer in the pan on a rack for 5 minutes. Turn the oven heat up to 375° F. Spread the brownie layer with the raspberry-liqueur mixture to within ½ inch of the edge of the pan. Sprinkle with mini–chocolate chips. Spread the hazelnut–egg white mixture over the top to within ½ inch of the edge.

6. Bake on the middle rack of the preheated oven for 25 to 30 minutes, until the top is firm and a tester comes out clean. Cool on a rack and cut into 36 bars. Serve at room temperature.

*B*LACK-BUTTER SHORTBREADS

Makes 48 walnut-sized balls
20 minutes to prepare
25 to 30 minutes to bake
2 large baking sheets

Melt in your mouth, crumbling, sweet, rich, redolent of almond, these cookies are too easy to taste this good. Use only unsalted butter for the best results. You may caramelize the butter hours before you want to make the cookies and hold it in the refrigerator. This makes the cookie baking just fly by. Never mind that the cookies will also fly out of the jar.

> 1 cup (2 sticks) unsalted butter
> About ½ teaspoon fresh lemon juice
> ¾ cup sugar
> 2 tablespoons milk
> 2 teaspoons vanilla extract
> 2 cups unbleached all-purpose flour
> 1 teaspoon baking powder
> ½ teaspoon salt

1. Place 1 oven rack in the upper third of the oven and 1 rack on the lower third of the oven. Preheat the oven to 300° F. Place the butter in a 4-cup glass measure and microwave it at 100% (high) for 7 minutes, until the solids begin to fall to the bottom, and the butter looks brown and smells like the richest caramel. Remove it from the microwave and add a few drops of lemon juice (about ½ teaspoon). Pour the butter into a flat metal pan with sides, taking care to scrape all those delicious brown solids into the pan, then place it in the freezer a few moments until the butter solidifies.

2. Once the butter is solid, use a rubber spatula to scrape it into the food processor bowl fitted with the steel blade, then add the sugar and process until the mixture is fluffy. Add the milk, vanilla, flour, baking powder, and salt and process just until the mixture forms a ball that begins to ride the blade around. Turn the ball out onto a lightly floured surface, knead a moment, then form into a ball again.

3. Using both your hands, a melon baller, or 2 teaspoons, remove walnut-sized pieces from the ball of dough, form them into small balls, and place them on an ungreased cookie sheet. Once all the balls are on the sheets, flatten each cookie with a fork (like old-fashioned peanut butter cookies). Bake in the preheated oven for 25 to 30 minutes, until the cookies are an even caramel color. For even baking, halfway into the baking period, rotate the baking sheets from top to bottom and front to back. Cool the cookies on the baking sheets for a few moments, then remove to a rack. Store in a tin.

Viennese Coffee

In a large microwavable mixing bowl, microwave on 100% (high) 1 ounce (1 square) semisweet chocolate or ¼ cup semisweet chocolate chips with 1 tablespoon of cream for every cup of coffee to be served just until melted. Whisk in 1 cup of hot coffee for each serving. Whisk until a light froth floats on the top, about 1 minute. Pour into cups. Top with additional whipped cream if desired and dust the tops with ground cinnamon or cocoa.

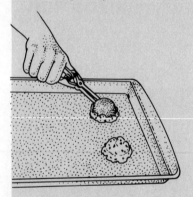
CHOCOLATE CHIP–PECAN COOKIES

Makes 24 cookies
15 minutes to prepare
17 to 20 minutes to bake
2 large baking sheets

Now, for about half the price and not much trouble, you can make your own version of the cookies that you find in the airport and exclusive shops. Real chocolate, fresh sweet butter, and pure vanilla are the secrets to the best cookies. Remember to watch them carefully the last few minutes of baking so they won't overcook and dry out.

½ cup (1 stick) plus 2 tablespoons unsalted butter, softened
½ cup dark brown sugar, packed
⅔ cup granulated sugar
1 large egg
1 teaspoon vanilla extract
1½ cups unbleached all-purpose flour
9 ounces (9 squares) good-quality semisweet chocolate, chopped into ½-inch chunks or 10-ounce package (1⅔ cups) large chocolate chips or chunks (see page 93 for mail-order source for chocolates)
¾ cup coarsely chopped pecans

1. Place 1 oven rack in the upper third of the oven and 1 in the lower third of the oven. Preheat the oven to 325° F. Coat 2 large baking sheets with cooking spray. In the food processor bowl fitted with the steel blade, combine the butter, sugars, egg, and vanilla. Process until light and fluffy, about 1 minute. Spoon the flour on top of the batter and pulse to mix with 3 or 4 pulses.

2. Stir in the chocolate and pecans with a wooden spoon. Drop large tablespoons of dough on the baking sheets about 3 inches apart. Bake for 17 to 20 minutes, until the tops look dry and the edges are lightly browned. For even baking, halfway into the baking period, rotate the baking sheets from top to bottom and front to back. Cool the cookies on the baking sheets for 5 minutes. Remove the cookies from the sheets to a rack to cool. Do not grease the cookie sheets again; repeat with the remaining dough.

COCONUT-LEMON SQUARES

Makes 18 squares
15 minutes to prepare
50 minutes to bake
13 x 9-inch glass baking pan

Always a special treat—as dessert, at an afternoon tea, or just for snacking. Dust lemon squares with confectioners' sugar or serve them plain. Dazzling yellow squares served on a white platter and garnished with edible blue and purple pansies from the garden—they look almost too good to eat, but not quite.

2 cups unbleached all-purpose flour
1 cup (2 sticks) unsalted butter
½ cup confectioners' sugar
4 large eggs
2 cups granulated sugar
1 cup gently packed shredded sweetened coconut
1 teaspoon baking powder
½ teaspoon salt
¾ cup fresh lemon juice (juice of about 3 large lemons)

1. Preheat the oven to 350° F. In the bowl of the food processor fitted with the steel blade, combine the flour, butter, and confectioners' sugar. Process for 15 seconds, until the butter particles are the size of small peas. Pat and press into the bottom of a 13 × 9-inch glass baking pan, building up a ½-inch rim around the edge to hold the filling. Bake on the middle rack of the preheated oven for 20 minutes.

2. Meanwhile, prepare the filling. With a whisk, beat the eggs, sugar, coconut, baking powder, salt, and lemon juice until the egg whites are thoroughly incorporated. Pour the filling over the hot crust. Return the pan to the oven and bake for an additional 30 minutes, until the center is set. Cool on a wire rack and cut into squares. Serve at room temperature. Coconut-Lemon Squares can be wrapped tightly with plastic wrap and stored in the refrigerator for several days. These do not freeze or travel well.

- For faster cleanup, bake the cookies on parchment paper–lined baking sheets. Sideless baking sheets allow the paper to slide off and on with ease.
- If you want a fatter cookie, let the dough chill, covered, in the refrigerator for 45 minutes before baking. The chilled dough will not spread as fast as the warm dough. If the dough gets too cold, flatten it slightly with the back of a spatula so the dough will spread more evenly.
- Always measure carefully. Pack the brown sugar into the cup. Scoop or spoon the flour into the cup and level the overflowing cup with a knife. Never pack or press the flour down into the cup.
- Rotate baking sheets for even baking. Before preheating the oven, place 1 rack in the upper third and 1 rack in the lower third of your oven. Halfway into the baking period, rotate the baking sheets from the top to the bottom rack and from the front to the back.
- Use the touch method to test for doneness. Open the oven door and carefully pull out the baking sheet. Touch the cookie lightly. If it sinks, it's underbaked and needs to be baked a few minutes longer. If the cookie sinks a little and springs back, it's perfect. If it's hard, it's overbaked.

MEXICAN WEDDING COOKIES

Makes 30 cookies
15 minutes to prepare
30 minutes to chill
15 to 20 minutes to bake
2 large baking sheets

In Texas pecan country we've seen hundreds of these light, pretty bites made for weddings, and no wonder, when you consider how easy they are to make.

1¾ cups pecan halves
1½ cups unbleached all-purpose flour
 ¾ cup (1½ sticks) unsalted butter, softened
 3 tablespoons granulated sugar
 ¼ teaspoon salt
1½ teaspoons vanilla extract
    Confectioners' sugar

1. In the bowl of the food processor fitted with the steel blade, add the pecans and chop until the pieces are about a fourth of their original size. Add the flour, butter, sugar, salt, and vanilla. Process until the ingredients are well incorporated and the pecans are finely chopped, about 1 minute. Cover and chill for 30 minutes.

2. Meanwhile, place 1 oven rack in the upper third of the oven and 1 rack in the lower third of the oven. Preheat the oven to 375° F. With lightly floured hands, squeeze the dough into balls about 2 inches in diameter. Use about 2 tablespoons of mixture per ball. Place the balls on 2 ungreased large baking sheets about 1 inch apart. Bake the cookies in the preheated oven for 15 to 20 minutes, until the cookies are set and the bottoms are lightly browned. For even baking, halfway into the baking period, rotate the baking sheets from top to bottom and front to back. Let the cookies stand on the cookie sheet for about 5 minutes before removing them to a rack. Roll the warm cookies in the confectioners' sugar and cool completely. Reroll the cookies in confectioners' sugar before serving.

*L*EMON DROPS

Makes 24 cookies
15 minutes to prepare
15 minutes to bake
2 large baking sheets

These cookies are nice and tart with a taste and texture similar to a lemon pound cake.

½ cup unsalted butter (1 stick), softened
3 large eggs
1⅓ cups granulated sugar
  Zest of 1 lemon, grated
3 teaspoons fresh lemon juice
¼ teaspoon lemon extract
2 cups unbleached all-purpose flour
¼ teaspoon salt
  Lemon Frosting (see sidebar)
  Pecan halves, for garnish (optional)

1. Place 1 oven rack in the upper third of the oven and 1 rack in the lower third of the oven. Preheat the oven to 375° F. Coat 2 large baking sheets with cooking spray.

2. In the bowl of the food processor fitted with the steel blade, add the butter, eggs, sugar, lemon zest, lemon juice, and lemon extract. Process until light and creamy, about 30 seconds. Spoon the flour and salt on top of the batter and pulse 3 or 4 times to combine.

3. Drop the cookies onto the sheets using 2 tablespoons of dough for each cookie. An ice-cream scoop (number 30) does a nice job of this. Bake in the preheated oven for 15 minutes, until the cookies are lightly ringed with brown and the middles spring back when lightly pressed with your finger. For even baking, halfway into the baking period, rotate the baking sheets from top to bottom and front to back.

4. Let the cookies cool for several minutes on the baking sheets and then remove them to a rack to cool.

5. When the cookies have cooled to room temperature, frost with the lemon icing and garnish with a pecan half if desired. Store at room temperature in an airtight container up to 4 days. Freeze for up to 2 months.

Lemon Frosting

This lemon icing is a breeze made in the food processor and helps the cookies maintain their moistness.

Zest of 1 lemon, grated
½ cup (1 stick) unsalted butter, softened
2¾ cups confectioners' sugar
1 large egg yolk
Pinch of salt
2 tablespoons fresh lemon juice or to taste

Place the zest, butter, confectioners' sugar, egg yolk, salt, and lemon juice in the bowl of a food processor fitted with the steel blade. Process until the icing is nice and smooth. Taste, and adjust tartness with additional lemon juice if you wish.

APRICOT–CREAM CHEESE MACAROONS

Makes 24 cookies
15 minutes to prepare
15 minutes to bake
2 large baking sheets

An especially moist cookie made with apricot jam, coconut, and pecans.

1¼ cups unbleached all-purpose flour
¼ cup granulated sugar
¼ teaspoon salt
1½ teaspoons baking powder
3 ounces cream cheese, room temperature
½ cup (1 stick) unsalted butter
½ cup apricot jam
½ cup lightly packed, sweetened shredded coconut
    Apricot Frosting (see sidebar)
24 pecan halves, for garnish

1. Place 1 oven rack in the upper third of the oven and 1 rack in the lower third of the oven. Preheat the oven to 350° F. Coat 2 large baking sheets with cooking spray. In the processor bowl fitted with the steel blade, combine the flour, sugar, salt, and baking powder. Pulse to blend. Add the cream cheese and butter and process until the fats are the size of small peas. Add the apricot jam and coconut and process until the mixture begins to mass around the blade.

2. Drop the dough by tablespoons onto the prepared cookie sheets. Bake the cookies for 15 minutes, until the cookies are set and the bottoms and edges are light brown. For even baking, halfway into the baking period, rotate the baking sheets from top to bottom and front to back. Cool the cookies on the baking sheets for 2 minutes and then remove them to a rack to cool.

3. Frost the cooled cookies with 2 teaspoons of icing per cookie and place a pecan half on each cookie for garnish.

COCONUT MACAROONS

Makes 40 macaroons
15 minutes to prepare
20 minutes to bake
2 large baking sheets

A busy-day favorite, these macaroons are chewy and sweet. If you like pecans, by all means stir them into the cookie dough. (For those of you who restrict your diets during Passover, these are strictly kosher.)

4 large egg whites
1 tablespoon fresh lemon juice or white wine vinegar
½ teaspoon almond extract
½ teaspoon vanilla extract
¼ teaspoon salt
1⅓ cups sugar
4 cups lightly packed, sweetened shredded coconut
½ cup finely chopped pecans (optional)

1. Place 1 oven rack in the upper third of the oven and 1 rack in the lower third of the oven. Preheat the oven to 325° F. Coat 2 large baking sheets with cooking spray.

2. Fit the processor bowl with the plastic or steel blade (see pages 19–20). Add the egg whites. Process until foamy, about 8 seconds. With the machine running, pour the lemon juice or white wine vinegar through the feed tube and process until the whites are stiff, about 1 minute. Add the almond extract, vanilla, and salt. With the machine running, gradually add the sugar to the egg whites through the feed tube. Spoon the egg whites into a large bowl and fold in the coconut and pecans, if desired.

3. Drop by rounded tablespoons onto the prepared baking sheets about 2 inches apart. Bake for 20 minutes, until lightly browned and firm to the touch. For even baking, halfway into the baking period, rotate the baking sheets from top to bottom and front to back. Cool for 5 minutes on the baking sheet and then remove them to a rack to cool completely.

These macaroons are great lunchbox treats; however, keeping them from getting crushed was proving difficult. Diana decided to pack them in recycled yogurt containers with lids before tucking them into the lunch pail. This works well for all cookies that must travel.

Chocolate-Raspberry Shortbread Bars

Makes eighteen 5 x 1½-inch bars
25 minutes to prepare
20 minutes to bake
13 x 9-inch glass baking pan

*Rich, exotic, spice laden, enrobed in dark chocolate, this shortbread
bar spread with a hint of raspberry jam will bring raves. You can
double the recipe easily. Just use a bigger pan, or 2 utility pans.*

SHORTBREAD CRUST

½ cup (1 stick) unsalted butter
¼ cup sugar
1 cup unbleached all-purpose flour
⅛ teaspoon salt

ALMOND-CHOCOLATE-RASPBERRY FILLING

½ cup almonds
½ teaspoon ground cinnamon
3 large egg whites
½ cup sugar
½ teaspoon vanilla extract
4 ounces (⅔ cup) semisweet chocolate chips
½ cup seedless raspberry jam

ALMOND–COCONUT–CHOCOLATE CHIP TOPPING

½ cup sliced almonds
½ cup sweetened shredded coconut
⅔ cup semisweet chocolate chips
½ cup (1 stick) unsalted butter, softened

1. Preheat the oven to 325° F. Spritz a 13 × 9-inch glass
baking pan with cooking spray. For the shortbread crust, in
the bowl of the food processor fitted with the steel blade,
combine the butter and sugar. Process until the mixture is
thoroughly blended. Open the lid and add the flour and salt.
Process until the mixture is as fine as sand.

2. Dump the mixture into the prepared pan and barely press down. Bake in the preheated oven until light brown, about 20 minutes. Remove pan to a rack.

3. Meanwhile, make the filling. Using the processor bowl with the steel blade, pulse to grind the almonds finely; add the cinnamon, then set the almonds aside. Wash and dry the processor bowl. Now, use a whisk attachment or the steel blade, and process the egg whites until foamy (see page 19–20), then with the motor running, add the sugar through the feed tube, a spoonful at a time, and whip the egg whites to soft peaks, adding the vanilla at the last minute.

4. While you're beating the eggs, melt the chocolate chips in a glass measure in the microwave at 100% (high) for about 30 seconds. Stir to mix them, then spoon the melted chocolate and ground almonds into the egg whites and fold to mix.

5. Spread the raspberry jam evenly over the crust, then spoon the almond-chocolate filling over that. Place in the oven and bake at 325° F until the chocolate filling sets and is shiny on the top, about 20 minutes.

6. For the topping, during the last 10 minutes of the baking time, spread almonds and coconut evenly over a buttered pan and place in the oven to toast. Stir a time or two so they'll brown evenly.

7. Once the shortbread is out on a rack, micro-melt the chocolate chips for the topping in the microwave set on 100% (high) for about 30 seconds, stir, then pour the melted chocolate over the soft butter and stir until the mixture is smooth. Spread the chocolate topping evenly over the baked chocolate bars. Sprinkle the top with the toasted almonds and coconut. Refrigerate until serving time, then cut into 5 × 1½-inch bars.

DEATH-BY-CHOCOLATE BROWNIES

Makes 24 brownies
15 minutes to prepare
25 to 30 minutes to bake
13 x 9-inch glass baking pan

Here are brownies so rich they will need to be kept under lock and key if you want to keep them around very long. Walnuts add contrasting taste and texture. Easy enough to have tonight.

1 cup (2 sticks) margarine
4 ounces (4 squares) unsweetened chocolate
2 cups sugar
4 large eggs
1 cup sifted unbleached all-purpose flour (do not eliminate sifting or the brownies will be soggy)
1 teaspoon baking powder
1 teaspoon vanilla extract
1 cup chopped walnuts (optional)

CHOCOLATE BROWNIE FROSTING

2 tablespoons unsalted butter
⅓ cup whipping cream
6 ounces (6 squares) semisweet chocolate, coarsely chopped
1 tablespoon plus 1 teaspoon sugar

1. Preheat the oven to 350° F and lightly grease a 13 × 9-inch glass baking pan. Place the margarine and chocolate in an 8-cup microwavable bowl. Microwave on 100% (high) for 2 minutes. Stir to melt any remaining bits.

2. Add the sugar, mixing thoroughly with a wooden spoon. Add the eggs one at a time, beating well after each.

3. Mix the sifted flour with the baking powder and add to the chocolate mixture. Add the vanilla and walnuts, if you like. Stir the mixture just until the dry ingredients are incorporated.

4. Spoon the batter into the prepared pan and bake on the middle rack of the preheated oven for 25 to 30 minutes, until a toothpick inserted in the middle comes out clean, with

a dry crumb. Cool on a rack until room temperature, and frost with the Chocolate Brownie Frosting.

5. Just before you are ready to frost the brownies, place the butter, cream, chocolate, and sugar in a small microwavable bowl. Microwave on 100% (high), stirring occasionally until the chocolate is partially melted, about 2 minutes. Remove the bowl from the microwave and stir the chocolate until it is smooth. Cool the frosting to room temperature. Frost the brownies. Cover and chill in the refrigerator for at least 1 hour before cutting and serving.

CHOCOLATE-RASPBERRY BROWNIES

Makes 18 brownies
10 minutes to prepare
30 minutes to bake
13 x 9-inch baking pan

Chocolaty, smooth, and rich best describe these brownies. Spangled with fresh raspberries and swirled with a best-quality raspberry sauce or your homemade raspberry jam, they are a sophisticated treat and the best in home baking.

½ cup (1 stick) plus 5 tablespoons (⅔ stick) unsalted butter
4 ounces (4 squares) unsweetened chocolate
1⅓ cups granulated sugar
½ cup packed brown sugar
4 large eggs
1 teaspoon vanilla extract
¼ teaspoon salt
1⅓ cups unbleached all-purpose flour
1 cup fresh raspberries (if raspberries are not in season, omit)
⅓ cup raspberry sauce, raspberry jam, or raspberry all-fruit spread

CHOCOLATE GLAZE

4 ounces semisweet chocolate or ¾ cup semisweet chocolate chips
2 tablespoons hot water

(continued)

(continued)

Raspberry Decadence Chocolate-Fudge Sauce

Diana's son Keith believes that chocolate is the bottom layer of the new food pyramid; even though he is only in the first grade, the boy knows what he likes, and he likes chocolate. He taught his first-grade class to make this sauce, and they sold it at their annual Christmas bazaar and were the top-earning class for the school. Skip the chocolate glaze on the Chocolate-Raspberry Brownies and serve them in a pool of this warm sauce for a nice surprise.

1 12-ounce package unsweetened frozen raspberries, thawed
⅔ cup whipping cream
⅔ cup unsweetened Dutch-process cocoa
¼ cup light corn syrup
1½ cups sugar
¼ cup (½ stick) unsalted butter, softened

1. Pass the raspberries through a strainer, reserving the juice. Discard the strained seeds and skin.

(continued)

2. In an 8-cup microwavable glass measure, whisk together the raspberry juice, whipping cream, cocoa, and corn syrup. Add the sugar and butter and mix until well blended. Microwave on 100% (high) for 4½ minutes, until the mixture comes to a boil, whisking after 2 minutes. Once the sauce begins to boil, lower the heat to 50% (medium-low) and let it continue to boil slowly for 6 minutes without stirring. Remove the sauce from the microwave and let it cool for 15 minutes if serving it hot, or pour it into a glass container and cover and refrigerate. The sauce will keep refrigerated for up to 6 weeks and may be reheated slowly in the microwave.

1. Preheat the oven to 350° F. Coat a 13 × 9-inch baking pan with cooking spray. In a 3-cup microwavable mixing bowl combine the butter and baking chocolate. Microwave at 100% (high) for 2 minutes. Remove from the microwave and stir to melt any remaining bits. Stir in the sugars with a wooden spoon and add the eggs, beating well after each.

2. Add the vanilla, salt, and flour to the chocolate mixture and mix thoroughly.

3. Pour the batter into the prepared pan and sprinkle with the fresh raspberries, if using. Dollop the top with tablespoons of the raspberry sauce or jam and swirl into the batter with the back of the spoon.

4. Bake on the middle rack of the preheated oven for 30 minutes, until a toothpick inserted into the chocolate mixture comes out clean. If the toothpick is inserted into the jam, it may come out wet, but the brownie will be done. Taste your toothpick to see what you have. Cool the brownies completely in the pan on a rack.

5. Just before you are ready to glaze the brownies, combine the chocolate and water in a microwavable 2-cup measure. Microwave at 100% (high) for 90 seconds and remove. Stir to melt any remaining bits. If your chocolate shows a bloom (has gray streaks running through it but is still perfectly fine to use), you may need to add a little more water to get the proper glaze consistency. Glaze the brownies by pouring a thin stream of chocolate back and forth across the top of them. Cut the brownies into 3 × 2-inch bars and serve. These are best served at room temperature and need to be covered for storage.

BUSY-DAY BROWNIES

Makes 9 brownies
5 minutes to prepare
25 to 30 minutes to bake
9-inch square baking pan

Here are brownies dense as fudge, deeper chocolate than a Hershey bar, and easy as pie. Hit the kitchen at a dead run. Turn the oven on. Throw the ingredients into a whirling food processor, and before you know it you've got a pan of brownies in the oven. Twenty-five to 30 minutes later, lift the pan out of the oven, sprinkle the top with chocolate chips you can spread into instant frosting as soon as they're melted, and you've made a mainline chocolate treat with no trouble at all and only 1 bowl to go into the dishwasher. That is a chocolate fix in a hurry. Pour yourself a tall glass of icy-cold milk to wash it all down.

½ cup chopped walnuts
2 large eggs
1 cup sugar
1 teaspoon vanilla extract
½ cup vegetable oil
¼ teaspoon salt
¼ teaspoon baking powder
⅓ cup unsweetened cocoa
½ cup unbleached all-purpose flour
3 ounces (½ cup) semisweet chocolate chips

1. Preheat the oven to 375° F. Coat a 9-inch square baking pan with cooking spray. Sprinkle the pan with the walnuts and set aside.

2. In the food processor bowl fitted with the steel blade with the motor running add the ingredients in order through the feed tube: eggs first, then sugar, vanilla, oil, salt, baking powder, and cocoa.

3. Turn off the processor, scrape down the sides with a rubber spatula, then sprinkle the flour evenly over the top of the mixture. Replace the lid, then pulse about 5 times, just until the flour is barely mixed in.

(continued)

Although the very idea of storing brownies is almost a joke in our kitchens, should you be fortunate enough to have leftovers, store them in the baking pan, tightly covered with foil or plastic wrap, for up to 5 days. You can also freeze them singly or by the panful in Ziploc bags for up to a month. Microwave a frozen brownie for 30 seconds at 100% (high), and you'll swear it's just baked.

4. Pour the mixture into the prepared pan, smoothing the batter evenly over the nuts. Bake in the preheated oven until the center is cooked, 25 to 30 minutes.

5. Remove the brownies from the oven and sprinkle with the chocolate chips. Once the chips have melted, smooth them evenly over the top with a spatula for the simplest icing you ever made. Cut the brownies into 9 equal squares and serve warm.

How to Soften Brown Sugar Bricks

How many times have you gone for the brown sugar only to find it hard as a rock? Once again your microwave comes to the rescue. Add an apple slice or a few drops of water to the sugar and then microwave, covered, on 100% (high) for a few seconds. If it's still not soft enough, repeat the heating once again.

OATMEAL-WALNUT-RAISIN CHEWIES

Makes 48 cookies
20 minutes to prepare
12 to 15 minutes to bake
2 large baking sheets

We discovered the secret for real oatmeal taste in an oatmeal cookie was to toast the oatmeal along with the nuts. The microwave toasts beautifully, but watch carefully and sniff the oatmeal to make sure it is toasting and not burning. It is better to have it a little underdone than burned. Remember, the oatmeal and nuts continue to toast a few moments after you remove them from the microwave. This makes one of our larger batches of cookies, great for sharing or giving as gifts to friends.

  2 cups chopped walnuts
  1 cup rolled oats (not instant)
  1 cup granulated sugar
  1 cup dark brown sugar
  1 cup (2 sticks) unsalted butter, softened
  2 large eggs
  1 teaspoon vanilla extract
1⅔ cups unbleached all-purpose flour
  1 teaspoon baking soda
  1 teaspoon baking powder
  ½ teaspoon salt
  2 cups raisins
1½ cups unsweetened nut-and-grain granola (unsweetened granola
      is not as sweet and is usually not as shiny as sweetened)

1. Place 1 oven rack in the upper third of the oven and 1 rack in the lower third of the oven. Preheat the oven to 375° F. Coat 2 large baking sheets with cooking spray. On a microwavable plate, spread the walnuts and rolled oats. Microwave on 100% (high) for 2 minutes. Stir and check for toasting. Microwave for an additional 2 minutes on 100% (high) and stir. The nuts and oatmeal should now be nicely toasted. Dump into a large bowl.

2. In the food processor bowl fitted with the steel blade, combine the sugars, butter, eggs, and vanilla. Process until smooth and creamy, about 30 seconds. In a small bowl, combine the flour, baking soda, baking powder, and salt. Stir to mix. Spoon the flour mixture on top of the batter. Pulse 3 or 4 times to mix.

3. Scrape the batter into the walnut-oatmeal mixture. Add the raisins and granola. Fold the ingredients together.

4. Drop the cookies onto the sheets using 2 tablespoons of dough for each cookie. An ice-cream scoop (number 30) does a nice job of this. Bake in the preheated oven for 12 to 15 minutes, until the tops are just beginning to brown but the middles still look a little soft. For even baking, halfway into the baking period, rotate the baking sheets from top to bottom and front to back. Cool on the baking sheets for a few minutes and then with a metal spatula remove to a rack to finish cooling. Store in an airtight container at room temperature for 1 week or in the freezer for 3 months.

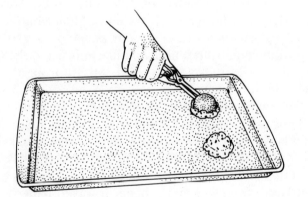

How to Soften Refrigerated and Frozen Stick Butters and Cream Cheese in the Microwave

To soften refrigerated ¼-pound stick butter in the microwave, place one stick of cold butter in the microwave on a saucer. Microwave on 20% (low) for 10 seconds (20 seconds for frozen butter). Turn the butter over and microwave on 20% (low) for an additional 5 seconds (20 seconds for frozen butter). Gently squeeze; the butter should just give a little. Let it stand for 5 minutes on the saucer, and the butter will be perfect room temperature.

To soften cream cheese in the microwave, place a cold, unwrapped 8-ounce brick of cream cheese on a saucer. Microwave on 100% (high) for 10 seconds. Turn the cream cheese over and microwave on 100% (high) for an additional 5 seconds. Frozen and thawed cream cheese tends to crumble; therefore, we don't recommend freezing it.

CRISPY OATMEAL THINS

Makes 15 cookies
10 minutes to prepare
15 to 17 minutes to bake
2 large baking sheets

A simple cookie that is crisp and chewy at the same time. Be sure to have parchment paper or waxed paper for baking these, because it is next to impossible to remove them from anything else. After baking, they can be rolled into a cigar shape if you let them cool just to the point where they are still warm but pliable. Flat or rolled, they are delicious.

¾ cup (1½ sticks) unsalted butter
1½ cups rolled oats (not instant)
¾ cup sugar
1 tablespoon unbleached all-purpose flour
1 teaspoon vanilla extract
½ teaspoon salt
1 large egg, lightly beaten

1. Place 1 oven rack in the upper third of the oven and 1 rack in the lower third of the oven. Preheat the oven to 325° F. Place the butter in a large microwavable mixing bowl and microwave at 100% (high) for 1 minute, until thoroughly melted. Cool the butter for 5 minutes. Meanwhile, cover 2 large baking sheets with parchment paper or waxed paper.

2. Add the oats, sugar, flour, vanilla, and salt to the melted butter. Mix well, then add the egg. Mix thoroughly with a wooden spoon.

3. For each cookie, place 1 tablespoon of the batter on the parchment or waxed paper–lined baking sheet. Leave at least 3 inches between cookies. Bake for 15 to 17 minutes, just until golden brown. For even baking, halfway into the baking period, rotate the baking sheets from top to bottom and front to back. Remove the parchment sheets or waxed paper with the cookies from the baking sheets to a rack to cool. Line the baking sheets with new parchment paper and repeat the baking and cooling process until all the cookies are baked. When the cookies are cool, peel them from the parchment paper and store them in an airtight container for up to 1 week.

JOAN'S MOTHER'S COOKIES

Makes 48 cookies
10 minutes to prepare
15 minutes to bake
Large baking sheet

Joan was one of those assigned college roommates that we'd just as soon forget. Her only redeeming feature was that her mother sent a box of cookies every week. For a couple of these spicy melt-in-your-mouth cookies, we were willing to forgive all.

They're easy to make because you just form long baguette shapes and bake them all on 1 cookie sheet. If you're out of raisins and/or nuts, simply cake granulated sugar onto the rolls before baking. Either way, cut the rolls into biscotti shapes after they're baked while they're still hot, and you've made cookies quickly.

½ cup vegetable shortening
½ cup granulated sugar
 1 large egg
 2 tablespoons mild honey
 2 tablespoons molasses
 2 cups unbleached all-purpose flour
½ teaspoon salt
 1 teaspoon baking soda
 1 teaspoon ground cinnamon
½ teaspoon ground nutmeg
 2 tablespoons water or enough to make a soft dough
½ cup golden raisins
½ cup chopped walnuts

QUICK WHITE FROSTING

½ cup confectioners' sugar
 3 tablespoons milk or enough to make a thick paste

1. Preheat the oven to 375° F. In the food processor fitted with the steel blade combine the shortening, sugar, egg, honey, and molasses. Process until blended. Add the flour, salt, baking soda, cinnamon, and nutmeg and pulse to mix. Add the water and process just until you have a soft dough that rides the blade around. Stop!

(continued)

If the honey in your pantry has crystallized into sugar, you can easily bring it back to a perfectly clear liquid by removing the metal lid from the jar and placing the glass jar of honey in the microwave. Heat at 70% (medium-high), stirring every 15 seconds until the honey is liquefied.

2. Remove the lid and steel blade and sprinkle the raisins and walnuts over the dough. Mix them into the dough with a rubber spatula. Remove the dough from the bowl to a lightly floured surface and knead a moment, then divide the dough into 3 equal parts.

3. Roll each part between your palms into a strip about 2 × 12 inches long. Lay these strips on a large ungreased baking sheet, leaving at least 3 inches between each strip. Flatten with the palm of your hand. Bake in the preheated oven for 15 minutes, until the tops begin to crack. Remove to a cutting board.

4. While the cookies are baking, make the frosting by combining the confectioners' sugar with the milk to make a thick paste. Once you have the cookies out of the oven and onto the cutting board, use a teaspoon to drizzle the frosting onto the hot cookies. Cut the cookies into ½-inch-thick pieces while still warm.

*B*UTTER PECAN BARS

Makes 24 bars
20 minutes to prepare
35 to 45 minutes to bake
9-inch square baking pan

Think of a finger of the richest pecan pie you ever tasted, and you'll begin to see the wisdom of a shortbread base with a rich buttery pecan topping. Don't substitute margarine. The loss in taste is too great.

SHORTBREAD CRUST

½ cup unsalted butter
½ cup packed dark brown sugar
1 cup unbleached all-purpose flour
⅛ teaspoon salt

CINNAMON-PECAN TOPPING

1 cup packed dark brown sugar
2 large eggs
1 teaspoon vanilla extract
2 tablespoons unbleached all-purpose flour
1 teaspoon ground cinnamon
½ teaspoon baking powder
¼ teaspoon salt
2 cups chopped pecans

1. Preheat the oven to 400° F. Spritz a 9-inch square baking pan with cooking spray.

2. To make the crust, combine the butter, brown sugar, flour, and salt in the food processor bowl fitted with the steel blade. Process until the mixture resembles coarse meal.

3. Dump the mixture into the prepared baking pan and press down lightly with the back of a large spoon. Bake in the preheated oven until the crust is lightly browned, 15 to 20 minutes.

4. Meanwhile, make the topping. In the processor bowl fitted with the steel blade combine the brown sugar, eggs, vanilla, flour, cinnamon, baking powder, and salt. Process until thoroughly mixed and aerated, about 1 minute. Add the chopped pecans and pulse twice to mix them in.

5. Pour the topping ingredients onto the baked crust, smoothing evenly. Replace in the oven. Reduce the temperature to 350° F and bake until browned, 20 to 25 minutes. Remove from the oven and cut into bars. Store in a tin.

❖　　❖

Alternately, instead of 2 cups chopped pecans, you can use a cup of pecans and a cup of sweetened shredded coconut. Once the bars are out of the oven, dust the tops with sifted confectioners' sugar.

In fact, this shortbread base is so good, you could top it with other things: a cup of nuts and a cup of granola. How about tossing in some chocolate chips?

This is one of those easy, everyday cookies that you can use when you wish to just grab something out of the pantry and make a fine cookie fast.

De-salting Nuts

Sometimes it's not easy to find exactly what you're looking for in the supermarket, especially if you live in a small town. When we had a difficult time finding unsalted macadamia nuts, we solved the problem by rinsing the salted nuts in a colander with hot tap water for about a minute. We then rubbed them dry with paper towels to remove any remaining salt.

WHITE CHOCOLATE, COCONUT, MACADAMIA COOKIES

Makes 24 cookies
20 minutes to prepare
15 to 17 minutes to bake
2 large baking sheets

A crispy, buttery cookie fresh from the oven is one of life's greatest pleasures.

½ cup (1 stick) unsalted butter, softened
½ cup packed light brown sugar
¼ cup granulated sugar
1 teaspoon vanilla extract
1 large egg
1⅓ cups unbleached all-purpose flour
¼ teaspoon salt
½ teaspoon baking soda
8 ounces white chocolate, coarsely chopped
1½ cups lightly packed, sweetened shredded coconut
¾ cup coarsely chopped unsalted macadamia nuts

1. Place 1 oven rack in the upper third of the oven and 1 rack in the lower third of the oven. Preheat the oven to 350° F. Lightly grease 2 large baking sheets. Fit the food processor with the steel blade. In the food processor bowl, combine the butter, sugars, vanilla, and egg. Process until light and fluffy, about 1 minute.

2. In a medium bowl, stir together the flour, salt, and baking soda. Spoon over the batter. Pulse 4 or 5 times to mix, just until combined. Spoon the cookie dough into the medium bowl. By hand, stir in the chocolate, coconut, and macadamia nuts.

3. Drop the cookies, using approximately 2 tablespoons of dough for each cookie, onto the baking sheets. Bake the cookies for 15 to 17 minutes, until lightly golden around the edges. For even baking, halfway into the baking period, rotate the baking sheets from top to bottom and front to back. Cool on the baking sheets for 5 minutes and then carefully remove them to a rack to cool. Wrap to store in an airtight container for up to 1 week.

SHORTBREAD DIAMONDS IN THE ROUGH

Makes 1½ pounds, about 48 diamonds
5 minutes to prepare
1 hour to bake
Large baking sheet

Satisfying to make and to eat, these cookies are so easy because you cut a whole sheet of baked shortbread with a pizza wheel. The aroma of baking butter is never to be forgotten. You may note that people who walk into your kitchen while you're baking these cookies get that stupid, glazed look of sheer ecstasy.

2 cups unbleached all-purpose flour
⅓ cup cornstarch
⅔ cup sugar
1 cup (2 sticks) butter

1. Preheat the oven to 275° F. Coat a large baking sheet with cooking spray and set aside.

2. Combine in the processor bowl fitted with the steel blade the flour, cornstarch, and sugar. Whack the butter into pieces on top of the dry ingredients. Close the lid and process until the dough is well blended and beginning to cling to the sides of the bowl, about 20 seconds.

3. Dump the mixture onto the baking sheet and pat it down into a ¼-inch-thick rectangle. If you can't stand all those handprints, roll over the top of it with a rolling pin or glass to smooth it out. Pop it into the preheated oven and bake for 1 hour.

4. Remove from the oven. The shortbread will be barely golden. Cut the shortbread into diamonds while it's still hot, using a pizza cutter or a sharp knife.

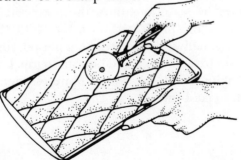

◆ ◆

Here's your chance to be an artist without too much training. We made a State of Texas Shortbread by tracing a map, then laying it atop the still hot cookie and cutting along the edges with a pizza cutter.

If you really want to get literal, write your kid's name in red-hots, raisins, or chocolate chips on the top. Then cut the hot cookie into jigsaw pieces and let your child put the puzzle back together once it's cold. We sent Linda's college kid one of these cookie jigsaw puzzles for finals week. Each piece was wrapped in red cellophane, then the whole cookie was packed in popcorn. When he put it all together, the red-hots spelled "Good luck!" Except Jay told us his roommate ate the "Go" piece before he got it put together, so he thought we'd wished him "od luck." Oh, well. It's the thought that counts.

Or, you could slather these cookies with royal icing made easily in the food processor.

◆ ◆

Instant Royal Icing

Makes about 1⅓ cups

1 large egg white
¼ teaspoon fresh lemon juice
2 cups confectioners' sugar

1. Fit the food processor with the steel blade. Process egg white and lemon juice until frothy. Add confectioners' sugar and continue processing until mixture forms stiff peaks, about 1 minute.

2. Slather icing onto cookies with a metal spatula.

These cookies are in that class of sweet that bakes but doesn't change color. Leave them in the oven too long, and they'll turn into rocks.

Emily says use your favorite kind of chocolate for them. Milk chocolate makes them chewier. Semisweet chocolate makes them denser and darker—perfect with coffee. When Emily uses only the semisweet chocolate, she uses dark rum instead of vanilla.

We know you'll make these cookies again and again.

EMILY'S FIRST FITTINGS COOKIES

Makes 24 to 36 cookies
10 minutes to prepare
10 to 12 minutes to bake
2 large baking sheets

Emily is an actress who knows how to get the best fit from her costumes. She bakes up a double batch of these cookies and takes them for the first fittings. Not only does she keep the costume designers busy, she knows she'll get a nice roomy fit. Emily is, by the way, a nice size 4, regardless of how many of these shiny on the outside, meltingly soft on the inside chocolate cookies she eats.

> 12-ounces semisweet or milk chocolate chips
> 1 14-ounce can sweetened condensed milk
> 1 tablespoon sugar
> ½ cup (1 stick) unsalted butter
> 1 cup unbleached all-purpose flour
> ¼ teaspoon baking powder
> ¼ teaspoon vanilla extract or dark rum
> ½ cup pecan pieces or raisins (optional)

1. For even baking, place 1 oven rack in the upper third of the oven and 1 rack in the lower third of the oven. Preheat the oven to 350° F. Coat 2 cookie sheets with cooking spray. Combine in a microwavable bowl the chocolate chips, milk, sugar, and butter. Heat in the microwave set at 100% (high) for 2 minutes. Remove from the microwave and whisk with a balloon whisk to mix.

2. Dump in the flour, baking powder, and vanilla or rum, and whisk to mix thoroughly. Add the nuts or raisins, if desired.

3. Drop by teaspoons onto the prepared baking sheets, then bake in the preheated oven for 10 to 12 minutes. For even baking, halfway into the baking period, rotate the baking sheets from front to back and bottom to top. Cool the cookies on the baking sheets for several minutes, then remove them to a rack to cool further.

GRAPEFRUIT ZODIAC

Makes sixteen 2-inch squares
5 minutes to prepare
40 minutes to bake
8-inch square baking pan

Adapted from Neiman-Marcus's famous citrus squares, these puckery little bites make a splendid dessert following chicken or fish. Although they're at their best chilled, you can make them so quickly that you can have them on the table with coffee, even if you started them at the same time you started the dinner.

Remember to preheat the oven well before you start the shortbread dough. Otherwise, you'll get ahead of yourself.

1 cup plus 2 tablespoons unbleached all-purpose flour, divided
½ cup (1 stick) unsalted butter, cold, cut into bits
1 cup plus 1 tablespoon sugar, divided
2 large eggs
¼ cup fresh, frozen, or canned grapefruit juice
2 tablespoons grapefruit zest, chopped (optional)
½ teaspoon baking powder

1. Preheat the oven to 375° F. In the food processor bowl fitted with the steel blade, process 1 cup of the flour, the butter, and ¼ cup of the sugar until the mixture resembles coarse meal. Dump the mixture into an 8-inch square baking pan and pat down firmly. Bake in the preheated oven for 15 minutes, or until a pale-gold color all over.

2. Meanwhile, break the eggs into the processor bowl fitted with the steel blade, and process 1 minute, then add ¾ cup of the sugar through the feed tube and continue to process 1 minute. Add grapefruit juice and chopped zest and process 1 minute.

3. Once the base is cooked and out of the oven, add the remaining 2 tablespoons of flour and the baking powder to the grapefruit juice mixture and pulse to mix. Pour this mixture over the shortbread base and return it to the middle of the preheated oven for 25 minutes, until it is golden. Remove from the oven and dust the top with the remaining tablespoon of sugar. Cool in the pan, on a rack. Cut the dessert into 2-inch squares.

A Citrus by Any Other Name

Make these puckery bites with the citrus fruit of your choice. Substitute the grapefruit measure-for-measure with lemon, lime, orange, tangerine, mandarin, satsuma, pommelo, or tangelo.

Your choice will determine the color and tanginess of the citrus bite. If you are choosing one of the sweeter citrus fruits, you may wish to reduce the sugar by a tablespoon or so, or to taste.

To zest citrus easily, use a zester (see page 14) or a potato peeler. Remember to take only the colored portion of the skin. The white layer of peel under the colored skin is bitter and should be avoided.

6
ALMOST STORE-BOUGHT

e started this book after *Bread in Half the Time* was done, while we were sitting around a pine table over a bowl of Häagen-Dazs, saying to each other, Now what could be better than this?

Believe me, we had to think a long time to come up with an answer. The first thing we began experimenting with for this book was sauce for ice cream. In the microwave there's nothing quicker or better than homemade hot fudge sundae sauce. We also adore butterscotch, and rum raisin, and all the other good sauces you'll find in this chapter.

Look for those big waffle cones, and you can have a fine fruit and frozen yogurt dessert pronto. We include here, as well, another of our new finds: store-bought crepes. Using these ready-mades, found in the produce section and made by Frieda's Finest, we can produce homemade strata easily.

We include in the pie and tart chapter our discoveries using store-bought piecrusts—another boon to the half-time cook.

But basically, what we want to say here is that if you've gone to the trouble to make dinner for somebody, you shouldn't have to do much more than haul out the ice cream and maybe a handmade sauce. I mean enough is enough.

QUICK-AS-A-FLASH ICE-CREAM PARTY CAKE

Serves 8
15 minutes to prepare
30 minutes to freeze

Like a magician pulling a rabbit out of the hat, you can assemble this cake in 15 minutes, freeze it for half an hour, then pull it out of the freezer ready to eat—a total of 45 minutes! Decorate with fresh fruit, edible flowers, or candles.

Lemon pound cake stuffed with Häagen-Dazs peach ice cream, then garnished with fresh peaches and mint, is our favorite. For chocoholics, try chocolate pound cake stuffed with mint chocolate-chip ice cream, whipped-cream icing, then drizzled with a lazy chocolate-syrup pattern.

2 cups whipping cream, chilled
3 tablespoons confectioners' sugar
1 10-inch best-quality pound cake, chocolate pound cake, or angel food cake
1 quart best-quality ice cream, slightly softened
Fresh fruit
Edible flowers

1. Pour the whipping cream into the food processor bowl fitted with the steel blade (see page 17). Process until the cream begins to thicken. With the machine running, sprinkle the confectioners' sugar through the feed tube. Continue processing until the cream will hold stiff peaks. Refrigerate until ready to use.

2. Put the cake on a serving plate that can easily be placed in the freezer and then taken to the table. Horizontally, slice off the top 1 inch of the cake and reserve. With a sharp boning knife, remove the middle of the cake to form a "bowl" by scoring vertically all the way around inside of the cake, 1 inch from both sides and about 1 inch from the bottom, leaving a shell of a cake about 1 inch thick. With your hand pull out the insides of the cake. Reserve cake insides.

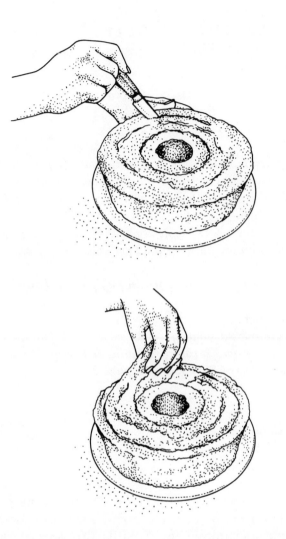

For an adult party cake, flavor the whipped-cream icing with a liqueur and fruit companion, zests, or chocolate. The possibilities are endless, just make sure they're complementary, like matching shoes and a bag.

2 cups whipping cream, chilled
½ cup confectioners' sugar
3 tablespoons Framboise with ½ cup fresh or drained frozen strawberries or raspberries
or
3 tablespoons crème de cacao, Tia Maria, or Kahlúa with 3 teaspoons unsweetened cocoa
or
2 tablespoons Triple Sec, Grand Marnier, or curaçao with 2 tablespoons grated orange zest
or
2 tablespoons Amaretto with ¼ cup finely chopped almonds

Pour the whipping cream into the food processor bowl fitted with the steel blade (see page 17). Process until the cream begins to thicken, about 10 seconds. With the machine running, sprinkle the confectioners' sugar through the feed tube. Continue processing until the cream holds stiff peaks. Add the liqueur and flavorings through the feed tube. Pulse twice to blend. Refrigerate until ready to use.

3. Working rather fast, fill the cake shell with the softened ice cream, packing lightly. Fill the hole in the middle of the cake with as many of the reserved cake pieces as possible. Place the top back on the cake.

4. Frost with the whipped cream. Freeze for at least 30 minutes or cover and freeze as long as 24 hours. Before serving, garnish with fresh fruit, edible flowers, or candles. Depending on how long the cake has been frozen, it may need to sit for 5 to 10 minutes to allow the ice cream to soften so that it can easily be cut.

Cherry Pitters

We found a new gadget being sold at the farmer's market during cherry season. It is a hand-held cherry pitter that works like a paper punch. Just place the cherry in the round holder and squeeze the handle. Out pops the pit! If these are not in your area, split the cherry with your fingers and scoop the pit out with your fingers or a small spoon.

CHERRY TURNOVERS

Serves 8
15 minutes to prepare
20 minutes to bake
Large baking sheet

These finest Cherry Turnovers are made with tender puff pastry that flakes into delicious leaves with each bite. The beauty of our turnovers is that we've developed a way to create these fabulous pastries quickly, without any fuss. Store-bought puff pastry doesn't require any rolling, folding of butter, or rest time like homemade. Thaw the pastry sheets on the top of the counter, fill, bake, and you're finished. Easy.

1 17¼-ounce package (2 sheets) frozen puff pastry, thawed
1 large egg
1 tablespoon water
8 teaspoons granulated sugar
1 21-ounce can best-quality cherry pie filling or 1 recipe Presidents' Day Sour Cherry Pie filling (see page 268)

GLAZE

½ cup confectioners' sugar
1 tablespoon milk
½ teaspoon vanilla extract

1. Preheat the oven to 450° F. Line a large baking sheet with parchment paper or spray the baking sheet with cooking spray. Separate and unfold the 2 puff pastry sheets. On a lightly floured surface, roll each sheet into a 12-inch square.

2. In a small bowl, beat the egg lightly with the water. Brush the egg mixture lightly over both pastry sheets, and reserve the remaining egg wash. Sprinkle each pastry sheet with 4 teaspoons of the sugar. Cut each pastry sheet into quarters to make four 6-inch squares.

3. Place 2 tablespoons of the cherry filling in the middle of each square. Fold each square into a triangle by folding one point over to the opposite diagonal point. Press the edges to seal. Brush the turnovers with the egg wash. Place the turnovers on the baking sheet.

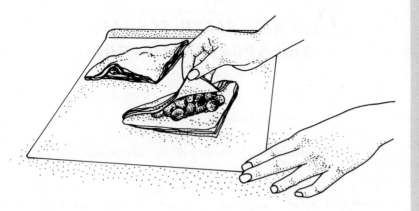

Make this recipe your own by varying the fillings. How about combining a little blueberry pie filling and topping it with a tablespoon of lemon pie filling? Or try vanilla or chocolate custard or pie filling with sliced bananas or raspberries. The combinations are endless.

4. Bake the turnovers on the middle rack of the preheated oven for 20 minutes, until the turnovers are nice and flaky and lightly browned. Remove the turnovers to a rack to cool on the parchment. The filling in these turnovers is extremely *hot*, be sure to let them cool for at least 20 minutes before you try them.

5. Meanwhile, for the glaze, mix the confectioners' sugar, milk, and vanilla. Drizzle the glaze over the turnovers as soon as they are cool enough to eat.

The best way to peel a big bunch of peaches is not to peel them with a sharp knife at all, but to blanch them first. Simply bring several quarts of water to a low boil on the stove and drop in 3 or 4 peaches. After 30 seconds remove them and drop them into cold water. Repeat with the remaining peaches. The skins will blister up when you pinch them. Then the peels will slip right off. This technique works well with tomatoes, too.

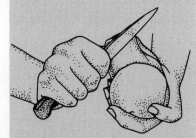

PEACHES, PEACH SCHNAPPS, AND SHORTBREAD FOOL

Serves 6 to 8
20 minutes to prepare
1 hour to chill
6 tall parfait glasses or balloon wineglasses

This old-fashioned combination of layered peaches, buttery shortbread, and whipped cream is simply delicious. Serve in tall parfait glasses or balloon wineglasses. Top each serving with a dollop of whipped cream and pass additional cookies.

4 pounds (8 large) fresh ripe peaches
⅔ cup granulated sugar
⅓ cup peach schnapps
1 6-ounce package shortbread cookies
¾ cup whipping cream, chilled
2 tablespoons confectioners' sugar

1. Peel peaches (see sidebar). Slice into wedges. Stir the peaches, sugar, and peach schnapps together in a microwavable 2-quart bowl. Microwave on 100% (high) for 5 minutes, until the peaches just start to simmer and the sugar is dissolved. Stir. Cover and refrigerate until well chilled, about 1 hour.

2. Meanwhile, in the bowl of a food processor fitted with the steel blade, process the cookies until they are crumbs, and set aside.

3. Rinse and dry the processor bowl and blade. Refit the blade in the processor bowl and add the cream (see page 17). Process for 30 seconds, just until the cream starts to thicken. Gradually add the confectioners' sugar and process until stiff. Set aside, covered, in the refrigerator until ready to use.

4. Spoon half of the peaches and syrup into the bottom of six glasses. Sprinkle with half of cookie crumbs. Top with the remaining peaches and syrup. Cover with the remaining cookie crumbs.

CHOCOLATE-RASPBERRY TART

Serves 6
10 minutes to prepare
25 minutes to bake
1 to 3 hours to chill
9-inch tart pan with removable bottom

Begin with a store-bought piecrust and this dessert goes together in 5 minutes. Prebake the crust, create a thin layer of chocolate, then top with raspberry-studded whipped cream. What could be simpler?

1 9-inch store-bought piecrust, unbaked
3 ounces (½ cup) semisweet chocolate chips
1 pint fresh raspberries or other berries
1 cup whipping cream
2 teaspoons sugar or to taste

1. Preheat the oven to 450° F. Place a prepared piecrust in a 9-inch tart pan with a removable bottom. Press the dough into the bottom and onto the sides of the pan. Push the heel of your hand against the dough overhanging the rippled edge of the pan to cut excess dough away. Prick the dough generously with a fork. Bake in the preheated oven until golden brown, about 15 minutes.

2. Remove the baked crust to a rack to cool. Immediately sprinkle chocolate chips evenly over the top. After a few moments, spread the melted chips all over the crust. Refrigerate the crust until serving time.

3. Pick over the raspberries or other berries and gently wash and drain them in a colander. Pour the cream into the food processor fitted with the steel blade or whisk attachment (see page 17). Process the whipping cream to soft peaks, adding the sugar by the teaspoon through the feed tube. Continue processing until the cream holds stiff peaks, no more than a minute or so. Use a rubber spatula to fold in the berries, then spoon the berries and cream onto the chilled crust. You may serve it immediately, or you may refrigerate it for up to 3 hours first.

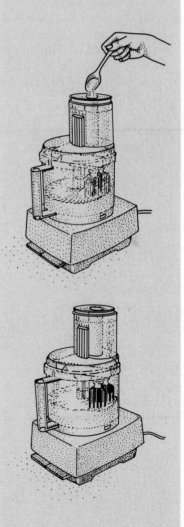

Make this dessert your own by using different kinds of chips and berries. How about white chocolate chips and boysenberries? Try milk chocolate and blackberries. Bittersweet chocolate and strawberries.

No berries available? No problem. Into the cream fold pecan pieces, or sweet cherries, or bits of navel orange.

You don't even have to know how to cook to make a great dessert. Using best-quality store-bought stuff, you can build dessert just like you'd build a house, from the bottom up.

On a best-quality base—say pound cake—you can build a fresh fruit layer then top with a shot of canned whipped cream. Sprinkle the top with sweetened shredded coconut or store-bought sprinkles: it's dessert in an instant.

Here are some of our favorite combinations:

For the base
• Graham cracker or cookie piecrust
• Pound cake
• Angel food cake
• Cookies (butter, vanilla wafers, chocolate)
• Frozen waffles and waffle cones and cups

For the filling
• Chopped fresh fruit
• Lemon curd
• Marmalade and jam
• Frozen yogurt and ice cream
• Nutella (chocolate hazelnut spread)
• Peanut butter
• Flavored cream cheese
• Marscapone

CINNAMON TORTILLA CRISPS WITH ORANGE DIP AND FRUIT SALSA

Serves 8
10 minutes to prepare
5 minutes to bake
2 large baking sheets

Teenagers having a slumber party? Here's a nearly store-bought dessert they can make themselves. It's low fat; it's sweet and crunchy; it's very nutritious. Crisp, ovenbaked flour tortillas are drenched in cinnamon sugar and served with an ad-lib mixture of fruits made into salsa and a luscious orange cream flecked with mint.

12 8-inch flour tortillas
½ cup sugar
1 teaspoon ground cinnamon
⅛ teaspoon unsweetened cocoa
1 8-ounce package Neufchâtel or low-fat cream cheese
½ cup fresh orange juice
2 tablespoons mild honey
4 tablespoons chopped fresh mint leaves plus 2 mint sprigs, for garnish
4 cups finely chopped mixed fresh fruit of your choice: bananas, strawberries, kiwi, papaya, oranges, apples, starfruit, seedless grapes

1. Preheat the oven to 500° F. Spritz 2 large baking sheets with cooking spray.

2. Cut the stack of tortillas into 6 equal wedges. Lay the tortillas out 1 layer deep on the countertop and spritz with cooking spray (this is great if you have olive oil spray).

3. Mix the sugar, cinnamon, and cocoa. Rub the mixture evenly over the tortillas. Turn them over and spritz the second side with cooking spray and coat that side with the sugar mixture.

4. Arrange the wedges on the prepared baking sheets in a single layer and bake in the preheated oven until crisp and golden, about 4 minutes. Take care not to burn them. Remove them to a serving tray.

5. Meanwhile, whisk together the cheese, orange juice, and honey. Season with 2 tablespoons mint. Pour the orange sauce into a bowl and decorate with a sprig of mint.

6. Peel, seed, and chop the fruit and mix it in a bowl. Add remaining 2 tablespoons chopped mint, then transfer the fruit to a serving bowl. Decorate the top with a sprig of mint. Add the bowl of sauce and fruit to your serving tray of warm tortilla chips and let your guests enjoy!

For the topping
- *Canned whipped cream*
- *Prepared sauces: hot fudge, caramel, fruit*
- *Marshmallow creme and marshmallows*
- *Frozen fruit and berries*
- *Fruit syrups*

For the final flourishes
- *Chopped nuts*
- *Chocolate chips*
- *Sprinkles*
- *Shredded sweetened coconut*
- *Crushed candy bars or hard candy*
- *Granola*
- *Vanilla sugar*

*N*EARLY STORE-BOUGHT STRATA

Serves 8
10 minutes to prepare

Of course you can make crepes at home, if you have the time and the inclination, but you can also buy them most anywhere in this country in the produce section of supermarkets—already made for you by Frieda's Finest. Grab a pack of Frieda's crepes. Some apricot jam. Vanilla ice cream. A pressure can of whipped cream and a bottle of maraschino cherries and some chopped walnuts. It's dessert.

16 store-bought crepes
1 12-ounce jar apricot preserves
½ cup chopped walnuts
1 pint best-quality vanilla ice cream
Whipped cream
Maraschino cherries

1. Place a crepe on each of 8 individual dessert plates. Spread each one with about a teaspoon of preserves, then sprinkle with chopped nuts. Top with the remaining crepes and spread with additional jam.

2. Top each crepe with a scoop of ice cream. Pipe whipped cream around the ice cream. Sprinkle with nuts and top with a cherry. Serve immediately.

❖   ❖

• For an instant dieter's dessert, spoon this hot sauce over nonfat frozen yogurt or 97% fat-free frozen ice milk.
• Make an impromptu dessert torte using homemade or frozen waffles or pancakes. Layer the cakes with ricotta cheese you've whizzed through the processor with a little milk to make it spreadable, then drizzle Orange Sauce overall, and garnish with fresh blueberries.
• Add a tablespoon of Triple Sec or Grand Marnier to the basic Orange Sauce and serve it over best-quality ice cream or a square of chocolate cake.
• Slice angel food cake and drizzle Orange Sauce over it for another low-fat dessert.
• Scoop out the membrane from the oranges you juiced, then place a scoop of ice cream in the orange shell, and top with Orange Sauce. A sprig of mint finishes the dessert.
• Spoon cold Orange Sauce on one side of a dessert plate and chocolate sauce on the other. Pass fresh fruit for your dinner guests to dip into the sauces: strawberries, kiwi, red-flame grapes, pear slices, apple slices, banana wheels, papaya, or melon balls.

Orange Sauce

Makes 1 pint
5 minutes to prepare
1½-quart microwavable bowl

With its intense orange flavor and color, this quick-as-a-wink sauce is great for topping ice cream, fruit, or cake.

⅓ cup sugar
2 tablespoons cornstarch
Zest of 1 medium orange
1 cup fresh or frozen reconstituted orange juice
Juice of ½ lemon

1. Combine in a microwavable 1½-quart bowl the sugar, cornstarch, orange zest and juice, and lemon juice. Stir to mix.
2. Heat in the microwave at 100% (high) for 2 minutes, whisk with a balloon whisk, then heat until thick and clear at 100% (high) power for an additional minute. Whisk.
3. Store, covered, in a sterile jar in the refrigerator for up to 2 weeks.

Hot Butterscotch Sauce

Makes 1 cup
5 minutes to prepare
4-cup glass measure

Poured like molten gold over vanilla ice cream, this makes a mouth-watering dessert. Store in the refrigerator where you can sneak out little bites with a long-handled spoon. Good hot or cold poured over ice cream, plain cake, or fresh fruit of the season. Over nectarines and plums, it's great.

1 cup packed light brown sugar
¼ cup half-and-half
4 tablespoons (½ stick) butter
2 tablespoons light corn syrup

1. Combine in a 4-cup glass measure the brown sugar, half-and-half, butter, and corn syrup. Stir to mix. Microwave at 100% (high) for 2 minutes, until it boils. Stir.

2. Pour into a sterile pint jar, cover, and store refrigerated for up to 1 month.

HOT CHERRY SAUCE

Makes 2 cups
20 minutes to prepare (includes 15 minutes to pit cherries)
8-cup glass measure

One of our favorite early summertime activities is a trip to the U-Pick orchards. Climbing high on the graceful fruit ladders we couldn't pick all the Bing and Queen Anne cherries we see if we picked a month of Sundays. Speaking of which—a jar of this will give you just that: a month of sundaes. Do invest in one of those little cherry-pitting doodads that looks like a pair of scissors with no blades. It cuts the work down to size. Serve this cherry sauce over ice cream, dessert waffles, on pancakes.

1 pound Bing or Queen Anne cherries, stemmed
¼ cup sugar
¼ cup water
1 tablespoon kirsch (optional)

1. Pit the cherries over an 8-cup glass measure to catch the juices. Stir in the sugar and water.

2. Microwave at 100% (high) for 6 minutes, or until thick. Pour into a sterile jar and store in the refrigerator, covered for up to 2 weeks.

Peach Melba

Makes 2 servings
10 minutes to prepare
9-inch glass pie plate

2 large fresh ripe peaches, peeled,
pitted, and halved
1 teaspoon fresh lemon juice
½ cup sugar
½ cup water
Vanilla ice cream
Melba Sauce

*1. Place the peaches cut side
down in a glass pie plate. Squirt
lemon juice over them, then sprinkle with sugar. Pour water in,
cover with plastic wrap, and microwave at 100% (high) for 5 to
6 minutes, until tender but not
mushy. Open the wrap carefully to
let out the steam. Let the peaches
stand 5 minutes.*

*2. Remove the peach halves to
dessert plates, then top with a
scoop of vanilla ice cream and a
drizzle of Melba Sauce.*

MELBA SAUCE

Makes 2 cups
15 minutes to prepare
4-cup glass measure

*For an August dessert, what could be better than fresh peaches with
Melba Sauce and vanilla ice cream, garnished with 1 perfect raspberry?*

¼ cup red currant jelly
1 pint fresh raspberries
2 tablespoons cornstarch
2 tablespoons cold water

1. In a 4-cup glass measure, spoon in the red currant jelly.
Microwave at 100% (high) for 1 minute, to boiling. Add the
raspberries, and microwave at 100% (high) for 2 minutes
more.

2. Meanwhile, dissolve the cornstarch in the cold water.
Stir it into the raspberry mixture. Stir thoroughly, then microwave at 100% (high) for 1 minute more, until slightly
thickened. Pour into a sterile pint jar, cover, and refrigerate
for up to a week.

GINGER-LIME SAUCE FOR A TROPICAL SUNDAE

Makes 1 cup sauce
10 minutes to prepare
4-cup glass measure

*Chopping crystallized ginger is a sticky job. We've found if you chill
the ginger in the freezer for 10 minutes or so before you start, then
whack it into a fine dice with a French chef's knife, it's not too
difficult.*

*For a terrific sundae, cut tropical fruits—including pineapple,
papaya, or mango—into balloon wineglasses. Scoop best-quality va-*

nilla ice cream over the fruit, drizzle the ginger-lime sauce over that, and finish with a sprinkling of toasted sweetened shredded coconut.

½ cup granulated sugar
½ cup packed light brown sugar
  Juice and zest of 1 lime (about ¼ cup juice)
 2 tablespoons water
¼ cup (½ stick) unsalted butter
 4 tablespoons chopped crystallized ginger

Combine in a 4-cup glass measure the sugars, juice and zest of the lime, water, butter, and ginger. Microwave at 100% (high) for 4 minutes. Pour into a sterile jar and store in the refrigerator, covered, for up to 1 month.

Mocha Sauce

Makes 2 cups sauce
5 minutes to prepare
4-cup glass measure

Make a fine sundae beginning with best-quality chocolate ice cream. Or start with a prepared graham cracker crust, and make a mocha pie. Layer in 1 pint of coffee ice cream, top with a layer of chocolate ice cream, then drizzle Mocha Sauce over that. Top with Heath bar bits, and you've made an instant ice cream pie.

 1 cup cold espresso or strong brewed black coffee
½ cup sugar
12 ounces (2 cups) semisweet chocolate chips
 6 tablespoons (¾ stick) unsalted butter

In a 4-cup glass measure combine the cold coffee and sugar. Microwave at 100% (high) for 1 minute and stir to thoroughly dissolve the sugar. Add the chocolate chips and butter and microwave at 100% (high) for 1 minute. Stir to blend thoroughly. Pour into a sterile jar, cover, and refrigerate until serving time, no more than 2 weeks.

Pear Melba

Peeled and cored whole pears can be poached the same way as peaches. Cut a slice off the bottom of each pear so that it will stand, then place each cooked pear in a scoop of ice cream, drizzle Melba Sauce over the top and finish with a sprig of mint.

There are several tests for a ripe pineapple. First, look at the pineapples. See if you can find one that's a deep green with some yellowing near the base. Pick that one up and take a deep whiff. It should smell aromatic, the way you remember pineapple. If there is no aroma, it may be immature. If it smells fermented, it's overripe.

Next pluck a leaf from the center of the pineapple. It should come out with little resistance. If the leaf clings tenaciously to the pineapple, it's probably immature.

Finally, squeeze the pineapple. It should be firm, with no soft spots.

Pineapples should be picked when they are ripe and not green. They won't ripen any more after being cut. Store the pineapple upside down to distribute the sugar throughout the meat and at room temperature if you plan on using it within a couple of days; otherwise, refrigerate the pineapple, and it will keep for 5 to 7 days.

PINA COLADA SAUCE

Makes about 2½ cups
5 minutes to prepare
Ovenproof glass dish
2-cup glass measure

If you can purchase fresh pineapple already peeled and cored, you can create this tropical dessert in less time than it takes to book a flight to Hawaii. Use canned pineapple chunks if you must, but be sure to drain them thoroughly first. Serve the hot pineapple chunks over your favorite ice cream. You may find, as we did, that the pineapple tastes so good, you can bag the ice cream and have a fine hot fruit dessert in fewer than 5 minutes.

1 pineapple, peeled, cored, and cut into large chunks (about 2 cups)
2 tablespoons unsalted butter
2 tablespoons brown sugar
2 tablespoons sweetened shredded coconut
2 tablespoons pecan pieces

1. Preheat the broiler. Arrange the pineapple chunks, 1 layer deep, in an ovenproof glass dish.

2. Combine the butter and brown sugar in a glass measure. Microwave at 100% (high) for 30 seconds, until the butter is melted. Stir to mix thoroughly.

3. Spread the butter mixture over the pineapple and place it under the broiler about 4 inches from the heat source. Heat until the topping is golden brown and bubbling, about 2 minutes.

4. Sprinkle the coconut shreds and pecan pieces evenly over the top, then broil until the coconut and pecans are toasted, about 30 seconds.

AMERICAN AIRLINES FIRST-CLASS HOT FUDGE SAUCE

Makes 1 cup sauce
3 minutes to prepare
4-cup glass measure

Serve with baseballs of best-quality vanilla ice cream, and you'll find dinner guests sighing with pleasure. This sauce, dark as death, not too sweet, growing chewier as it chills over the ice cream, will ensure you a home run.

The secret to the sauce is using dark brown sugar and Dutch-process cocoa. Accept, as they say, no substitutes.

This sauce goes together so fast, you ought to form the ice-cream balls and place them in dessert dishes in the freezer long before dinner. Then, after the main course, whip up the sauce and pour it over the ice cream while it's piping hot. Top with a jot of whipped cream, chopped pecans, and a long-stemmed cherry if you wish.

½ cup whipping cream
3 tablespoons unsalted butter
⅓ cup granulated sugar
⅓ cup dark brown sugar
⅛ teaspoon salt
½ cup unsweetened Dutch-process cocoa

1. Place the cream and butter in a 4-cup glass measure. Microwave at 100% (high) for 45 seconds, until the butter melts and the mixture boils.

2. Stir in both sugars until the crystals dissolve. Rub the mixture between your fingers to see if the graininess has disappeared. Add the salt and cocoa and whisk until smooth.

3. Microwave at 100% (high) for 45 seconds, until the mixture thickens. Pour immediately over ice cream and serve.

4. Pour the leftovers into a sterile jar, cover, and refrigerate for up to 2 weeks. Reheat in the microwave, after removing the cover, at 100% (high) for about 30 seconds, until the sauce is thin enough to pour. If it still seems too thick, stir in a few drops of hot water.

Miniature Liqueur Bottles

We used to be stopped by recipes that called for a spoonful of some expensive liqueur when we discovered that a fifth of many of them can cost $20 plus. Since most recipes use these liqueurs by the tablespoon, for enhancement of flavor, it seemed like a waste to be buying a lifetime supply.

But then, on an airplane trip, when we each got a different small liqueur bottle, it occurred to us that this was the ideal size for kitchen use. Miniatures are about the size of a bottle of vanilla and, in the kitchen, are used in much the same way.

Once back home, on a trip to the neighborhood liquor store, we stocked up on miniatures of Chambord, cognac, calvados, kirschwasser, Grand Marnier, Amaretto, curaçao, and whatever else we could grab that struck our fancy. Now our desserts are really spirited.

Crystallized ginger chopped and passed in a small bowl makes a satisfying dessert by itself. A cup of espresso, a bite of sweet, hot ginger, and you have ended your dinner with zip.

DOLCE SPAZIO (SWEET SAUCE)

Makes 1 pint
10 minutes to prepare
8-cup glass measure

Spoon this hot, dark, sweet sauce over best-quality vanilla ice cream, plain cake, fresh fruit, or orange sherbet.

½ cup unsweetened cocoa
1 cup sugar
1 cup light corn syrup
½ cup half-and-half
¼ teaspoon salt
3 tablespoons unsalted butter
1 teaspoon vanilla extract
¼ cup finely chopped crystallized ginger
    Zest of ½ orange, chopped

1. Combine the cocoa, sugar, corn syrup, half-and-half, salt, and butter in a 2-quart microwavable bowl. Stir to mix. Heat at 100% (high) power for 4 minutes.

2. Remove from the heat and stir in the vanilla, crystallized ginger, and orange zest. Pour into a sterile pint jar, cover, and refrigerate for up to 1 month.

CHOCOLATE SHELL

Makes 1 cup
2 minutes to prepare
2-cup glass measure

And you thought you had to make a trip to the ice-cream shop to get a dipped cone. Heck, no. You can make it yourself. You'll find coconut oil for sale in natural-food stores. If you don't use all the shell when you first make it, store it covered in the refrigerator, then warm it back to dipping liquid in the microwave for a few seconds.

6 ounces best-quality semisweet or milk chocolate bars, chopped or
   1 cup chips
6 tablespoons coconut oil

1. Combine the chocolate and coconut oil in a 2-cup glass measure. Microwave at 100% (high), just until the chocolate begins to melt, about 2 minutes. Stir to mix.

2. To serve, dip ice-cream cones into the hot shell, or pour the sauce over a dish of your favorite ice cream or fresh fruit. It hardens instantly.

MICROWAVE CHOCOLATE SAUCE

Makes 2 cups
5 minutes to prepare
4-cup glass measure

Serve this sauce at room temperature, spooned over ice cream, fresh fruit, or a little plain cake. If it seems too thick, whisk it to soften, or place it back in the microwave for a few seconds to warm.

¾ cup whipping cream
8 ounces (1⅓ cups) best-quality semisweet chocolate chips or bars,
   chopped
2 tablespoons unsalted butter
1 tablespoon liqueur of your choice—curaçao, Triple Sec, Cour-
   voisièr—or good-grade vanilla extract

1. Combine in a large microwavable bowl the cream, chocolate, and butter. Microwave at 100% (high) for 2 minutes, then remove from the microwave and add the flavoring. Whisk to blend thoroughly.

2. Pour into a sterile pint jar and store in the refrigerator, covered until ready to serve. This keeps for months in the refrigerator.

7

PANDOWDIES, GRUNTS, BETTIES, CRUMBLES, CRISPS, AND OTHER DESSERTS WITH FUNNY NAMES

K. We confess. This is the catch-all chapter. The one where we put all the old-fashioned desserts made in half the time that wouldn't fit in any other place.

Crisps, included here, are baked desserts with layers of sugared and spiced fruit interspersed between buttered bread crumbs or oatmeal. We needn't mention how thrifty such desserts can be. Here is the place to use up the stale heels of bread along with some barely flavorful fruits you bought at the grocery store, because you can pump up the flavor of the fruit with sugar and spice, and soon you'll have—using the food processor—everything nice.

Brown betties are sometimes known as *buckles* or *crumbles* and are simply another fruit-and-leftover-bread dessert. Jim Fobel's Apple Brown Betty is almost as American as you know what, and we highly recommend it to you.

Slumps and *grunts* are basically the same thing. Fruit or berries simmered in a black pot under a blanket of dumplings. Although conventional wisdom says the names come from the sound the gurgling fruit made as it cooked, slung in a black Dutch oven on a bracket over an open fire in the fireplace, we don't believe a word of it. We figure the slump was the posture assumed by the poor cook who had to stoop over to look in the pot to see how the dessert was progressing, and the grunt was the sound she made when she tried to straighten up, hanging on to that heavy pot full of berries and dumplings. Surely, after all that manual labor, she had slipped a disk. Or two.

Cobblers are, as you may have guessed, cobbled together in deep dishes filled with fruits, then topped with biscuitlike crusts. Baked in the oven, the mixture of fruit, sugar syrup, and flaky biscuits is hard to beat. Make the biscuits in the food processor, and you can cobble these up quicker than ever.

Pandowdies are fruit baked in a pan and topped with a crust that is pressed into the fruit—known as dowdying. Whiz up the topping in the food processor after you've sliced the fruit, and you'll have this in the oven in no time flat.

You can make brown betties of other fruits of the season. Field pears are perfect. Peaches and nectarines make a great August betty. You can also substitute brown bread if that's your preference. Then you'll get a double brown betty. Goes great with a double cappuccino for a fine fusion dessert.

JIM FOBEL'S APPLE BROWN BETTY

Serves 8
10 minutes to prepare
45 minutes to bake
15 minutes to cool
13 x 9-inch baking pan

Jim Fobel convinced us bread bakers that all we needed to begin this "American as . . ." dessert are slices of leftover homemade white bread and some tart green apples. We use the processor to slice the apples and crumb the bread. Quick work for the half-time cook.

About 6 slices leftover good-quality white bread
5 large (about 2½ pounds total) tart green apples of your choice:
    Granny Smiths, Baldwin, Pippins
Zest and juice (about ¼ cup) of ½ lemon
½ cup apple cider or apple juice
½ cup (1 stick) unsalted butter
¾ cup packed brown sugar
1 teaspoon ground cinnamon
½ teaspoon freshly grated nutmeg
¼ teaspoon salt
Whipping cream (optional)

1. Position the rack in the center of the oven and preheat to 375° F. Generously butter a 13 x 9-inch baking dish.

2. Fit the processor bowl with the steel blade, tear the bread into pieces, and arrange them in the bowl. Process to make bread crumbs. Measure out 3 cups of coarse fresh crumbs into a large bowl. (You can freeze any that are leftover in a clean jar for other uses.)

3. Fit the processor with the slicing disk. Core the apples but do not peel them. Cut the apples in half, then drop them through the feed tube, slicing them. Toss with the lemon zest and juice and the apple cider or juice.

4. In a large, heavy skillet melt the butter over moderate heat. Add the bread crumbs and, stirring frequently, toast them to a golden brown. Replace them in the bowl.

5. In a small bowl, stir together the brown sugar, cinnamon, nutmeg, and salt.

6. Sprinkle ¼ of the bread crumbs evenly over the bottom of the buttered dish. Arrange ⅓ of the apples and juice over the crumbs. Sprinkle with ⅓ of the brown sugar mixture. Repeat twice more. Pop the betty into the hot oven and bake 45 minutes, until bubbly and brown. Cool at least 15 minutes, then serve in dessert bowls with whipping cream pooled in the bottom of the bowl.

The Right Apple

Looking for great cooking apples? Try some of these alone or combine varieties in your favorite apple dishes.

> *Stayman-Winesap*
> *Cortland*
> *Jonathan*
> *Rhode Island Greening*
> *McIntosh*
> *Macoun*
> *York Imperial*
> *Northern Spy*
> *Newtown Pippin*
> *Yellow Transparent*

The following apples are considered all-purpose apples and may also be used for cooking: Rome Beauty, Baldwin, Wealthy, and Gravenstein.

CRISP APPLE STRUDEL THE EASY WAY

Serves 6
25 minutes to prepare
35 to 40 minutes to bake
12 x 18 x 1-inch baking sheet

Grandmother had to roll strudel dough so thin she could see her hand through it; however, with phyllo pastry you can eliminate this step. Also called filo or strudel leaves, this handy pastry is available in 1-pound packages in the frozen-food department of most supermarkets.

½ cup (1 stick) unsalted butter
⅓ cup chopped walnuts
1 teaspoon minced lemon zest
5 medium Granny Smith or other tart cooking apples
⅔ cup granulated sugar
¼ cup golden raisins
1 teaspoon ground cinnamon
6 sheets phyllo pastry, thawed
    Confectioners' sugar

1. Preheat the oven to 400° F. With cooking spray, lightly coat a baking sheet that has 1-inch sides and is at least 18 inches long.

2. Place the butter in a microwavable bowl and microwave at 100% (high) for 45 seconds, until the butter is completely melted. Set aside to cool.

3. Place the steel blade in the food processor and pulse to process the walnuts and lemon zest until finely chopped. Remove the mixture to a large bowl. Replace the steel blade with the slicing disk. Peel and core the apples. Slice the apples in the food processor. Remove the apples from the processor bowl and add them to the walnut–lemon zest mixture. Add the sugar, raisins, and cinnamon to the apples and toss to mix.

4. On a tea towel approximately the same size as the phyllo pastry, place 1 sheet of phyllo. Brush with approximately 1 tablespoon of the butter (keep remaining phyllo covered with plastic wrap to prevent drying). Repeat this process, stacking all 6 sheets of phyllo together.

5. Mound the apple mixture along the long side of the phyllo, 1½ inches in from the sides and ends. Fold short ends of phyllo in toward filling. Using the tea towel as a handle, gently roll up the strudel, enclosing the filling. When the strudel is rolled to the edge of the tea towel, pick up the towel and strudel and gently roll the strudel off the towel onto the prepared baking sheet. Brush the top and sides of the strudel with the remaining butter.

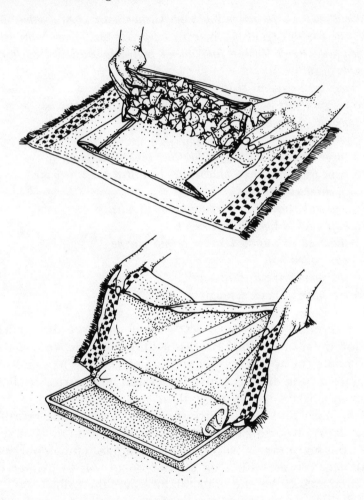

6. Bake on the middle rack of the preheated oven for 35 to 40 minutes, until golden. Cool in the pan on a wire rack. Sprinkle with confectioners' sugar and serve two 1-inch slices per person. Tightly wrap and store in the refrigerator.

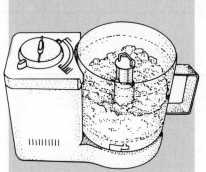

BLUE RIDGE APPLE-BERRY CRISP

Serves 6
10 minutes to prepare
30 minutes to bake
8-inch square baking dish

"Wow!" was all that was said by one kitchen tester when it came time to taste test this beautiful, crunchy crisp. He ran off with the pan when we weren't looking and didn't return it until 2 days later! Empty of course.

You can enjoy this crisp any time of the year because frozen blueberries work just as well as fresh. Remember, the fat is less than 2 teaspoons per serving.

2 large Granny Smith or other tart cooking apples
2½ cups fresh or frozen blueberries or pitted fresh or frozen sweet cherries
½ cup unbleached all-purpose flour, divided
⅓ cup packed light brown sugar
3 tablespoons unsalted butter or margarine
¼ cup rolled oats
½ teaspoon ground cinnamon
¼ teaspoon ground nutmeg

1. Preheat the oven to 400° F. Peel and core the apples. Chop them in the food processor fitted with the steel blade. Combine the apples and blueberries or cherries in an 8-inch square baking dish. Toss the apples and blueberries or cherries with 1 tablespoon of the flour.

2. Rinse and dry the processor bowl. Process the remaining flour, brown sugar, and butter or margarine until mixed thoroughly, about 15 seconds. Add the oats, cinnamon, and nutmeg. Process with 1 or 2 quick on-and-off turns, just to combine. Sprinkle the flour mixture over the fruit.

3. Bake on the middle rack of the preheated oven for 30 minutes, until bubbly. Remove to a rack to cool for 10 minutes. Serve warm.

DEEP-DISH CINNAMON-APPLE PANDOWDY

Serves 6 to 8
20 minutes to prepare
50 minutes to bake
9- or 10-inch deep-sided cake pan

Bring a copy of this recipe with you when you share this apple crisp with friends, because they will probably ask for it. Packed with apples and pumped up with a little applejack, it's irresistible.

6 Granny Smith or other tart cooking apples, peeled, cored, and
   sliced in the food processor
3 tablespoons applejack liquor
½ cup firmly packed light brown sugar
2 tablespoons unbleached all-purpose flour
2 tablespoons water
1 teaspoon ground cinnamon
½ cup coarsely chopped pecans

CRUMB TOPPING

1 cup unbleached all-purpose flour
½ cup (1 stick) butter
1½ cups packed light brown sugar

1. Preheat the oven to 350° F. With cooking spray lightly coat a 9- or 10-inch deep-sided cake pan. In a large bowl, toss together the apples, applejack, brown sugar, flour, water, and cinnamon. Spoon into the prepared pan and sprinkle with the chopped pecans.

2. For the crumb topping, in the processor bowl fitted with the steel blade, process the flour, butter, and brown sugar until crumbly. Sprinkle evenly over the apple mixture, press down with the back of a spoon, and bake on the middle rack of the preheated oven for approximately 50 minutes, until brown and bubbly.

Fried Apple Pies

Makes 8 pies to serve 8

If you happen to have any extra apple crisp leftover, you may want to make these quick and delicious Fried Apple Pies. Use a candy thermometer to check the temperature of the fat. Be patient and don't use it until it reaches 365°F. Fry no more than three at a time and let the temperature return to 365°F before frying the second and third batches.

Fat, for deep frying
2 9-inch unbaked piecrusts,
   homemade or store-bought
2 cups leftover Deep-Dish
   Cinnamon-Apple Pandowdy

Heat the fat (at least 3 inches deep) to 365°F. Roll the piecrust ⅛ inch thick and cut into eight 6-inch circles. Place ¼ cup apple filling in the center of each. Dampen the edges lightly with water, fold over, and seal well. Fry for 2 to 3 minutes, turning as needed, until golden brown. Drain on paper toweling and roll in sugar. Serve warm.

APPLE-WALNUT-CHEDDAR CRUMBLE

Serves 6
15 minutes to prepare
30 minutes to bake
2-quart deep-dish casserole

The Jewel Tea man brought treasures with the foodstuffs when he made his rounds to rural households during the Great Depression. One of our most treasured objects from that time is Grandmother's deep-dish casserole. Remember what this pottery looked like? Cream colored with a gold-and-red chevron design, made to withstand the onslaught of dishes washed in a tin sink; the piece we have is still free of chips, shiny as new, and as precious as memories of home.

What we're glad we don't have to do now is laboriously hand grate apples and cheddar the way grandmother did: an operation guaranteed to put a little cook's blood in the blend. This is an old-fashioned dessert that requires little of your attention, only the processor bowl and the casserole to wash, and will yield up a golden, cheese-flecked, steamy crumble crust over tart, sweet apples, raisins, and walnuts. Serve in individual bowls in a pool of whipping cream and it's heaven.

> *3 large (about 1½ pounds) green apples (Granny Smiths or Pippins work well)*
> *Zest and juice of ½ lemon*
> *½ cup chopped walnuts*
> *½ cup golden raisins*
> *1 cup sugar*
> *1 tablespoon ground cinnamon*
> *1 teaspoon freshly grated nutmeg*
> *3 ounces (1 cup) shredded sharp cheddar cheese*
> *⅔ cup unbleached all-purpose flour*
> *¼ cup (½ stick) unsalted butter or margarine, cold*

1. Preheat the oven to 375° F. Core but don't peel the apples, then shred them in the food processor fitted with the steel shredding blade.

2. Place the shredded apples in a 2-quart deep-dish casserole and stir together with the lemon juice and zest. Stir in the walnuts, raisins, sugar, cinnamon, and nutmeg.

3. Still using the steel shredding disk in the food proces-

sor, shred the cheese. Replace the shredder with the steel blade. Add the flour to the cheese, cut the cold butter into pieces, and add. Pulse to mix until the mixture resembles coarse crumbs. Sprinkle the mixture over the apples.

4. Bake on the middle rack in the preheated oven until the topping is golden and the apples are tender, about 30 minutes.

5. Remove the casserole to a wire rack to cool 5 to 10 minutes.

RED RHUBARB–BING CHERRY BETTY

Serves 6
20 minutes to prepare
40 minutes to bake
9-inch square baking dish

The tartness of rhubarb and the sweetness of cherries makes an old-fashioned betty with a bite. Serve with homemade vanilla ice cream if there's time; if not, top-quality store-bought will do. Choose see-through stemware for serving, because the swirling red rivers melting the ice cream create a beautiful color contrast.

1 pound (about 3 or 4 stalks) fresh red rhubarb
3 cups stemmed and pitted fresh Bing cherries or thawed and
    drained frozen Bing cherries
1 cup packed light brown sugar
1/8 teaspoon ground cloves
1/2 teaspoon ground cinnamon
1/3 cup fresh orange juice
1/4 cup (1/2 stick) unsalted butter
    **Enough fresh best-quality white bread or day-old cake, such as
    pound cake, to make 3 cups lightly packed crumbs**
1 pint vanilla ice cream

(continued)

Rhubarb

Crisp, tender rhubarb is generally available April through June in local farmstands and April through September in the produce section of large grocery chains. Carefully discard any leaves or roots from the rhubarb stalk as they are poisonous to humans and animals alike.

Look for stalks that are pink or red, however, don't be reluctant to use green-stalked rhubarb instead of the red, if that's what you find; simply peel off the tough outer skins, chop, and proceed as for the tender red stalks.

1. Preheat the oven to 350° F. Trim and clean the rhubarb. Cut the rhubarb into 1-inch pieces and toss in a large bowl with the cherries. In a small bowl, mix the brown sugar, cloves, and cinnamon. Reserve 2 tablespoons of the mixture and mix the rest in with the fruit, then add the orange juice.

2. Microwave the butter at 100% (high) for 20 to 30 seconds, until the butter is melted. In the food processor bowl fitted with the steel blade, pulse the bread or cake until crumbs are formed. Remove the lid and measure 3 cups of crumbs. Remove the extra crumbs and store in an airtight container or feed them to the birds. Return the measured crumbs to the bowl and fit with the lid. With the machine running, add the melted butter slowly through the feed tube and process until all the crumbs are moistened with the butter.

3. Pat half the buttered crumbs into the bottom of a glass 9-inch square baking dish. Add the fruit mixture. Top with the remaining crumbs. Sprinkle the top with the reserved sugar-spice mixture.

4. Cover the betty loosely with foil and bake on the middle shelf of the preheated oven for 20 minutes. Uncover and bake for another 20 minutes, until the rhubarb is tender and the bread crumbs are nicely browned. Spoon the warm betty over vanilla ice cream and serve.

RASPBERRY-RHUBARB CRISP

Serves 6
20 minutes to prepare
45 minutes to bake
11 x 7 x 2-inch glass baking dish

Serve this crisp warm with a side of vanilla ice cream or topped with sweetened whipped cream.

1½ pounds fresh red rhubarb, cut into 1-inch pieces (about 4 cups)
¾ cup granulated sugar
   Zest of 1 large orange, minced
⅓ cup fresh orange juice
 2 cups unsweetened frozen raspberries
 1 cup plus 2 tablespoons unbleached all-purpose flour
½ cup packed light brown sugar
½ teaspoon ground cinnamon
½ cup (1 stick) unsalted butter, cut into quarters
½ cup rolled oats (not instant)

1. Preheat the oven to 350° F. In an 11 × 7 × 2-inch glass baking dish combine the rhubarb, sugar, orange zest, orange juice, raspberries, and 2 tablespoons of the flour. Stir to combine. Set aside.

2. In the food processor bowl fitted with the steel blade, combine the remaining 1 cup flour, brown sugar, and cinnamon. Process for 5 seconds. Add the butter pieces and process until the butter is incorporated into the dry ingredients and no longer visible, almost 20 seconds. Add the oats and with an on-off turn, pulse once to combine.

3. Spoon the flour mixture evenly over the surface of the fruit. Bake on the middle rack of the preheated oven for 45 minutes, until the topping is brown and the juices are bubbling. Cool slightly before serving.

BLACKBERRY COBBLER WITH AN EASY FLIP-FLOP CRUST

Serves 6 to 8
25 minutes to prepare
45 minutes to bake
14 x 10 x 3-inch baking pan

There are many methods for preparing cobblers; some require dumplings or biscuits be used on the top of the filling with nothing on the bottom. Our favorite gives you crust on the bottom and top. A simple 2-crust piecrust is rolled out just a little bigger than the pan, the filling is added, and the pastry edges are flopped over onto the top. Simple. Almost any berry or combination of berries can be substituted for the blackberries in this recipe.

1 __double__ recipe (2 crusts) Basic Butter Crust (see page 56),
    unbaked
9 cups fresh blackberries or thawed and drained frozen berries
1⅓ cups sugar
¼ cup unbleached all-purpose flour
¼ cup (½ stick) unsalted butter

1. Preheat the oven to 425° F. Roll out the crust into a rectangle, big enough to line a 14 × 10 × 3-inch baking pan and flop over the top. (This crust will not completely cover the top.) Line the pan with the crust.

2. In a 3-quart mixing bowl, mix the berries, sugar, and flour together thoroughly. Dump the berries into the prepared pan. Dot the berries with small chunks of the butter. Flip the edges of the pastry up and over the berries. There will probably be a small hole in the center.

3. Bake on the middle rack of the preheated oven for 45 minutes, until the crust is nicely browned. Serve warm or at room temperature.

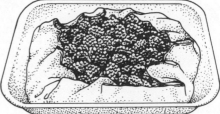

BLUEBERRY GRUNT

Serves 8
10 minutes to prepare
25 minutes to bake on top of the stove
10-inch cast-iron skillet

Although there may be fierce arguments over the virtues of tiny Maine blueberries versus giant Oregon ones, there can be no question about the merits of an old-fashioned berry dessert cooked in a black cast-iron skillet under a blanket of dumplings.

¾ cup unbleached all-purpose flour
½ cup sugar, divided
1 teaspoon baking powder
⅜ teaspoon salt, divided
3 tablespoons unsalted butter or shortening
3 tablespoons milk
1 quart fresh blueberries
Zest and juice of ½ lemon
1½ cups water
Ground cinnamon to taste
Whipping cream

1. In the food processor bowl fitted with the steel blade, combine the flour, 2 tablespoons of the sugar, baking powder, and ¼ teaspoon of the salt. Pulse to mix. Cut the butter or shortening into pieces and arrange on the top. Process to incorporate until the mixture resembles coarse meal, about 10 seconds.

2. Sprinkle the milk over the surface, then pulse to mix, just until the dry ingredients are moistened. (The dough will be sticky.) Set aside.

3. In a 10-inch cast-iron skillet, combine the remaining sugar with the blueberries. Sprinkle with the remaining ⅛ teaspoon salt, lemon zest and juice, water, and cinnamon. Stir well. Raise to a boil over medium heat.

4. Reduce the heat to a simmer and cook, uncovered, 5 minutes. Drop the dough by the tablespoon onto the blueberries. Cook uncovered for 10 minutes, then cover and cook an additional 10 minutes. Serve warm in dessert bowls in a pool of whipping cream.

Blueberries

Fresh blueberries are available June through August in most areas of the United States. We freeze or dehydrate them to use in the winter. Look for large berries that are dark blue, plump, and wrinkle free. Discard any green berries or berries with mold. Dried blueberries have a concentrated blueberry flavor and are delicious when mixed in with frozen berries in your favorite muffin recipe.

Ripe Peaches

To ripen peaches more quickly, place them in a brown paper bag that has several holes poked in it to allow the fruit to breathe. Store the bag at room temperature in a well-lit area. Domed plastic ripening bowls work well and are available in the produce department of most supermarkets or in specialty kitchen shops. (See sidebar, page 229 for a discussion of peach varieties.)

Georgie porgie,
pudding and pie,
Kissed the girls and
made them cry;
When the boys came
out to play
Georgie Porgie ran away.

GEORGIE PEORGIE'S PEACH PUDDING

Serves 8
10 minutes to prepare
40 minutes to bake
13 × 9-inch glass baking dish

As much as we love peach puddings and cobblers, we are always a little sad when we shelve the peach recipes after fresh peaches are out of season in August. Come about January, we get desperate for peaches and finally start opening our home-canned peaches, or, if we were lazy the previous summer and didn't put any by, we reach for the cans, feeling guilty all the while.

This recipe is so easy, simple, beautiful, and good you will not believe it could be so fast.

½ cup (1 stick) unsalted butter
5 cups peeled (see sidebar, page 168) sliced fresh ripe peaches and their juice or 3 1-pound cans peaches in light syrup
1 cup unbleached all-purpose flour
1½ cups sugar, divided
1 tablespoon baking powder
¾ cup milk
1 teaspoon vanilla extract
Vanilla ice cream (optional)
Whipped cream (optional)

1. Preheat the oven to 350° F. In a 13 × 9-inch glass baking dish heat the butter in the microwave on 100% (high) for 50 seconds, until melted. Arrange the fresh peaches in a single layer on the bottom of the pan, or drain 2 cans of peaches and add the contents of all 3 cans (1 can undrained) to the pan.

2. In a medium mixing bowl, whisk together the flour, 1 cup of the sugar, baking powder, milk, and vanilla. Pour this batter over the peaches. Sprinkle the batter with the remaining ½ cup sugar. Bake on the middle rack of the preheated oven for 40 minutes, until the pudding is puffed and golden brown. Serve warm over vanilla ice cream or topped with whipped cream if desired.

MICROWAVE PEAR-CHEDDAR CRISP

Makes one 10-inch pie to serve 8
10 minutes to prepare
10 to 12 minutes to microwave
5 minutes to broil
9- or 10-inch deep-dish glass pie pan

For a quick fall dessert, microwave pears under a blanket of oats and cheddar, then run the whole thing under the broiler for a golden-brown finish. Serve warm in a pool of whipping cream.

**6 large ripe pears, peeled and cored
 Zest and juice of ½ lemon
1 teaspoon vanilla extract
2 ounces (¾ cup) shredded sharp white cheddar cheese
½ cup unbleached all-purpose flour
½ cup rolled oats (not instant)
½ cup packed brown sugar
4 tablespoons (½ stick) unsalted butter, softened
 Whipping cream**

1. Generously butter a 9- or 10-inch deep-dish glass pie pan. Slice the pears in the food processor using the slicing disk. Toss the pear slices with the lemon zest, juice, and vanilla. Arrange the pear slices in the pan. Top with the grated cheese.

2. Mix the flour, oats, and brown sugar. Cut in the butter using a fork, until the mixture looks like crumbs. Sprinkle over the pears.

3. Preheat the broiler. Microwave at 100% (high) for 10 to 12 minute, until the pears are tender. Run the dish under the broiler, about 4 inches from the heat, until the top is bubbly and brown, about 3 minutes. Watch it. Don't let it burn.

Pears of different types are sold at different times of the year and in different parts of the country. For the most part, pears from the West Coast states of Washington, Oregon, and California find their way into markets all across the country.

Use them interchangeably. But remember, pears are always picked green. Let pears stand a few days in a warm room, and they'll get sweeter and softer. The skin color may not change, however. To test for ripeness, hold the pear in the palm of your hand and press on the stem end. It should yield slightly. If it's hard, put it back.

8
CUSTARDS, PUDDINGS, MOUSSES, AND FLANS

earn to make milk-based desserts in the microwave, and you will never do them in a double boiler again. We thought of calling this chapter "What to Do When the Recipe Calls for a Bain Marie." We will tell you this. In any cookbook or food magazine, when you see the instructions "Cook in a double boiler," let the light bulb go off over your head. Think *microwave*.

Nothing is easier to do than make pudding in the microwave. If the thickener is cornstarch, all you have to do is combine the ingredients in a large microwavable bowl, microwave at 100% (high), whisk with a balloon whisk to thoroughly mix, and, before you know it, you've got pudding.

Working on this chapter, we learned what a friend to cornstarch the microwave is. It cooks cornstarch-based foods to perfection, so that you never get that lumpy, raw, wallpapery taste.

There is one caveat to microwaving cornstarch-thickened sauces and puddings. If the recipe calls for cooking an acid such as cherry juice or lemon juice with the cornstarch, the mixture must not heat above 170° F. The simple solution to that problem is to keep the microwave set at 70% (medium) for the entire cooking period.

And once again, use your judgment. Rely on the way the pudding looks. If the recipe says to cook and whisk at 30-second intervals, stop microwaving the moment the pudding or sauce begins to thicken. The microwave energy will keep bouncing around, cooking the mixture for 5 minutes or so. Just let it stand a few moments. It will thicken right up.

If you find that you've overheated a pudding and it stubbornly won't thicken, stick it in the refrigerator to cool to room temperature, then try it again, using a lower setting on your microwave.

Egg-based custards can be made successfully in the microwave as well. Again, take care not to let the mixture get too hot. Custards will curdle. Turn your microwave down to 70% (medium) or lower, use the minimum time recommended in the recipe, then test for doneness the same way you would if you'd baked the custard in a hot-water bath in the oven: Insert a table knife in the middle of the custard. If it comes out clean, the custard is cooked through.

Always remember that in microwave cooking the food continues cooking for about 5 minutes after you've removed it from the oven. Therefore, it is always advisable to undercook rather than overcook puddings and custards to avoid the risk of curdling.

HOME-ALONE CHOCOLATE PUDDING

Instead of cocoa, you could use 3 tablespoons of chocolate chips. Stir them into the hot pudding with the vanilla. Instead of vanilla, try grating some orange zest on top. Or for plain vanilla pudding, skip all the chocolates, and simply dust the top of the pudding with cinnamon before refrigerating.

Makes one 12-ounce mug
3 minutes to prepare
3 minutes to cook
1 hour to chill
2-cup glass measure

Feeling sorry for yourself? Need Mama in a mug? Make pudding in the microwave. Make the pudding in a 2-cup glass measure, because it boils up to twice the volume and can make the inside of your microwave look like the foothills of Mount Etna if you don't use a big enough container to begin with. Then pour the hot pudding into your favorite mug to cool.

  1 tablespoon cornstarch
  2 tablespoons unsweetened Dutch-process cocoa
  3 tablespoons sugar
  ¾ cup milk
  ¼ teaspoon vanilla extract

1. In a 2-cup or bigger glass measure, dissolve the cornstarch, cocoa, and sugar in the milk. Stir thoroughly.
2. Microwave at 100% (high) for 90 seconds, whisk, then microwave again at 70% (medium) until the mixture boils and thickens, just under a minute and a half.
3. Stir in the vanilla extract. Whisk to mix thoroughly. Pour into your favorite mug. Refrigerate at least an hour.

THE PRINCE OF CHOCOLATE PUDDINGS

Serves 4
10 minutes to prepare
30 minutes to chill
8-cup microwavable batter bowl

No childhood is complete without chocolate pudding. Now with the microwave it's faster than ever.

2 tablespoons cornstarch
1 cup sugar
¼ teaspoon salt
2 cups milk
2 ounces (2 squares) unsweetened chocolate
2 large egg yolks
1 teaspoon vanilla extract
2 tablespoons unsalted butter
Sweetened whipped cream (optional)
Chocolate Curls (optional; see sidebar, page 202)

1. In an 8-cup microwavable batter bowl blend together the cornstarch, sugar, and salt. Slowly pour in the milk and add the chocolate squares. Microwave on 100% (high) for 6 minutes, whisking every 3 minutes until the mixture is smooth and the chocolate is melted.

2. Meanwhile, in a small bowl beat the egg yolks slightly. Stir ½ cup of the milk-and-chocolate mixture into the egg yolks. Return the egg mixture to the pudding and whisk well. Microwave the pudding on 90% (medium-high) for 2 minutes, whisking after 1 minute until the pudding is smooth and thickened. Whisk in the vanilla and butter until the butter is melted. Pour the hot pudding into pretty stemmed dessert dishes. Refrigerate for at least 30 minutes. Garnish with sweetened whipped cream and chocolate curls or serve plain.

Variation: Vanilla Princess Pudding

To make Vanilla Princess Pudding omit the chocolate and decrease the sugar to ¾ cup. Proceed as in main recipe.

❖   ❖

Homemade Vanilla Extract

Years before vanilla was discovered, brandy and cognac were used to flavor cakes. Not only do they help preserve the cake and add their own spirited taste, they have a leavening power that makes the product lighter.

Pure vanilla extract is sublime and very easy to make. Ounce for ounce it's cheaper than commercially prepared "pure" vanilla extract.

To make 5 ounces of vanilla, you will need 2 vanilla beans, ½ cup plus 2 tablespoons of 190-proof grain alcohol, and an airtight, sterile glass container. Slit the vanilla beans lengthwise to expose the hundreds of black seeds. Then cut the beans crosswise into 1-inch pieces. Add the beans and the alcohol to the container and seal. Shake the bottle every other day for 2 to 3 weeks. The vanilla beans may be used again for 2 or 3 more batches; after that toss the beans and start over with fresh ones. Store at room temperature for up to 6 months.

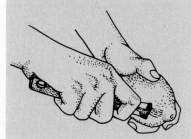

LEMON MOUSSE CHARLOTTE

Serves 6 to 8
20 minutes to prepare
2½ hours to chill
2-quart charlotte mold and pastry bag with decorative tip

Crisp and airy ladyfinger cookies allow you to prepare this elegant dessert in only 20 minutes. Ladyfingers are a dry, egg-white-based cookie that should be in everyone's half-time pantry. They can be the base for desserts such as this or Chocolate Mighty Mousse (see page 112) or you can serve them simply as a side with ice cream. Ladyfingers are available by mail order from California Cuisine, 3501 Taylor Dr., Ukiah, CA 95482, or by calling their toll-free number, (800) 753-8558.

24 ladyfingers
8 large eggs, separated
1 cup granulated sugar
    Zest of 3 lemons, minced
½ cup fresh lemon juice
2 tablespoons (2 envelopes) Knox or other unflavored gelatin
½ cup cold water
2 teaspoons lemon juice or white wine vinegar
1 cup whipping cream
1 tablespoon confectioners' sugar
    Fresh mint leaves (optional)
    Fresh violets (optional)

1. With cooking spray coat the charlotte mold (this is to keep the plastic wrap flat against the sides of the mold). Line the mold with a layer of plastic wrap, leaving a 2-inch border of plastic wrap around the outside. Line the bottom and sides of the mold with the ladyfingers. Set aside.

2. In an 8-cup microwavable measure, using a stainless or Teflon-coated whisk, beat the egg yolks with the sugar, lemon zest, and ½ cup lemon juice. Microwave on 70% (medium) for 2 minutes. Stir. Microwave on 70% (medium) for an additional 2 minutes. Stir. Microwave on 70% (medium) for 1 minute.

3. Meanwhile, add the gelatin to the cold water and let it stand for 2 minutes to allow the gelatin to soften. Whisk the gelatin into the thickened cooked custard until smooth. Cover the custard with plastic wrap and refrigerate just until cool, about 30 minutes.

4. Meanwhile, place the egg whites in the bowl of the food processor fitted with the plastic or steel blade (see page 00). Process the egg whites for 10 seconds, until foamy. With the machine running, add 2 teaspoons lemon juice or white wine vinegar through the feed tube and process until the egg whites are stiff (they will just tip over when a small amount is lifted with a spoon). Fold the egg whites into the chilled lemon custard. Pour the mousse into the charlotte mold. Cover and refrigerate until the mousse has jelled, about 2 hours (the top will spring back when lightly touched with your finger). The charlotte may be refrigerated up to 24 hours at this point.

5. Right before serving, pour the whipping cream into the bowl of the food processor fitted with the steel blade. Process the cream until it begins to thicken. Add the confectioners' sugar through the feed tube and continue processing until stiff. Using the overhanging plastic wrap on the outside of the charlotte mold as a handle, gently pull and loosen the charlotte from the mold and invert the charlotte onto a serving platter. Place the whipped cream in a pastry bag and pipe it decoratively around the bottom of the charlotte and onto the top. Garnish with mint leaves and violets, if desired. Serve immediately, or refrigerate for up to 4 hours.

Variation: Lime Mousse Charlotte

To make, follow the directions for Lemon Mousse Charlotte; however, substitute the grated and minced zest of 2 limes and ⅓ cup plus 1 tablespoon of lime juice for the lemon zest and lemon juice. The egg whites can be processed with either 2 teaspoons lime or lemon juice.

CHOCOLATE MOUSSE

Serves 8
15 minutes to prepare
1 hour to cool
8 stemmed goblets

A perfect fast finish for any occasion.

12 ounces (2 cups) semisweet chocolate chips
½ cup half-and-half
 4 large eggs, lightly beaten
 2 cups whipping cream
⅓ cup confectioners' sugar
 1 tablespoon Irish cream, Chambord (raspberry liqueur), or Triple Sec (optional)
 Sweetened whipped cream, for garnish (optional)
 Chocolate Curls, for garnish (optional; see sidebar)

1. Pour the chocolate chips and the half-and-half into an 8-cup microwavable bowl. Microwave on 100% (high) for 2 minutes. Remove the bowl from the microwave and stir the mixture until smooth. Add the eggs and whisk until smooth. Cool to room temperature.

2. Fit the processor bowl with the steel blade. Add the whipping cream and process until thickened. Gradually add the sugar through the feed tube and process until stiff, about 90 seconds.

3. Gently fold the whipped cream into the chocolate mixture. Fold in the liqueur if you like. Spoon ¾ cup of mousse into each of 8 stemmed goblets. Refrigerate for at least 1 hour. Serve chilled, garnished with additional whipped cream and Chocolate Curls, if desired.

CREME BRULEE

Serves 4
10 minutes to prepare
4 hours to chill
4-cup glass measure
4 broilerproof ⅔-cup ramekins or glass custard cups

A classic dessert made simple in the microwave. Serve it for any occasion or time of year. Crème Brûlée is nothing more than sweetened cream and eggs blended together with just a whiff of nutmeg and vanilla. Beautiful simplicity. Plus, you can make this at your convenience: in the morning, the night before, even 2 days ahead.

2 cups whipping cream
4 egg yolks
3 tablespoons granulated sugar
⅛ teaspoon salt
½ teaspoon vanilla extract
⅛ teaspoon freshly grated nutmeg
3 tablespoons packed light brown sugar

1. Pour the cream into a microwavable 4-cup glass measure. Microwave on 100% (high) power for 3 to 4 minutes, just until small bubbles start to form around the edge.

2. Meanwhile, in a small bowl whisk together the egg yolks, sugar, and salt. Carefully remove the hot cream from the microwave and slowly whisk it into the egg-yolk mixture. Whisk until smooth.

3. Microwave at 50% (medium-low) for 4 to 5 minutes, whisking every minute or so until the mixture thickens slightly. Remove from the microwave and stir in the vanilla extract and grated nutmeg. Pour the cream into 4 individual broilerproof ramekins or custard cups and refrigerate for 3 hours, until well chilled.

4. Set the oven rack to the broiler position. Preheat the broiler. Meanwhile, with a spoon push the brown sugar through a sieve or strainer onto the cream. Set the dishes on the broiler rack and broil for 4 to 6 minutes, until the sugar caramelizes and becomes shiny. Refrigerate for 1 hour to allow caramel to harden. This can be made 1 or 2 days ahead if need be. Store covered in the refrigerator.

Blowtorch Cooking

A favorite piece of cooking equipment in restaurant kitchens is the blowtorch, used for singeing the hair off of game birds and caramelizing the topping on brûlées. Small propane blowtorches can be purchased for home use. Light the blowtorch according to the manufacturers' instructions and adjust the flame to its lowest setting. Pass the nozzle back and forth across the top of the brûlée until the sugar is melted, shiny, and light brown. Handle the brûlées with hot pads or mitts until completely cool.

BLACK BRULEE

If you don't have espresso powder, grind espresso coffee beans to a powder in your coffee grinder and substitute measure for measure.

Serves 4
10 minutes to prepare
4 hours to chill
4 broilerproof ⅔-cup ramekins or glass custard cups or a
3- to 4-cup broilerproof serving dish

An elegant dessert for special occasions is this dark chocolate pudding or brûlée.

  6 ounces semisweet chocolate or 1 cup semisweet chocolate chips
1½ cups whipping cream
1½ teaspoons instant espresso powder
  5 large egg yolks
1½ tablespoons coffee liqueur
  ¼ cup chopped pecans
  1 tablespoon plus 1 teaspoon sugar

1. Place the chocolate in a 2-quart microwavable bowl and microwave on 100% (high) for 3 minutes to melt semisweet chocolate squares and 2 minutes to melt semisweet chocolate chips. Stir to melt any remaining bits and add the whipping cream. Whisk to combine. Microwave the chocolate mixture on 100% (high) for 2½ to 3 minutes, until bubbles start to form around the edge.

2. Meanwhile, in a small bowl whisk together the espresso powder, egg yolks, and coffee liqueur. Whisk in half of the chocolate mixture. Return the chocolate–egg yolk mixture to the larger bowl and whisk thoroughly. Microwave on 50% (medium-low) for 2 minutes. Remove from the microwave and whisk to smooth. Pour the brûlée into 4 individual broilerproof ramekins or custard cups or a 3- to 4-cup broilerproof serving dish.

3. Cool to room temperature and refrigerate for at least 3 hours. Two hours before serving, preheat the broiler. Sprinkle the top of the brûlée with the chopped pecans. With the back of a spoon, press down lightly so the nuts are just under the surface of the brûlée. Sprinkle evenly with the sugar. Be sure the nuts are submerged completely so they will not burn.

Broil 2 inches from the heat source until the sugar caramelizes, watching carefully, for about 30 seconds. Refrigerate until cold, about 1 hour.

MICROWAVE FLAN ALMENDRA

Serves 4
Four ⅔-cup ramekins or glass custard cups

Making custards in the microwave is simple, provided you remember to turn the power back to 50%. Use a too-hot setting, and the custard will curdle. You can flavor this basic egg custard with other things besides almonds, if you wish. Lemon or orange zest. A whiff of espresso. Any way you make it, this is easy comfort.

1¼ cups milk
4 large eggs
⅓ cup sugar
1 teaspoon vanilla extract
1 teaspoon almond extract (optional)
4 tablespoons slivered almonds, divided (optional)

1. Place the milk in 1-quart microwavable bowl and microwave at 100% (high) for 2 minutes.

2. Meanwhile, in another bowl, whisk together the eggs, sugar, vanilla, and almond extract, if using. Pour the hot milk into the egg mixture and stir to mix.

3. If you wish, place a tablespoon of slivered almonds in each of four ⅔-cup ramekins or glass custard cups. Pour the custard into the ramekins or cups. Arrange the ramekins or cups evenly on the carousel. Microwave at 50% (medium) for 6 to 7 minutes, until firm.

4. Remove from the microwave and cool. Serve at room temperature or chilled.

Even though the almonds you buy for this recipe will probably come from California, Europeans in Portugal and Spain first planted the trees by the orchard full around the beginning of the Renaissance. These and other Mediterranean cooks began using almonds in nougat, marzipan, and countless other dishes.

Buy the freshest almonds you can locate. If you're limited to those little packages of slivered almonds, check the pull date. They don't last long.

If, like us, you live in an area where fresh California almonds are sold in bulk, by all means, buy them that way. Sneak a taste from the bin to guarantee that these whole almonds are fresh, then scoop up a supply and take it home.

For this recipe, you can sliver the almonds either by hand, using a sharp knife and a cutting board, or use the finest slicing blade on your food processor and pulse to slice them into the work bowl. A sliver, a slice? There's little difference in taste.

If you insist on removing the skins (get real, this is the nineties—who has time). Drop whole almonds in boiling water a few seconds, then drain them and the skins should slip off (easier said than done let us assure you). Want our advice? Use almonds skin and all.

BING HASTY PUDDING WITH RASPBERRY SAUCE

Makes 6 servings
20 minutes to prepare
45 minutes to bake
8-cup 3-inch-deep casserole dish

We start this luscious pudding with homemade French or Italian bread, made in the bread machine. Barring that, you can use any good-quality white bread, crusts trimmed, and cut into ½-inch-thick slices. Fresh or frozen cherries work equally well in this dessert, and if you're really in a hurry, skip the raspberry sauce and just heat up a little raspberry jam in the microwave, then thin it with Kirsch.

½ cup (1 stick) unsalted butter
¾ pound good-quality white bread, crust trimmed, cut into ½-inch-
    thick slices, then cut into triangles
2 cups milk
½ cup whipping cream
1½ cups granulated sugar, divided
2 large egg yolks
1¼ cup fresh or frozen pitted Bing cherries, thawed and drained
2 tablespoons kirsch or Chambord (raspberry liqueur)

WHIPPED TOPPING

1 cup whipping cream
2 tablespoons confectioners' sugar
1 recipe Raspberry Sauce (optional; see sidebar)

1. Preheat the oven to 350° F. Butter an 8-cup 3-inch-deep casserole, and butter the bread slices on both sides. Arrange half the bread over the bottom of the casserole dish.

2. In a quart-sized microwavable bowl, combine the milk, cream, and ½ cup of the sugar. Microwave at 100% (high) for 4 minutes, then stir until the sugar dissolves. Remove from the microwave and set aside.

3. In a large mixing bowl, lightly beat the egg yolks; stir them into the hot cream mixture. Pour half this custard onto the bread in the casserole.

4. Combine the cherries, remaining 1 cup sugar, and the kirsch or Chambord in a small bowl, mixing thoroughly. Spoon this mixture over the bread in the casserole, reserving a few cherries to garnish the top.

5. Layer the remaining half of the bread in the dish and pour the remaining custard over the top. Lightly press the top bread slices down with the back of a spoon to make sure all the bread slices are moistened. Place the remaining cherries artfully on top.

6. Bake on the middle rack of the preheated oven for 45 minutes, until the pudding is set and lightly browned. Remove to a rack to cool.

7. Just before serving, whip the cream. Place the cream and sugar in the food processor bowl fitted with the steel blade (see page 17). Process just until the cream forms stiff peaks, about 2 minutes.

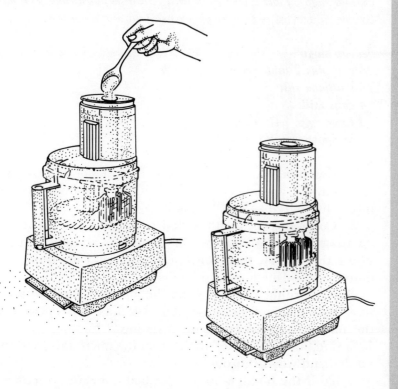

8. Serve the pudding warm or at room temperature in a pool of Raspberry Sauce, if desired, and with a dollop of whipped cream on top.

But good dog Tray is happy now;
He has no time to say "Bow-wow!"
He seats himself in Frederick's chair
And laughs to see the good things there:
The soup he swallows, sup by sup—
And eats the pies and puddings up.

—*HEINRICH HOFFMAN*
(1809–1874)
Cruel Frederick

Vanilla Sugar

To make Vanilla Sugar, simply bury a vanilla bean in a pint of sugar and leave it there for at least 2 weeks. Good sprinkled on fruit, sugar cookies, and custard.

No-BLANCH BLANCMANGE

Serves 6
15 minutes to prepare
1 hour to bake
Six ⅔-cup ramekins or custard cups

Beginning home-ec students in junior high schools have made gallons of this fabled French pudding—as plain and white and simple sounding as can be. Made the classic way, it demands attention from the cook—standing and stirring until the cornstarch changes from that raw-as-wallpaper taste you remember from home-ec blancmange to a subtle, smooth-as-silk, simple, sweet dessert. Made in the microwave, blancmange is foolproof. Serve it plain or dusted with cinnamon or vanilla sugar. Pour it over fresh fruit or a little plain cake. You may become as devoted to this simple French pudding as we are.

½ cup sugar
¼ cup plus 2 tablespoons cornstarch
¼ teaspoon salt
4 cups milk
2 large eggs, well beaten
1 teaspoon vanilla extract

1. Combine the sugar, cornstarch, and salt in a 2-quart microwavable bowl. Gradually whisk in the milk until the mixture is lump-free and well mixed.

2. Cover the bowl with waxed paper and place it in the microwave oven. Microwave for 5 minutes at 100% (high). Whisk thoroughly, then continue by microwaving 3 minutes more at 70% (medium-high).

3. Remove the pudding from the microwave and whisk in the 2 eggs, mixing thoroughly. Re-cover the bowl, replace it in the microwave, and finish microwaving 2 minutes more at 70% (medium-high). Remove it from the microwave, add the vanilla, and whisk thoroughly.

4. Pour the pudding into individual ramekins, or custard cups, cover, and refrigerate to chill.

SWEET LARRY'S NANNER-NANNER

Serves 8
15 minutes to prepare
1 hour to chill

Sweet bananas and juicy pineapple are a delicious combination of flavors in this yummy pudding, which is poured over vanilla wafers. A refreshing dessert made in no time.

¼ teaspoon salt
2 tablespoons cornstarch
¾ cup sugar
2 cups whole milk
2 large egg yolks
2 tablespoons unsalted butter
1 teaspoon vanilla extract
1 15-ounce can crushed pineapple, drained
4 firm ripe large bananas
40 vanilla-wafer cookies
   Sweetened whipped cream (optional)

1. In a 4-cup glass microwavable mixing bowl, combine the salt, cornstarch, and sugar. Stir well to combine. Gradually stir in the milk. Microwave on 100% (high) for 6 to 7 minutes, whisking every 3 minutes, until the mixture is smooth, thick, and clear.

2. In a small mixing bowl, lightly beat the egg yolks. Whisk a small amount of the hot pudding into the egg yolks. Return the egg yolk mixture to the pudding and mix well. Microwave on 70% (medium-high) for 2 to 3 minutes, until smooth and thickened. Add the butter and vanilla.

3. Add the pineapple to the hot pudding. Slice the bananas and set aside.

4. On the bottom of an 8-cup or larger glass bowl, arrange a layer of 20 vanilla wafers. Cover with half of the banana slices. Pour half of the pudding over the bananas. Repeat, beginning with the vanilla wafers. Chill for at least 1 hour, allowing the pudding to soften the wafers a bit. Garnish with sweetened whipped cream, if desired.

Variation: Chocolate Nanner-Nanner

For a chocolate-banana pudding, prepare the pudding as directed in Sweet Larry's Nanner-Nanner, except increase the sugar to 1 cup and add 2 squares unsweetened chocolate along with the milk. Omit the pineapple. Layer as directed, and for a grand finale, place a paper doily over the top of the finished pudding. Sprinkle the top of the doily with sifted confectioners' sugar and carefully remove the doily. The sugar should now look stenciled on top of the chocolate pudding.

Blueberry Sauce

Makes 2 cups sauce
8-cup microwavable batter bowl

1 cup sugar
1 cup water
Dash of salt
1 quart fresh or frozen blueberries, thawed

Place the sugar, water, and salt in a 8-cup microwavable measure and microwave at 100% (high) for 2 to 3 minutes, until the mixture boils. Boil for 2 minutes. Carefully remove the sugar-water mixture from the microwave and add the cleaned and picked-over blueberries. Replace in the microwave and heat at 100% (high) for 2 minutes, just until the blueberries begin to pop and open. Remove the blueberries from the microwave and allow to cool. Serve the cooled sauce over ice cream. (Any remaining sauce is great served the following morning over pancakes.)

ORANGE ICE CREAM WITH FRESH BLUEBERRIES AND MINT

Serves 6
20 minutes to prepare
25 minutes to chill
30 minutes to freeze
Ice-cream freezer

Although we rarely attempt to compete with Ben and Jerry or Häagen Dazs, this is one time we can't resist. Haul out the ice-cream freezer. It's worth it.

For a refreshing summer cooler try this tried-and-true combination of orange and blueberries. The bright-orange ice cream looks beautiful served in stemware and sprinkled with fresh blueberries. Blueberry sauce as a crown and a twig of mint for garnish is another beautiful topping.

2 teaspoons grated orange zest
½ cup milk
¼ cup light corn syrup
Dash of salt
¼ cup sugar
2 large egg yolks
1⅔ cups fresh orange juice
½ cup whipping cream
1 cup fresh or frozen blueberries, thawed
Prepared blueberry sauce or 1 recipe homemade Blueberry Sauce (optional; see sidebar)
Fresh mint leaves, for garnish (optional)

1. Place the orange zest and milk in a 1-cup microwavable measure. Microwave at 100% (high) for 70 seconds, until tiny bubbles form around the edge of the cup.

2. Meanwhile, in a 4-cup microwavable measure whisk the corn syrup, salt, sugar, and egg yolks together. Slowly add the milk mixture to the corn syrup mixture and stir thoroughly.

3. Place the milk-and-sugar base back in the microwave and microwave at 50% (medium-low) for 3 minutes, stirring after the first 2 minutes. Remove the mixture from the microwave oven and stir. The base should now be able to coat

the back of the spoon. Add the orange juice and whipping cream and stir well. Place the mixture into the freezer compartment of your refrigerator and chill until very cold and ice crystals just begin to form around the edge of the container, about 25 minutes.

4. Pour the mixture into the container of an ice-cream freezer and freeze according to the manufacturer's directions. To serve, spoon into dessert dishes and sprinkle with the fresh or frozen, thawed blueberries. Garnish with fresh mint leaves if you like. Serve immediately.

*B*RIOCHE BREAD PUDDING WITH BOURBON SAUCE

Serves 6 to 8
10 minutes to prepare
45 minutes to bake
8½ x 5-inch loaf pan
Deep ovenproof pan

Bread pudding is no better than the bread you begin with. Start with day-old brioche, either homemade or from your finest neighborhood bakery, and you'll soon have a bread pudding to remember. Drizzle Bourbon Sauce over all.

  6 to 8 day-old brioches
  Unsalted butter
⅓ cup golden raisins
⅓ cup pecan halves
1½ cups milk
  2 large eggs
  2 egg yolks
¼ cup bourbon
⅓ cup sugar
  1 teaspoon vanilla extract
  1 recipe Bourbon Sauce (see sidebar)

(continued)

Bourbon Sauce

Makes 1½ cups
5 minutes to prepare
2-quart microwavable batter bowl

Try Bourbon Sauce over ice cream or curried fruits. A fine old Southern tradition.

4 egg yolks
⅓ cup sugar
⅓ cup bourbon

1. *Combine the egg yolks, sugar, and bourbon in a microwavable 2-quart batter bowl. Beat until light with a balloon whisk.*
2. *Microwave at 100% (high) for 30 seconds. Whisk thoroughly, then repeat for 30 seconds more. Repeat, microwaving and whisking at 30-second intervals until the sauce is thick and creamy. Pour into a sterile jar, cover, and refrigerate until serving time. Serve cold. Keeps for up to 2 weeks, refrigerated.*

1. Preheat the oven to 350° F. Fill a quart microwavable container with water, and microwave at 100% (high) for 5 minutes to boil. Generously butter an 8½ × 5-inch loaf pan.

2. Meanwhile, slice off the brioche tops (hats) and set them aside. Slice the brioches into ½-inch-thick slices. Lightly butter the slices, then fit them into the prepared pan, covering the bread layer with a sprinkling of raisins and pecan halves. Repeat the layers until you have used all the bread, raisins, and pecans.

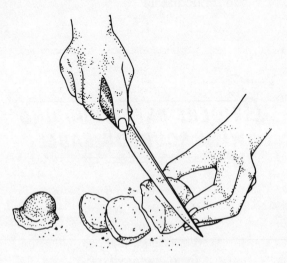

3. In a large mixing bowl, whisk together the milk, eggs, egg yolks, bourbon, sugar, and vanilla. Slowly pour this mixture over the layered brioche, allowing the bread time to absorb all the milk. When the milk reaches 1 inch below the top of the loaf pan, stop adding. Butter the undersides of the brioche hats and artfully arrange them atop the pudding.

4. Place the loaf pan in the middle of the deep ovenproof pan. Pour the boiling water from the microwave into the large pan until the water reaches halfway up the sides of the loaf pan. Place the pans in the center of the preheated oven and bake until the pudding is set, about 45 minutes. Lift the loaf pan from its water bath and cool on a rack.

5. Cut in thick slices and serve warm with a dollop of Bourbon Sauce atop. Good cold, leftover, for breakfast the next morning, too.

BIG PEARL'S APPLE-TAPIOCA PUDDING A LA MODE

Serves 6 to 8
15 minutes to prepare
15 minutes to cook
8-cup microwavable bowl

Tapioca is the starch from cassava roots made into granules. If you are using quick-cooking tapioca, the granules will be small. Fish-eye tapioca is round and comes in medium- and large-pearl sizes. The three are not interchangeable, as the larger granules take longer to soften and cook.

In this quick-to-cook recipe, the apples and their juice are thickened with the tapioca. The tapioca lends body to the cooked fruit and makes it the perfect hot apple compote to spoon over vanilla ice cream, cinnamon ice cream, or frozen yogurt.

4 large Granny Smith or other tart cooking apples, peeled, cored, and sliced
1 cup packed light brown sugar
⅓ cup quick-cooking tapioca
2 cups water
2 tablespoons unsalted butter
2 tablespoons fresh lemon juice
½ teaspoon ground cinnamon
½ teaspoon salt
1 quart vanilla ice cream

1. In an 8-cup microwavable bowl, mix the apples, brown sugar, tapioca, water, butter, lemon juice, cinnamon, and salt. Let stand for 5 minutes.

2. Microwave the mixture uncovered on 100% (high) for 6 minutes, until it starts to boil. Stir. Reduce the heat to 70% (medium) and microwave for 8 minutes, stirring after every 4 minutes, until the apples are easily pierced with a fork.

3. Spoon the ice cream into serving dishes and ladle the hot apple compote over the top. Serve immediately.

Using Tapioca

Small-granuled, quick-cooking tapioca can replace cornstarch and flour used for thickening fruit in pies and desserts. Use slightly less tapioca than the amount of flour or cornstarch called for in the recipe.

Makes 2 cups
20 minutes to prepare
4-cup glass measure
Sterile jar

To fancy up your service, pool Easy Rum-Raisin Sauce on a dessert plate, then add a square of kugel and top with a fan of fresh sliced pear, cut in half, cored, then sliced thin up to but not including the stem, so that you can fan the pear half out over the kugel square.

Stored in a sterile jar, this sauce keeps in the refrigerator for up to a month. Pour it over vanilla ice cream or plain yellow cake as well as over kugels and other fruits and puddings.

1½ cups water
½ cup golden raisins
⅓ cup brown sugar
2 tablespoons margarine or butter
1½ tablespoons cornstarch
2 tablespoons cold water
2 tablespoons rum

1. In a 4-cup glass measure, combine the water with the raisins. Microwave at 100% (high) for 4 minutes, until the mixture comes to a boil. Set it aside for 10 minutes.

2. Now stir the brown sugar and margarine or butter into the raisins, replace in the microwave, and cook at 100% (high) for 4 minutes, until the mixture comes to a boil.

(continued)

NORTHWEST NOODLE KUGEL

Serves 6
15 minutes to prepare
6 minutes to bake in microwave;
1 hour to bake in conventional oven
8-inch square glass baking dish

A kugel is basically a pudding made famous by Jewish cooks that can be made savory or sweet, with or without milk, but always with eggs.

Kugels are good to add to your repertoire of half-time recipes because the ingredients are not expensive and—once you learn to cook a kugel in the microwave—you can knock the preparation time down to no more than 15 to 20 minutes.

Kugels can be made from noodles, matzo meal, carrots, or potatoes as well as pears, prunes, or other fruits. But always the base ingredient is combined with beaten eggs and, for a dairy meal, you may add milk, cottage cheese, or sour cream. Dessert kugels are sweetened with sugar and heightened in flavor with vanilla and cinnamon. Kugels fall into the category of comfort food, regardless of your religious persuasion, and are a good thing to know how to make.

8 ounces (4 cups dry) wide egg noodles
4 quarts boiling, barely salted water
3 large eggs
⅓ cup sugar
2 cups low-fat milk
1 teaspoon vanilla extract
2 tablespoons margarine
½ teaspoon salt
1 teaspoon ground cinnamon
⅓ cup golden raisins
1 large Comice pear, peeled, cored, and chopped

1. Spritz an 8-inch square glass baking dish with cooking spray. If you're planning to bake the kugel in the conventional oven, preheat it to 300° F.

2. Cook the egg noodles in barely salted boiling water for 4 minutes in a large sauce pot. Meanwhile, in a medium bowl beat the eggs and sugar together until the mixture looks foamy, about 2 minutes. Stir in the milk, vanilla, margarine,

salt, and cinnamon. Pour into the prepared baking dish. Now add the raisins and chopped pear and stir to mix.

3. Once the noodles are cooked, drain and pour them into the prepared baking dish. Bake the kugel fast in the microwave, covered with plastic wrap, at 100% (high) for 6 minutes. Let it stand 5 minutes, then remove the plastic. Alternately, bake uncovered in the preheated conventional oven, for 1 hour, until browned. Serve warm or at room temperature, cut into squares.

CARAMELIZED PEAR FLAN

Serves 6
15 minutes to prepare
12 minutes to microwave
10-inch black cast-iron skillet
Six ⅔-cup ramekins or glass custard dishes

Nothing caramelizes quite so deliciously as a black skillet, so brown the fruit in the skillet first, then divide into ramekins and finish the custards in the microwave for a fast, complex-flavored dessert.

3 ripe Comice or Anjou pears (1½ pounds), peeled, cored, and
   quartered
   Juice and zest of ½ lemon
2 tablespoons unsalted butter
¼ cup sugar, divided
2 large eggs
1 large egg yolk
½ cup whipping cream
   Generous grating (about ½ teaspoon) fresh nutmeg

1. Place a glass 10- to 12-inch round or square dish with 2-inch sides in the microwave. Pour in about 1 inch of water. Heat to boiling in the microwave at 100% (high), about 3 minutes to make a hot water bath. Leave it in the microwave oven with the door closed.

(*continued*)

3. Meanwhile, dissolve the cornstarch in the cold water. Stir the cornstarch solution into the hot sauce. Microwave for 45 seconds at 100% (high), until the mixture thickens. Remove from the microwave and stir in the rum. Pour into a sterile jar, cover and store in the refrigerator until needed, for up to 1 month.

❖   ❖

You can substitute apples for pears with equal luck. Apples yield less liquid than pears and will caramelize more quickly. Stir carefully.

2. Meanwhile, slice the pear quarters into ¼-inch-thick slices in the food processor fitted with the slicing disk, then toss with the lemon juice and zest.

3. Preheat the black cast-iron skillet over medium-high heat, then add the butter and melt. Spread the pear slices over the bottom of the pan, sprinkle with 2 tablespoons of the sugar, and cook without turning until the pears begin to brown, about 5 minutes. Reduce the heat and continue to cook until the pears are tender and nicely caramelized. Notice that heavenly aroma that wafts up your nose. Keep turning the pears so they won't burn.

4. Meanwhile, add the eggs, yolk, and remaining sugar to the food processor bowl fitted with the steel blade. Process about 3 minutes.

5. While the eggs and sugar are processing, heat the cream in a glass measure placed in the hot water bath in the microwave to just under boiling, at 100% (high) for about 1 minute. Then with the food processor motor still running, pour the hot cream through the feed tube and continue processing until well blended with the egg-sugar mixture, about 30 seconds. Season with the nutmeg. Stir the cooked pears and sauce into the bowl.

6. Divide the mixture among six ramekins or ⅔-cup glass custard cups. Arrange the cups in the large pan of water in the microwave. Microwave at 100% (high) until the custard sets, about 6 minutes. Remember the custard will continue to cook about 5 minutes after you remove it from the microwave. Better to undercook than overcook, when the custard could separate. So don't worry if the custard still jiggles when you take it out of the microwave.

FROZEN GINGER CUSTARD

Makes ½ gallon
20 minutes to prepare
2 hours to chill
30 minutes to freeze
Ice-cream freezer

Also known as soft ice cream, this rich, pungent frozen custard punctuates an Oriental dinner with an exclamation point. Use one of those porcelain ginger graters to speed up that job, and forget about peeling ginger.

We like to serve Shortbread Diamonds in the Rough (see page 159) with this pure-white creamy custard that's freckled with crystallized ginger. The flavor combination of hot fresh ginger in smooth-as-silk frozen custard makes a perfect foil for crumbly butter shortbreads.

½ cup water
¾ cup sugar, divided
3 tablespoons grated fresh ginger
1 quart half-and-half
3 large eggs, lightly beaten
2 tablespoons finely chopped crystallized ginger (see page 21)

1. In a 2-cup glass measure combine the water, ½ cup of the sugar, and grated ginger. Microwave, uncovered, at 100% (high) for 5 minutes. Set aside to steep.

2. In a 2-quart microwavable batter bowl, add the half-and-half and remaining sugar. Stir to dissolve the sugar. Microwave, uncovered, at 100% (high) for 4 minutes. Now whisk in the eggs, using a balloon whisk, until the mixture is smooth.

3. Microwave the custard, uncovered, at 100% (high) for 2 minutes, until a custard forms that will coat the back of a spoon. Remove from the microwave and strain in the ginger syrup. Stir the grated ginger in the strainer so that you get all the good ginger-infused syrup. Discard the grated ginger.

4. Stir in the chopped crystallized ginger. Chill the custard—either in the refrigerator or in an ice-water bath (see sidebar). Once the custard is cold, prepare ice cream according to the directions for your ice-cream maker.

Speed Chilling with an Ice-Water Bath

Use your microwave oven to guarantee perfect custard, then speed-chill in an ice-water bath if you want the ice cream fast. Simply employ a restaurant technique for cooling down the custard before freezing.

Once the custard is cooked, instead of putting it in the refrigerator to cool, place the bowl inside a larger bowl filled with ice cubes and water. Paddle the custard until it cools. You'll be surprised at how fast it chills, stuck in an ice-water bath.

❖   ❖

When buying fresh ginger, look for firm, heavy tubers with papery tan skins. Reject soft, withered, or dry ginger. Unless the skin is exceptionally crusty, there's no need to peel. Just grate, mince, sliver, slice, or julienne right from the knob. Store fresh ginger in plastic wrap in the refrigerator for a couple of weeks. For longer periods, chunk ginger root into a jar and cover with dry sherry. Cover and refrigerate. Keeps for months, and the ginger-infused sherry makes a terrific scent addition to other desserts. Sprinkle it over fresh fruits or ice cream. Yum.

9
FRESH FRUIT DESSERTS

lthough a perfectly ripe Comice pear, split in half and eaten with a spoon, is, perhaps, the ideal dessert with simply no competition at all, we did try to devise other ways to enjoy fresh fruits in desserts that would be simple to make, mouth-watering to look at, and healthy besides.

Something as simple as Spiced Strawberries will finish off an elaborate dinner in a rare and luscious way. This putting pepper onto fruit is an old Southern trick that seems to work on the taste buds to enhance the sweet perfume of the fruit.

We also love compotes of fresh and sometimes dried fruits. Compotes, simply mixtures of fruits, are a good way to use fruits that may not be as flavorful as you'd hoped when you bought them. Combine fruits of varying colors, textures, and tastes, marinate them with spirits, and you've got dessert.

The microwave is ideal for poaching fresh fruits. Choose perfectly ripe fruits, heavy with perfume, wash and core them, then place them in the microwave with water or wine, and before you know it you have poached fruit that has retained its natural color, heightened its natural flavor, and is ready for dessert in less than 10 minutes.

We also recommend to you Rick and Mona's Pineapple Surprise. This makes a flashy finish to dinner, in that each diner gets a quartered pineapple boat brimming with broiled pineapple chunks studded with cloves. It's quick. It's easy. And it tastes great.

Choosing peaches from the supermarket can be tricky, especially in
the off-season when the peaches are
usually imported from South
America. To be sweet and juicy, a
peach must be allowed to ripen on
the tree. Check the fragrance of the
peach—does it have that special
"peachy" aroma? Fragrance is an
indicator of ripeness. The color
should be a creamy gold with pink
blush and no hint of green. Give a
gentle squeeze near the stem; it
should give just a little and not be
rock hard.

CHINA PEACH

Serves 4
20 minutes to prepare
Large nonstick skillet

Diana created this recipe to be served on a blue-and-white delft plate
for a photo shoot. It tastes heavenly, and makes a stunning presentation on any blue-and-white china.

**4 large fresh ripe peaches, skinned (see sidebar, page 168), pit-
ted, and sliced**
1 cup whipping cream
2 tablespoons confectioners' sugar
2 tablespoons Amaretto
¼ cup (½ stick) unsalted butter
¾ cup granulated sugar
¼ cup sliced almonds (optional)

1. Bring 2 quarts of water to a boil in a large saucepan.
Blanch the peaches in the water for 1 minute. Remove the
peaches from the water and carefully peel the skin off, trying
not to nick the peach flesh. Slice the peaches in half and
remove the pit.

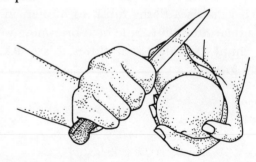

2. Fit the processor bowl with the steel blade and add the
whipping cream (see page 17). Process until the cream thickens. Add the confectioners' sugar and Amaretto through the
feed tube a spoonful at a time. Process just to blend, as the
cream does not need to be stiff. Refrigerate until ready to use.
3. Melt the butter in a large nonstick skillet over medium
heat. Add the granulated sugar and stir to dissolve. Cook the

sugar-and-butter mixture until it is light brown, about 3 to 5 minutes.

4. Add the peaches, cut side down. Increase the heat to medium-high and cook until the peaches are well caramelized, no more than 5 minutes.

5. Remove the pan from the heat and arrange 2 peach halves on each of four blue-and-white or other brightly colored dessert plates, cut side up. Spoon Amaretto cream on one side of the peaches and the caramel sauce on the other. Sprinkle the middle of the peaches with sliced almonds if desired. Serve immediately.

*H*OT GINGERED PAPAYA

Serves 4
5 minutes to prepare
20 minutes to bake
Large baking sheet

Want your Caribbean or other tropical dinner to go out in style? Serve a dead-ripe, golden, fresh papaya baked with crystallized ginger, lime juice, and a dash of cayenne.

2 firm ripe papayas
2 tablespoons unsalted butter
2 tablespoons fresh lime juice
   Zest of ½ lime
   Cayenne pepper
2 tablespoons chopped, crystallized ginger

1. Preheat the oven to 350° F. Cut the papayas in half, lengthwise, scooping out and discarding the seeds. Arrange the fruits on a large baking sheet. In the hollow of each fruit, place a pat of butter, a squeeze of lime, some zest, a whiff of cayenne, and a dab of crystallized ginger.

2. Bake in the preheated oven for 20 minutes, until golden brown and bubbly. Baste a time or two if you think of it.

Picking Papayas

Papayas are available in American markets from late spring to fall. Called "pawpaws" in the British Caribbean tropics, they're not to be confused with the American pawpaw that grows in the South. Ripe papayas are yellow, sometimes with an orange blush. You can eat them chilled, like a melon, by simply scooping out the seeds and eating with a spoon. You can add a dab of vanilla ice cream to the center if you wish.

Green papayas are really bright green and are used as a vegetable in the tropics. They make a terrific chutney or relish, but won't do for dessert. If you can only find green ones in the market, buy them and place them in a fruit-ripening bowl or under a glass dome. They'll color up and ripen in much the way that green avocados do.

SABLE OF FRESH BERRIES AND CREME FRAICHE

Serves 10
15 minutes to prepare
10 minutes to bake
Large baking sheet
3-inch cookie cutter

Fresh berries topping crisp sweet pastry on a pool of crème fraîche. What could be better or more beautiful? Be sure to serve these on your prettiest dessert plates.

2 prepared 9-inch pie crusts, unbaked
2 tablespoons sugar

CREME FRAICHE

½ cup whipping cream
2 tablespoons sugar
½ cup sour cream

BERRY SAUCE

5 cups assorted fresh berries of your choice: strawberries, blueberries, blackberries, or raspberries, hulled
1 12-ounce package unsweetened frozen raspberries, thawed or 2 cups fresh raspberries
1 cup seedless raspberry preserves or strawberry preserves
2 tablespoons raspberry liqueur, such as Chambord

Fresh mint leaves, for garnish (optional)

1. Preheat the oven to 400° F. Open the piecrust sheets onto a lightly floured surface. Using a 3-inch round cookie cutter, cut out a total of 10 rounds. Place the cutouts on a baking sheet and sprinkle evenly with the 2 tablespoons of sugar. Bake for 10 minutes on the middle rack of the preheated oven until the rounds are lightly browned. Cool.

2. Meanwhile, prepare the crème fraîche. In the processor bowl fitted with the steel blade, process the cream until it

thickens (see page 17). With the machine running, slowly add the sugar until stiff peaks form. Fold in the sour cream. Transfer to a glass bowl. Cover and refrigerate.

3. For the berry sauce, in a large bowl combine all of the fresh berries. In the bowl of the food processor fitted with the steel blade, process the fresh or frozen raspberries and preserves for 10 seconds, until smooth. Strain the puree through a sieve over the bowl of fresh berries. Stir in the liqueur and toss gently.

4. To serve, spread 2 tablespoons of crème fraîche on each serving plate. Top with a *sablé* cookie, spoon on ½ cup berry sauce. Garnish with fresh mint, if desired. Serve immediately.

*S*PICED STRAWBERRIES

Serves 4
15 minutes to prepare
2 hours to chill

When early summer rolls around, put on your sunbonnet and go strawberry picking. Two for us and one for the pail! They're great eaten out of hand. Try these spiced berries with a splash of vinegar and a dash of pepper. The vinegar heightens the berry flavor, and the pepper makes them seem even sweeter.

2 cups fresh ripe strawberries
2 teaspoons balsamic vinegar
Freshly fine-ground black pepper to taste

Wash and hull the strawberries. Slice them in half vertically. In a glass bowl combine the strawberries and vinegar. Toss to mix. Cover and chill in the refrigerator for 2 hours, stirring occasionally. Spoon the strawberries equally into serving dishes and sprinkle with freshly ground pepper to taste. Serve immediately.

With refrigerated containers now being used to transport perishables by truck and plane, you are likely to find strawberries in the marketplace almost year-round, and often at a good price. Buy the berries in bulk, if possible, so that you can handpick each berry, inspecting it for mold or mushiness in the process. If you must buy them in the basket, check for bruised berries or leakage on the bottom. Sort them as soon as possible, tossing any questionable ones.

PAULA CUTTER'S FRESH FRUIT CUPS WITH CINNAMON-YOGURT DRESSING

Serves 4
15 minutes to prepare
4 dessert plates

A dessert so beautiful it looks like a painted still life: the green of the kiwi, against the ruby-red raspberries, nestled against the gold of the peaches, layered against the texture of the waffle cup. All napped with cinnamon-yogurt dressing or crème fraîche.

3 kiwis, peeled and thinly sliced
1 cup fresh raspberries
1 cup thinly sliced firm ripe banana rounds
1 cup peeled, thinly sliced fresh peaches
½ cup (4 ounces) plain yogurt or crème fraîche (see sidebar)
3 tablespoons sugar (use only 2 tablespoons if using crème fraîche)
1 tablespoon cinnamon (freshly ground is best)
4 waffle ice-cream cups or large waffle cones
Fresh mint leaves

1. Toss the prepared fruit together lightly in a medium mixing bowl.

2. In a small mixing bowl, mix together the yogurt or crème fraîche, sugar, and cinnamon.

3. Place 1 waffle cup on each of 4 of your prettiest dessert plates, or if you're using waffle cones, wrap the bottom of each cone with a pretty paper doily or a favorite cloth or colorful napkin. Divide the fruit equally among the 4 cups or cones. Nap the top with the dressing and garnish with mint leaves. Serve immediately.

Fresh Berries in Orange-Yogurt Cream

Serves 4
10 minutes to prepare
30 minutes to chill
2-cup glass measure
4 footed parfait dishes or balloon wineglasses

Here's a fruit dessert that tastes as good as the sweet berries you find, then naps them in an aromatic orange yogurt, fat-free and fine. Use raspberries, strawberries, dewberries, blackberries, olallieberries, whatever you can find that's bursting with flavor and sweet enough on its own to require little if any sugar. Serve the colorful berries and the pale-orange cream in footed dessert dishes or balloon wineglasses. Top with a sprig of mint if you've got it.

1 pint fully ripe berries
Sugar (optional, only to enhance sweetness of berries)

ORANGE-YOGURT CREAM

Zest and juice of 2 oranges
¼ cup sugar
½ cup (4 ounces) plain nonfat yogurt
Fresh mint leaves (optional)

1. Pick over the berries, rinse, then taste for sweetness. If they don't seem quite sweet enough, sprinkle with a little sugar, then cover and refrigerate until serving time.

2. For the orange-yogurt cream, in a 2-cup glass measure, combine the zest, orange juice, and sugar. Microwave at 100% (high) for 4 minutes, until the mixture is reduced by half. Stir the yogurt into the orange essence, cover, and refrigerate for 30 minutes or until serving time.

3. To serve, puddle orange-yogurt cream in the bottom of 4 parfait dishes or balloon wineglasses, and pile high with sweet berries. Serve at once.

The Color of Raspberries

A bright-red raspberry may be tempting to the eye, but raspberry growers assure us that the sweetest berries are those that have been allowed to ripen on the vine a little longer. The vine-ripened berries will be darker in color, almost a purple-red or magenta color. These berries will begin to appear on the market 2 to 3 weeks after the season starts.

Remember that stone fruits, including peaches, apricots, and plums, do not continue to ripen once they're plucked from the tree. When you're looking for stone fruits, try to buy them as close to the orchard as possible. Take a deep whiff of the outside of the fruit. If the fruit perfume doesn't take your breath away, put the fruit back. If it doesn't smell good, it probably tastes like a potato.

FORTY-NINERS' PEACH SNOW

Serves 8
10 minutes to prepare
1 hour to chill
8-cup microwavable batter bowl

For about 2 weeks in August, here in the Rogue Valley of Oregon, we get peaches known as forty-niners that are so desirable, they're whisked all over the country by fast shippers filling Fruit-of-the-Month Club orders.

Each peach is bigger than a boxer's fist, sweet, yet tart and perfumed. Besides eating them whole, out of hand, on the back porch, where you can enjoy the juice dripping down to your elbow, we think this is the second-best way to enjoy them, and the very best way we know to stretch these heavenly peaches to serve more people.

Use any fresh peach you can find, and you'll be happy, so long as the peach is truly ripe and perfumed. Garnish the snow with the best berries you can find, raspberries, dewberries, marionberries, or blackberries.

1 pound (about 2 medium) fresh peaches
Juice of ½ lemon
1 cup water
1 cup sugar
½ teaspoon vanilla extract
1 pint best-quality vanilla frozen yogurt or ice cream
1 tablespoon crème de cassis
Dewberries, raspberries, marionberries, or blackberries, for garnish
Fresh mint leaves, for garnish

1. Peel, pit, and cut the peaches into several chunks in a bowl. Pour lemon juice over all and set aside.

2. Combine the water and sugar in an 8-cup microwavable batter bowl. Stir to mix, then heat in the microwave at 100% (high) for 3 minutes. Stir to mix until the sugar is completely dissolved.

3. Add the peaches to the sugar-water syrup, place in the microwave, and heat for 2 minutes. Remove from the microwave, stir in vanilla, cover, and refrigerate for at least 1 hour.

4. At serving time, scoop yogurt or ice cream into the food processor bowl fitted with the steel blade, lift the poached peaches from their cooking syrup into the bowl, and puree until you have a smooth mixture.

5. Stir crème de cassis into the reserved peach-poaching syrup. Scoop peach snow into dessert dishes, garnish with fresh berries and mint leaves, then drizzle the reserved poaching syrup over all, and serve at once.

*F*RESH PEACHES WITH AMARETTO AND COOKIES

Serves 4
15 minutes to prepare
2 hours to marinate
4 footed dessert dishes

We begin anticipating the perfectly ripe peach at the beginning of summer. This sweet juicy fruit is one of our favorites, whether eaten the simplest way, out of hand, or dressed up a little. Some of our favorite light desserts begin with this fruit, available to us only 2 weeks in August.

4 large ripe peaches *(about 1½ pounds) peeled, pitted, and sliced*
3 tablespoons *Amaretto*
12 small **amaretti** *cookies*
Fresh mint leaves (optional)

1. In a medium bowl combine the peaches with the Amaretto and cover. Refrigerate for 2 hours.

2. Meanwhile, fit the processor bowl with the steel blade and process the cookies until they are large crumbs. Set aside.

3. Just before serving, spoon the peaches and Amaretto into footed serving dishes. Sprinkle with cookie crumbs and garnish with mint leaves, if desired. Serve immediately.

Use this same poaching technique for pears. Choose firm Bosc or Comice pears. Try poaching the pears in red wine instead of water, and skip the bourbon. A great winter dessert.

MICRO-POACHED PEACHES IN BOURBON SAUCE

Serves 4
10 minutes to prepare
15 minutes to cook
2 hours to chill
9-inch pie pan or soufflé dish

When the peach harvest is at its height, and you can pick up a peach that's heavy with perfume in the market, make this ultimate peach dessert. Choose peaches that weigh about a half pound apiece, with a nice blush over about a quarter of their cheeks. Serve each peach in a pool of syrup with a dollop of unsweetened whipped cream you've touched with a little Frangelico on top, and a mint-leaf garnish, and people will drop their spoons. It's that good.

    4 fresh ripe peaches (about 8 ounces each)
    Juice of ½ lemon
    2 tablespoons sugar
    1 cup water
    1-inch piece cinnamon stick
    1 whole clove
    ¼ cup bourbon (optional)
    ½ cup whipping cream
    1 tablespoon Frangelico (optional)
    Fresh mint leaves, for garnish

1. Peel (see sidebar, page 168) and pit the peaches. Cut a small bit away from the bottom of each peach so that it will stand without falling over, then slip it into a bowl of water to cover in which you have squeezed the lemon juice. Set aside.

2. In a 4-cup glass measure combine the sugar, water, cinnamon stick, and clove. Microwave, uncovered, at 100% (high) for 1½ minutes.

3. Cover this syrup with plastic wrap and microwave at 100% (high) for another 3 minutes. Carefully remove the plastic wrap.

4. Arrange the peaches in a microwavable 9-inch pie pan

or soufflé dish, pour the syrup over the peaches, cover with plastic wrap, and microwave at 100% (high) for 4 minutes. Carefully lift the plastic wrap and spoon the syrup over the peaches. Add the bourbon, if using. Re-cover and microwave at 100% (high) for 4 more minutes. Uncover and cool to room temperature. Cover and refrigerate for 2 hours or until serving time.

5. Pour the cream into the food processor bowl fitted with the steel blade or whisk attachment and process to soft peaks (see page 17). Sprinkle with Frangelico if desired. Stir to mix.

6. Serve each peach in a pool of bourbon-flavored syrup, top with whipped cream, and finish with mint leaves.

BRANDIED PEACHES FLAMBE

Serves 4
10 minutes to prepare
4 dessert plates

A dessert meant for that evanescent late-summer dinner when the peach harvest is at its height.

2 large ripe peaches
Best-quality vanilla ice cream
½ cup brandy or other 80-proof liquor

1. Peel, pit, and cut the peaches into halves. Set 1 peach half on each of 4 dessert plates. Place a scoop of ice cream beside each peach. Line the dessert dishes up at the head of the dining room table.

2. Heat the brandy or other liquor in a small saucepan to just under boiling. At the dining table set the liquor alight with a match and pour the flaming liquor over the peaches and the ice cream. Serve at once.

Peach Varieties to Look For

Forty-niner peaches are yellow meated freestones sometimes as big as a boxer's fist and twice as potent. Look for them for about 2 weeks in August. Our favorite for eating, for putting on or in ice cream, and for poaching.

Redhavens are also August peaches, yellow meated freestones a tad smaller than forty-niners but perfumed, sweet, and mouth-watering to eat plain or to poach or preserve.

Elbertas come last, somewhere around September; they're equally good for eating, for poaching, or for canning.

There are several tests for a ripe pineapple. First, look at the pineapples. See if you can find one that's a deep green with some yellowing near the base. Pick that one up and take a deep whiff. It should smell aromatic, the way you remember pineapple. If there is no aroma, it may be immature. If it smells fermented, it's overripe.

Next pluck a leaf from the center of the pineapple. It should come out with little resistance. If the leaf clings tenaciously to the pineapple, it's probably immature.

Finally, squeeze the pineapple. It should be firm, with no soft spots.

Pineapples should be picked when they are ripe and not green. They won't ripen any more after being cut. Store the pineapple upside down to distribute the sugar throughout the meat and at room temperature if you plan on using it within a couple of days; otherwise, refrigerate the pineapple, and it will keep for 5 to 7 days.

RICK AND MONA'S PINEAPPLE SURPRISE

Serves 4
10 minutes to prepare
5 minutes to broil
Broiler pan

The surprise is that not only can you serve this Caribbean delight for dessert, but it also goes onto a main-dish plate alongside something tropical, like Curaçao-style red snapper and barefoot rice, with equal aplomb. Whenever you serve this, make sure you're with your most intimate friends. It only tastes right when eaten with your hands. No forks, please.

1 large pineapple
Whole cloves
¼ cup mild honey
¼ cup white wine

1. Quarter the whole pineapple, cutting down through the leaves and skin. Cut the core out and discard. Now, using a thin-bladed sharp knife, cut away the meat of the pineapple, and cut it into bite-sized chunks. Stud each pineapple chunk with a clove.

2. Place the 4 pineapple shells onto a baking sheet. Heap the chunks of pineapple onto each quarter. Mix the honey and white wine and drizzle evenly over the quarters. This can be made up to this point early in the day, covered, and refrigerated.

3. Broil the pineapple about 4 to 6 inches from the heat source for 5 minutes, until hot and bubbly. Serve after 5 minutes. This you eat with your hands.

*F*RESH FRUIT WITH CHEESE DATE DIP

Serves 6
15 minutes to prepare

You don't have to be an artist to make this dip tantalizing to the eye and palate. Simply spoon the dip into a pretty serving bowl and surround with the season's freshest fruit as dippers.

½ cup pitted whole dates
1 8-ounce can crushed pineapple
1 8-ounce package cream cheese or Neufchâtel cheese, room temperature
4 to 6 cups assorted fresh fruit dippers of your choice: strawberries, apple and pear wedges, grapes, etc.

1. Place the steel blade in the bowl of the food processor. With the machine running, drop the dates in through the feed tube and process until coarsely chopped, about 3 seconds (if the dates seem extremely sticky, lightly toss with a tablespoon or so of flour before processing to keep them from sticking to the blade).

2. Remove the dates from the food processor bowl, set aside, and wipe the bowl clean with a paper towel. Return the bowl to the processor base. Drain the pineapple, reserving 2 tablespoons of juice.

3. Place the pineapple, the reserved juice, and the cheese in the processor bowl and process until well blended and smooth. Scoop the cheese mixture into the serving bowl and stir in the chopped dates. Surround the cheese mixture with the fresh fruit, and serve.

Strawberry Angels

Strawberry Angels are a fast and easy garnish to make. They can garnish individual desserts or whole desserts or be placed on mounds of whipped cream.

To make Strawberry Angels, choose firm, ripe berries with long stems and caps, if possible (Drexel strawberries are raised in California specifically for this purpose). Starting at the tip, cut almost to the stem, making several slices in each berry. Gently spread the slices to form wings.

PORTED FIGS STUFFED WITH RICOTTA

Serves one, can be multiplied
10 minutes to prepare
Overnight to soak
2-cup glass measure

For a winter dessert, plump some dried figs in port overnight, then just before serving, stuff them with ricotta and top each with a whole roasted hazelnut or macadamia nut. Serve 3 to the dessert bowl. They're gorgeous. They're easy and they're done.

3 dried mission figs
¼ cup water
⅛ cup port wine
2 ounces (¼ cup) ricotta cheese
3 whole toasted hazelnuts (see page 22) or macadamia nuts per serving

1. Place the dried figs in a 2-cup glass measure with ¼ cup water, cover with plastic wrap, and microwave at 100% (high) for 2 to 3 minutes. Remove from the microwave, pour the port over the dates, cover, and refrigerate overnight or until serving time.

2. At serving time, lift the soft purplish figs from their nectar, cut an X pattern into the bottom of each, open each one, and spoon in a generous tablespoon of ricotta cheese. Top with a nut, arrange 3 to the dessert bowl, and serve in a pool of the reserved port nectar.

RICOTTA-LEMON FRITTERS

Serves 4
3 minutes to prepare
3 minutes to fry
10-inch skillet

Ricotta is used in Italian meals from antipasto to dessert. For a luscious hot bite, you can whip up these fritters in no time flat.

4 ounces (½ cup) ricotta cheese
1 large egg
2 tablespoons unbleached all-purpose flour
1 tablespoon butter
  Zest of ½ lemon
  Vegetable oil, for frying
  Confectioners' sugar

1. Combine the ricotta, egg, flour, butter, and lemon zest in the food processor fitted with the steel blade. Process to mix.

2. Heat 1-inch-deep oil over medium-high heat in a 10-inch skillet until water flicked onto the surface leaps off sizzling, then drop the batter by the teaspoon into the hot oil. Don't overcrowd the pan. Boil in oil until the fritter floats to the top and becomes golden on one side (about 1 minute), then flip and brown the second side. The fritters will puff into balls the size of a big marble. Drain on paper towels. Dust with confectioners' sugar and serve hot.

How to Zest and Juice a Lemon

The easiest way to use zest and juice from the same lemon is to zest the yellow skin first, then cut the lemon(s), squeeze, strain, and measure the juice.

BROILED GRAPEFRUIT

Serves 4
10 minutes to prepare
8 minutes to broil
Medium baking pan with sides

Another almost-instant dessert, Broiled Grapefruit is best served in midwinter and early spring when good Texas pink grapefruits have made it to your local supermarket.

2 large pink grapefruits, cut in half
4 teaspoons unsalted butter
2 teaspoons rum
4 tablespoons mild honey
  Banana leaf or kale

1. Arrange the grapefruit halves, cut side up, on a baking pan with sides. Cut segments free using a grapefruit knife. Dot each half with 1 teaspoon of butter, ½ teaspoon rum, and coat with 1 tablespoon of thick honey.

2. Refrigerate, covered, until it's time for dessert, then pour ½ inch of water into the baking pan and run the grapefruit halves under the broiler until bubbly and brown, about 8 minutes.

3. Serve each grapefruit on a dessert plate over a large, green leaf. In Florida they use banana leaves. You could use kale if you live in more northern latitudes. Splash each grapefruit with more rum if you desire. Now's the time to dredge up those grapefruit spoons you got for a wedding present.

Sweet Potato Compote
or Beta Carotene Made Easy

Serves 6
20 minutes to pre-bake potato;
10 minutes to prepare; 30 minutes to bake
9-inch pie pan

Although sweet potatoes can appear on the menu from appetizers to desserts, one of our favorites is this dessert we serve all year-round.

We know that the orange-colored vegetables provide beta carotene: carrots, pumpkins, sweet potatoes. It's just that we seem to get kind of stuck when it comes to figuring out what to do with those orange starchy vegetables once we get them home from the market. Here's a delicious solution.

1½ pounds sweet potatoes or yams
½ cup (1 stick) butter or margarine
½ cup brown sugar
  Zest and juice of 1 orange
¼ cup brandy (optional)
1 apple, cored and cut into thin rings
2 firm ripe bananas, peeled and thinly sliced into rounds
¼ cup pine nuts

1. Pierce the sweet potato or yam skins with a fork, then cook the sweet potatoes or yams in the microwave or conventional oven until tender (20 minutes in the microwave at 100% [high], or about 1 hour in a 375° F oven), or until tender when pierced with a fork. Cool to room temperature.

2. Then in a 2-cup glass measure, melt the butter or margarine in the microwave for 1 minute. Combine the melted butter or margarine with the brown sugar and orange zest and juice, then add the brandy, if desired. Set aside.

3. Peel the cooked cool sweet potatoes, then cut them into thin slices and arrange them on a 9-inch pie pan you've spritzed with cooking spray. Arrange apples over the sweet potato, then the bananas. Top with the pine nuts. Pour the butter mixture over all. Bake in 350° F oven for 30 minutes. Serve in bowls, warm.

How to Cook Sweet Potatoes

1. Bake them on a cookie sheet at 375° F for up to 1 hour and 15 minutes, or until tender when pierced with a fork.

2. Boil them in a saucepan, barely covered with water, for about 35 minutes, until tender when pierced with a fork. Peel and serve.

3. Microwave them on a microwavable plate. First, pierce them in several places, then microwave at 100% (high) power for about 20 minutes, or until tender when pierced. Let them stand 5 minutes before cutting them open.

BANANAS FOSTER

Serves 4
10 minutes to prepare
10-inch skillet

This spectacular dessert is easier than you might expect. Butter-glazed bananas are nestled in a rich coconut-pecan sauce and napped with banana liqueur. Showcase this dessert by spooning the sauce over vanilla ice cream in your prettiest dessert bowls.

½ cup (1 stick) unsalted butter
¼ cup packed light brown sugar
4 firm ripe bananas, peeled and sliced lengthwise
½ teaspoon ground cinnamon
⅓ cup small pecan halves
3 tablespoons banana liqueur
3 ounces rum
1 pint vanilla ice cream

1. In a 10-inch skillet over medium-high heat, melt the butter. Stir the brown sugar into the butter until melted. Add the bananas and sauté until tender and barely brown, about 3 minutes on each side. Sprinkle with the cinnamon and pecan halves.

2. Pour the banana liqueur and rum over the bananas. Raise the liquid to a boil. Strike a match, light the liquid, and then baste the bananas with the flaming sauce until the flame dies out.

3. Meanwhile, scoop the ice cream into 4 bowls. Pour the bananas and sauce over the ice cream, and serve immediately.

BENEDICTINE COMPOTE FLAMBE

Serves 4
5 minutes to prepare
Large skillet

You've heard of serving the sizzle without the steak—well here's dessert without much planning. Using a combination of the best fruits of the season you can pick up, combined with dried fruits and nuts you find in the pantry, simply cut the fresh fruits into big bites, sauté them in butter with dried fruits and nuts, then flambé in Benedictine at the table. Your diners will be dazzled. Your dinner will be done . . . in style.

4 pieces fruit of the season of your choice: peaches, apricots, apples, kiwi, bananas, pears, plums, or figs
2 cups dried fruit of your choice: raisins, currants, prunes, dried apricots or peaches
¾ cup Benedictine, divided or other 80-proof liquor
2 tablespoons butter
1 cup nuts of your choice: hazelnuts, pecans, walnuts, or macadamia nuts

1. Peel, seed, and cut the fresh fruit into large chunks over a bowl, saving the juice, then set aside.

2. Place the dried fruit in a 2-cup glass measure with ½ cup of the liquor. Cover with plastic wrap and microwave at 100% (high) for 1½ to 2 minutes to rehydrate. Set aside.

3. In a large skillet, heat the butter over medium-high heat, then sauté the fresh fruits until they begin to brown. Add the rehydrated dried fruits, the nuts, and reserved fruit juice and continue to toss until all the fruits are soft and sizzling. Divide the fruits among dessert dishes and put them on the dining room table before the diners.

4. In a small saucepan, heat the remaining liquor to just under boiling. Quick as a flash, return to the dining room table, set the liquor alight with a match, then pour the flaming liquor over the hot fruits. Voilà!

Easy Hard Sauce
Makes 1 cup

If you can think ahead, say about 5 minutes ahead, Easy Hard Sauce makes a great accompaniment. It's also a natural over store-bought plum puddings and other dark fruitcakes. It keeps, covered in the refrigerator, for a week or so.

½ cup (1 stick) unsalted butter, softened
½ cup confectioners' sugar
2 tablespoons Benedictine or other good brandy

Whip the butter and sugar together in the food processor fitted with the steel blade, then add the brandy and pulse to incorporate. Transfer to a small bowl, cover, and chill until serving time.

Judy's Apple Dumpling Crust

Makes 6 dumpling crusts
5 minutes to prepare
20 minutes to chill

Judy's crust is light and flaky and puffs just a bit because of the addition of baking powder.

2 cups unbleached all-purpose flour
1 teaspoon salt
2 teaspoons baking powder
¾ cup vegetable shortening, chilled
½ cup milk

1. In the bowl of the food processor fitted with the steel blade, combine the flour, salt, and baking powder. Pulse to blend. Add the cold shortening and process until the shortening is incorporated and the size of small peas, about 10 seconds. With the machine running, pour the milk through the feed tube and process just until the pastry forms a ball, about 20 seconds.

2. Carefully remove the pastry from the machine and press into a 1-inch-thick flattened disk. Wrap in plastic wrap and chill for at least 20 minutes. On a well-floured surface, roll the dough into a rough rectangle, ¼-inch thick, and cut into 6 pieces. Proceed with the remainder of the recipe beginning with step 2.

JUDY TARPENNING'S FAMOUS APPLE DUMPLINGS

Makes 6 dumplings
20 minutes to prepare
35 minutes to bake
9 × 12 × 3-inch baking pan

Judy made these tender dumplings on a camping trip in the tiny kitchen of her camper, and they were the hit of the campground. We've substituted prepared piecrusts for Judy's original recipe; however, we offer her recipe, if you have time—it is certainly worth the trouble.

For added color, fiber, and texture, don't peel the apples, just scrub them well and core.

2 9-inch unbaked piecrusts store-bought or 1 recipe Judy's Apple Dumpling Crust (see sidebar), unbaked
6 large Granny Smith or other tart cooking apples, peeled and cored
2⅔ cups sugar, divided
1¾ teaspoons ground cinnamon, divided
2 cups water
¼ teaspoon freshly grated nutmeg
¼ cup (½ stick) unsalted butter or margarine

1. Preheat the oven to 375° F. On a well-floured surface, roll each prepared crust into a round, ¼-inch thick. Cut each crust into 3 equal triangle-shaped pieces. Proceed to step 2 if using Judy's Apple Dumpling Crust (see sidebar).

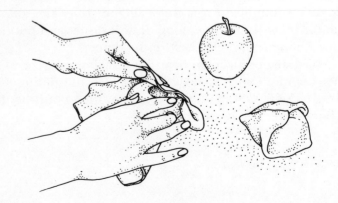

2. Place 1 apple on each piece of dough. Mix ⅔ cup of the sugar and 1 teaspoon of the cinnamon in a small bowl. Fill the hollowed-out core of each apple with the sugar-cinnamon mixture. Fold and wrap the dough around each apple to completely enclose. Place the apples in a large baking dish with sides at least 3 inches deep.

3. In a large 2-quart microwavable bowl, combine the remaining sugar, water, remaining ¼ teaspoon cinnamon, nutmeg, and butter or margarine. Microwave the mixture on 100% (high) for 4 minutes, until it starts to boil. Lower the heat to 70% (medium) and boil for 5 minutes. Pour the hot syrup over the apples.

4. Bake on the middle rack of the preheated oven for 35 minutes, until the apples are tender when pierced with a fork and the crust is golden brown. Remove to a rack to cool until just warm and serve.

ƷINFANDEL PEARS IN SWEET CREAM

Serves 4
15 minutes to prepare
25 minutes to bake
2-quart glass baking dish

Luscious port-colored pears are the perfect finale to a hearty meal. Serve them on simple white dessert plates floating in a pool of wine sauce and topped with a dollop of sweetened whipped cream. Garnish with mint leaves.

1 lemon
2 large just-ripe Comice pears, still slightly firm to the touch
1 cup zinfandel wine
½ cup granulated sugar
½ cup whipping cream
2 tablespoons confectioners' sugar
8 small fresh mint leaves

(continued)

Is this Pear Ripe?

A good way to tell if your pears are "just ripe" is to give them one of two tests. Hold the pear in the palm of your hand and give a gentle squeeze; the pear should just give with pressure, and your fingers should not poke through the skin; that's a too-ripe pear.

The second test only works if the pear still has some of its stem. Hold the pear in one hand and pull on the stem with your other hand. If the stem pops out, the pear is perfect for eating or baking.

Stolen sweets are always
sweeter,
Stolen kisses much completer,
Stolen looks are nice in
chapels,
Stolen, stolen, be your apples.

—JAMES HENRY LEIGH HUNT
(1784–1859)
Song of Fairies Robbing an
Orchard

1. Preheat the oven to 400° F. Carefully slice the yellow-colored zest away from the lemon. Slice the zest into thin strips. Then measure out 1 tablespoon and set aside. Peel the pears and cut in half lengthwise. Carefully cut out and remove the cores. Cut the lemon in half and rub the cut side of the lemon over the pears. Place the pears in a 2-quart glass baking dish.

2. Pour the wine into a 4-cup glass measure and add the sugar. Microwave the wine and sugar at 100% (high) for 2 minutes. Stir until the sugar dissolves. Add the lemon strips. Pour the wine mixture over the pears.

3. Bake the pears, uncovered, on the middle rack of the preheated oven, basting every 5 minutes with the wine sauce for 25 minutes, until the pears are easily pierced with a fork. Cool the pears in the sauce for 5 minutes.

4. Meanwhile, in the bowl of the food processor fitted with the steel blade (because of the small quantity, a small food processor works well here), process the cream until it begins to thicken (see page 17). Add the confectioners' sugar and process until stiff, about 1 minute. Serve the pears on 4 dessert plates surrounded with several tablespoons of sauce and topped with whipped cream. Place 2 mint leaves on the end of the pear where the stem used to be as a garnish.

𝓕AST AND FANCY FRUIT DESSERTS IN 5 MINUTES

Serves 2
5 minutes to prepare
no time to wait

Nothing is quite so fancy as a perfect piece of fruit, unadorned, sitting in the middle of a fine dessert plate with nothing more than the proper cutlery to accompany it. But sometimes we like to gild the lily—just a bit. Sometimes the results are silly, sometimes sweet, but always easier than the proverbial pie.

- Peel 2 bananas, cut them in half, and place them on dessert plates. Add a scoop or two of vanilla ice cream, drizzle with your favorite chocolate sauce (see index), and top with a dollop of crème fraîche (see sidebar, page 224) or sour cream. The rich sweet, sour, cold, dark taste beats the heck out of a banana split.

- Halve 2 bananas and place them on a pie plate. Sprinkle with rum, brown sugar, and lemon juice, then run them under the broiler until they're bubbly and hot, about 3 minutes. Give them a shot of whipped cream and serve on dessert plates.
- Peel 2 perfectly ripe pears, core, and cut off the bottom so they'll sit up straight. Drizzle them with Poire William, a pear liqueur, top with vanilla ice cream, and hit them with Hot Fudge Sauce (see page 96).
- Gouge out melon balls of several colors: from cantaloupe, honeydew, watermelon, Persian, casaba. Toss the balls with fresh mint leaves and champagne. Then sprinkle them with sugar and cognac and serve.
- Peel 2 oranges, section, then dip them in chocolate sauce (see index) and serve. Or dip them in cognac. Add a dollop of vanilla ice cream.
- Peel and cut up bananas, apples, and oranges, then toss them with toasted coconut and fresh orange juice.
- Toss strawberries in balsamic vinegar and pepper lightly.
- Cut a wedge of fine blue cheese, place it in a bed of blueberries, then drizzle all with port. Offer thin-sliced French bread.
- Pour a little rum in the bottom of a dessert plate. Peel and slice mangoes, papayas, and/or kiwi and serve as a base for a snowball of vanilla ice cream rolled in toasted coconut.

Toasting Coconut

To toast sweetened shredded coconut in the microwave, sprinkle the coconut evenly into a 9-inch glass pie plate. Microwave at 70% (medium) for 4 to 5 minutes for 1 cup flaked coconut, until the coconut begins to turn a light brown. It continues to cook once you've removed it from the microwave, so don't overdo it. Toss it with a fork a time or two while it's cooking and once or twice after you've removed it from the microwave. Store in an airtight container for up to a month.

10
SWEET BREADS, PANCAKES, AND WAFFLES

SWEET BREADS

east breads and quick breads both make satisfying desserts. In this chapter you'll learn the Micro-Rise method for baking yeast breads as well as some easy-to-make quick breads that are leavened with baking powder and/or baking soda.

Actually, the Micro-Rise method is what turned us into half-time cooks in the first place. When we perfected the revolutionary new way to make yeast breads, using the food processor to knead the dough in 1 minute and the microwave oven as a proofing cabinet to raise the dough to double in bulk in a quick 15 minutes, we realized we'd invented a new cooking craft.

We discovered, in testing our last book, *Bread in Half the Time*, that with the Micro-Rise method, yeast breads could be made from flour to finished product in about 90 minutes.

And, as you might guess, dessert breads made with yeast were some of our favorite discoveries. What could be better? Something sweet and ready in a hurry, and as a bonus your house is perfumed with the yeasty aroma of baking bread. It makes a house a home.

In fact, for shortcut parties that are sure to please, why not simply serve espresso and a yeasty sweet to guests? A piece of fruit, the perfume of just-baked bread, maybe a piece of cheese: it's all you need to say *welcome*.

MICRO-RISE YEAST BAKING: AN OUTLINE

First off, before you start to machine knead yeast dough, look at your food processor. A heavy-duty, 8-cup-capacity-bowl machine is desirable. Both Braun and Cuisinart make food processors with motors suitable for machine kneading dough. Using either one, you can knead enough dough to make a 1½-pound loaf of sweet bread in one minute flat.

Second, to Micro-Rise yeast dough, you'll need a 500-watt or better microwave oven with a mid- to large-capacity cavity. Preferably, your machine should have ten power settings, but five will do. You can raise dough to double in bulk in a short 15 minutes, once you learn to use your microwave for a proofing cabinet.

Finally, you may have to practice a little kitchen science yourself to determine the appropriate Micro-Rise setting for your particular microwave oven. If you just want to jump in without a test, set your microwave at 10% power. Put an 8-ounce glass of water in the back. Cover the kneaded dough with plastic wrap and Micro-Rise our standard way. Heat 3 minutes, rest 3 minutes, heat 3 minutes, and rest 6 minutes. That's a total of 15 minutes. Look at the dough in the food processor bowl. It should be doubled in bulk.

If you want to find the absolute best setting for your microwave, we'll show you how.

MICRO-RISING BREAD DOUGH: LEARNING HOW TO SET YOUR MICROWAVE

1. Read your instruction book. Determine the wattage and capacity of your microwave. If you can't find the book that came with the machine, look for the serial-number plate on the back or bottom of the machine. It usually tells the wattage of the machine.

- For 600- to 700-watt microwave ovens, the setting is generally somewhere between 10% and 35% power, or around 250 watts, to Micro-Rise yeast dough.
- A 500-watt oven usually requires the lowest setting, 10% power.
- Small-cavity ovens, regardless of the wattage, may require the lowest setting, 10% power, and may require a shortened heating time, 2 minutes.

2. To test your microwave oven, make a recipe for plain bread in the food processor. Remove the steel blade. Cover the bowl of dough with plastic wrap and put it into the microwave. Set an 8-ounce glass of water in the back of the microwave. Set the microwave oven at 10% power. Then follow the Micro-Rise process: that is, heat 3 minutes, rest 3 minutes, heat 3 minutes, and rest 6 minutes. This is a total of 15 minutes.

Remove the dough from the microwave and examine it. Ask yourself these questions: Did the dough double in bulk? Now pull the dough out of the bowl—is it too hot to handle? Can you hold the dough in your hand comfortably? Take the dough's temperature if you've got an instant-read thermometer. It should read no more than 112° F. Ideally, the dough should be somewhere under 110° F.

3. If the dough is too cold, make adjustments in your microwave setting, raising it to 20% power. Punch the dough down, put it back in the food processor bowl, and repeat the test. If the dough is too hot, drop the time back to 2 minutes. If the dough doesn't rise at all and feels hot to the touch, you have probably killed the yeast. Mix up another packet of yeast with warm water and a little flour, knead it into the dough, and repeat the test, shortening the cooking time and/or lowering the setting.

4. In testing your microwave, always begin with the lowest setting and work your way up. We know people who use this lowest setting and have never made any effort to see if they could raise it, because they're perfectly content with the results.

Remember, all you are doing is creating a "warm, draft-free place" in your kitchen that is scientifically temperature and humidity controlled. You've made your microwave oven into a proofing cabinet just like a professional baker uses, and now you'll have the control over yeast baking that the professionals have always had.

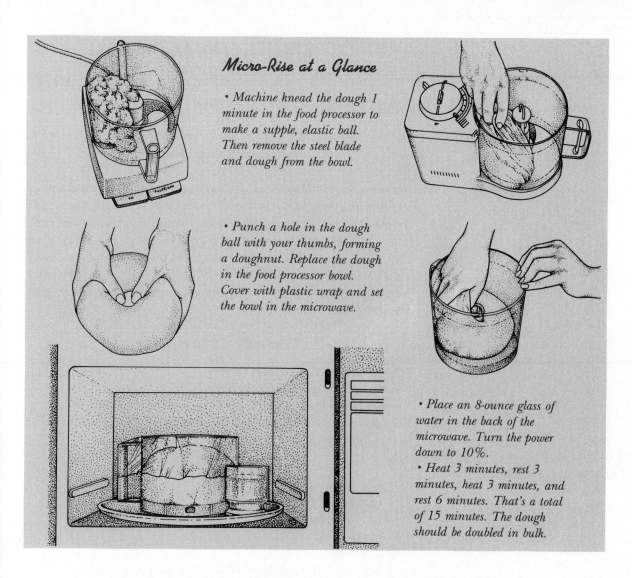

Micro-Rise at a Glance

• *Machine knead the dough 1 minute in the food processor to make a supple, elastic ball. Then remove the steel blade and dough from the bowl.*

• *Punch a hole in the dough ball with your thumbs, forming a doughnut. Replace the dough in the food processor bowl. Cover with plastic wrap and set the bowl in the microwave.*

• *Place an 8-ounce glass of water in the back of the microwave. Turn the power down to 10%.*
• *Heat 3 minutes, rest 3 minutes, heat 3 minutes, and rest 6 minutes. That's a total of 15 minutes. The dough should be doubled in bulk.*

MAKING QUICK BREADS IN THE FOOD PROCESSOR

We've found the same procedures work for both cakes and quick breads made in the food processor. The main idea is not to overmix the batter, which will give you those strange tunnels in the final product that come from overmixing.

First off, combine the fat, sugar, eggs, and liquid in the food processor bowl fitted with the steel blade. Process to mix thoroughly. Then pour the dry ingredients in on top and pulse to barely mix, no more than five or six off-on pulses. Use a rubber spatula to fold into the mixture the last bit of dry ingredients clinging to the sides of the bowl. Fold in raisins, fruits, or nuts either by barely pulsing or using a rubber spatula. Quickly pour the batter into a prepared pan and bake as directed. These breads are good for dessert, brunch, and special occasions as well.

60-MINUTE CINNAMON ROLLS

Serves 6
25 minutes to prepare
33 to 35 minutes to raise and bake
Large baking sheet

On your mark, get set, bake! With the new 50% faster yeast, baking is faster and more fun than ever. These rolls require just 1 short rising period of 15 minutes (which can be accomplished by using a hot-water bath or the Micro-Rise method) and are then baked. Prepare the glaze while they are baking, and you have real, honest-to-goodness home-made bread on the table in 1 hour flat! We love these for Christmas morning, after the gifts are unwrapped, to feed the hordes while we make a fine Christmas dinner.

CINNAMON-SUGAR FILLING

½ cup packed light brown sugar
½ cup golden raisins
½ cup coarsely chopped walnuts, or pecans
1 tablespoon freshly ground cinnamon (we clean out the coffee grinder and grind cinnamon sticks in it)

SWEET-ROLL DOUGH

3¼ cups bread flour
¼ cup granulated sugar
1 teaspoon salt
1 large egg
5 teaspoons (2 packages) 50% faster active dry yeast
3 tablespoons unsalted butter, divided
1 cup hot water

GLAZE

2¾ cups confectioners' sugar
½ cup (1 stick) butter
1 large egg yolk
Pinch of salt
1 teaspoon vanilla extract
2 tablespoons milk or more for the desired consistency

1. Preheat the oven to 375° F. Lightly coat a large baking sheet with cooking spray. Meanwhile, for the cinnamon-sugar filling, combine the brown sugar, raisins, nuts, and cinnamon in a small bowl and set aside.

2. For the dough, in the processor bowl fitted with the steel blade, combine the flour, sugar, salt, egg, yeast, and 2 tablespoons of the butter. Pulse for 10 seconds to blend.

3. With the processor motor running, slowly add the 1 cup hot water to the dry ingredients, holding back the last portion of the water to see if the dough will form a ball.

4. When the dough leaves the sides of the bowl and forms a ball, knead with the motor running for 60 seconds. Use the last portion of water only if necessary. Pinch up a piece of the dough; it should feel soft, tacky, smooth, elastic, and warm.

5. Remove the dough from the bowl to a lightly floured surface, then knead by hand a few seconds, adding flour as necessary if the dough seems sticky. With a rolling pin, roll the dough into a 14 × 10-inch rectangle.

6. Spread the dough with the remaining butter. Sprinkle with the filling ingredients. Roll up the dough from the long side, and seal the seams by pinching together. Cut the rolls into 12 equal-sized slices and place on the baking sheet, leaving 1 to 2 inches around each roll. Cover lightly with plastic wrap. Micro-Rise the dough (see pages 243–245) or pour 6 cups of boiling water into a shallow 9 × 12-inch baking dish and set the baking sheet on top. Let the dough rise for 15 minutes. Bake the rolls on the middle rack of the preheated oven for 18 to 20 minutes, or just until they are beginning to turn light brown. Remove them from the oven and allow them to cool slightly on the baking sheet.

7. Meanwhile, prepare the glaze. Place all of the glaze ingredients in the bowl of a food processor fitted with a steel blade. Process until smooth, adding more milk if necessary for a nice, spreadable consistency. Spread on the warm rolls. Serve warm. These rolls will keep for 1 or 2 days if stored in an airtight container at room temperature.

For easy slicing of any long roll or tube of dough, try using a piece of strong thread or unwaxed dental floss. Slide the thread under the dough to the desired thickness, then loop the thread over into a knot and pull through. This makes a nice even cut through the dough. Repeat with the remaining dough.

SUGAR-CRUSTED GALLETTE

Makes one 16-inch flat cake
45 minutes to prepare
15 minutes to bake
16-inch pizza pan

A French flat bread, buttery, crunchy, and sweet, topped with granulated sugar, this simple-to-start Micro-Rise bread comes from Perouges, a medieval city near Lyons.

1¾ cups bread flour
2½ teaspoons (1 package) 50% faster active dry yeast
½ cup sugar, divided
⅓ teaspoon salt
¾ cup (1½ sticks) unsalted butter, divided
¼ cup hot water
1 large egg
  Zest of ½ lemon

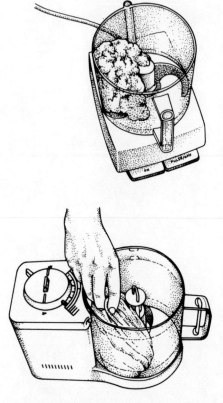

1. In the processor bowl fitted with the steel blade, combine the flour, yeast, 3 tablespoons of the sugar, and salt. Pulse to mix. Now cut ½ cup of the butter in finely and pulse to blend so that it almost disappears.

2. Combine the hot water and egg in a glass measure. Whisk together with a fork, then with the processor motor running, *drizzle the liquid very slowly* into the dry ingredients, holding back the last portion of liquid to see if the dough will form a ball.

3. Process until the dough begins to leave the side of the bowl, forming a ball. Add the last liquid only if necessary. Knead in the food processor for 60 seconds, adding flour as necessary if the dough seems sticky. Pinch up a piece of the dough. It should feel soft, tacky, smooth, elastic, and warm. Add the lemon zest and pulse to mix.

4. Remove the dough and the steel blade and prepare to Micro-Rise. On a lightly floured surface, knead the dough by hand a few seconds, then form it into a ball. With your thumbs, punch a hole to make a doughnut shape and replace the dough in the processor bowl. Cover loosely with a damp tea towel or plastic wrap. Put the dough in the microwave.

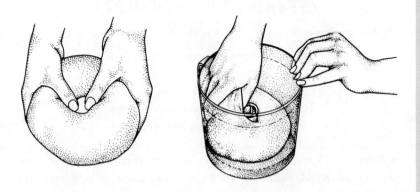

5. Place an 8-ounce glass of water in the back of the microwave. Lower the microwave to 10% power or the appropriate Micro-Rise setting (see page 244). Place the dough in the microwave. Heat for 3 minutes. Rest for 3 minutes. Heat for 3 minutes. Rest for 6 minutes, until the dough has risen to about double in bulk.

6. Remove the dough to a lightly floured surface and knead by hand a few seconds. Roll out into a circle about 12 inches in diameter, cover with a damp tea towel or plastic wrap, and let it rest for 10 minutes.

7. Generously butter a 16-inch pizza pan. Preheat the oven to 425° F. Place the dough in the pizza pan, and pat and stretch the dough to fill the pan. Pinch up the edge to make a slight lip. Dot the top of the galette with the remaining ¼ cup butter, first by cutting the butter into 24 pieces, then distributing the butter evenly over the surface. Sprinkle the top of the galette with the remaining 5 tablespoons of sugar.

8. Bake in the preheated oven for 12 to 15 minutes, until evenly browned. Cut into wedges while warm. Wrap in plastic to store. This bread is best eaten the day it's baked.

BREAD AND CHOCOLATE

Makes 4 mini-loaves or 1 dozen buns
30 minutes to prepare
25 minutes to bake
Four 2½ × 4-inch miniature-loaf pans
or a 12-cup Texas-size muffin tin

A favorite with French schoolchildren for hundreds of years, this sweet yeast bread enfolded around best-quality chocolate and raspberry jam or orange marmalade makes a surprisingly simple and good dessert.

   2 tablespoons granulated sugar
   3 tablespoons nonfat dry milk
   ½ teaspoon salt
   2½ cups plus 2 tablespoons bread flour
   2½ teaspoons (1 package) 50% faster active dry yeast
   ¼ cup (½ stick) unsalted butter
   1 large egg
   1 cup minus 1 tablespoon hot water
   ½ tablespoon lemon zest
   ¼ cup raspberry jam or orange marmalade
   3 ounces (½ cup) semisweet chocolate chips
   1 large egg, whisked with 1 tablespoon milk
   Turbinado or brown sugar

1. In the food processor bowl fitted with the steel blade combine the sugar, dry milk, salt, flour, and yeast. Pulse to mix. Add the butter and process until the mixture resembles coarse meal.

2. In a 2-cup glass measure combine the egg and hot water. Whisk together with a fork, then with the processor motor running, *drizzle the liquid very slowly* into the dry ingredients, holding back the last portion of liquid to see if the dough will form a ball.

3. Process until the dough begins to leave the side of the bowl, forming a ball. Add the last liquid only if necessary. Knead in the machine for 60 seconds, adding flour as necessary if the dough seems sticky. Pinch up a piece of the dough. It should feel soft, tacky, smooth, elastic, and warm. Add the lemon zest and pulse to mix.

4. Remove the dough and the steel blade and prepare to Micro-Rise. On a lightly floured surface, knead the dough by hand a few seconds, then form the dough into a ball. With your thumbs, punch a hole to form a doughnut shape and replace the dough in the processor bowl. Cover loosely with a damp tea towel or plastic wrap. Put the dough in the micro-wave.

5. Place an 8-ounce glass of water in the back of the microwave. Lower the microwave to 10% power or the appropriate Micro-Rise setting (see page 244). Place the dough in the microwave. Heat for 3 minutes. Rest for 3 minutes. Heat for 3 minutes. Rest for 6 minutes, or until the dough has risen to double in bulk.

6. Remove the dough to a lightly floured surface and knead by hand a few seconds. It will be quite soft. Form into a ball, cover with the food processor bowl, and let the dough rest for 10 minutes.

7. Meanwhile, preheat the oven to 350° F. Then coat with cooking spray four 2½ × 4-inch miniature-loaf pans or a 12-cup Texas muffin tin.

8. Roll the dough into a 10 × 8 × ¾-inch rectangle. Cut into 4 or 12 equal pieces. Spread with jam or marmalade, then scatter chocolate chips evenly over the surface of each rectangle. Roll up the loaves or buns, jelly-roll fashion.

9. Place each miniature loaf, seam side down, in a loaf pan (place buns in muffin tins with the rolled seam showing, like pinwheels). Set aside in a warm, draft-free place to rise until almost doubled in bulk, about 25 minutes.

10. Brush the egg-milk glaze gently on the raised loaves or buns. Sprinkle the tops of the loaves or buns with turbinado or brown sugar. Bake the loaves or buns in the preheated oven for about 25 minutes, until golden brown.

11. Carefully turn out onto a rack to cool for about 10 minutes before serving. Slice each miniature loaf into several pieces. Quarter the buns and serve warm.

• A citrus zester shaves off just the yellow rind, not the bitter white pith that is underneath.
• To get the most lemon juice from lemons, use a lemon reamer; it gets every drop.
• Need just a little lemon juice? Roll the lemon on the countertop to soften and pierce one end twice with a toothpick or ice pick. Squeeze gently.
• To get the most juice from a lemon, pierce the lemon several times with the tip of a sharp knife or stab it with a fork and then microwave on 100% (high) for 30 seconds. A warm lemon will now give more juice.

✧   ✧

Lemon Extract

Keep lemon extract in your cupboard as a backup to lemon juice when you want added lemon flavor. A drop or two added to buttermilk pancake or waffle batter will fortify the buttermilk taste.

Add ½ teaspoon or so to reconstituted frozen lemonade concentrate for a zesty, fresh lemon taste and aroma. Add a little more and you can stretch the concentrate with more water when making lemonade for a crowd.

Don't try to substitute extract for fresh juice when being used to prevent darkening of fruit, such as in jam making or pie making. Fresh juice contains citric acid that prevents darkening. Lemon extract does not.

ZESTY LEMON BREAD

Makes one 8-inch loaf
20 minutes to prepare
50 minutes to 1 hour to bake
30 minutes to soak
8 × 4-inch glass loaf pan

A quick bread soaked in lemon-sugar syrup, Zesty Lemon Bread is a real treat for the lemonphile in your family. We serve this luscious, light bread for breakfast or tea or as a snack before bedtime.

½ cup walnut halves
⅓ cup unsalted butter
1 cup sugar
2 large eggs
  Zest of 1 lemon, minced
1 tablespoon fresh lemon juice
1 teaspoon lemon extract
½ cup milk
1½ cups unbleached all-purpose flour
1 teaspoon baking powder
1 teaspoon salt

LEMON SYRUP

½ cup fresh lemon juice (about 2 lemons)
1 cup sugar

1. Preheat the oven to 350° F. Coat a 8 × 4-inch glass loaf pan with cooking spray.

2. Fit the processor bowl with the steel blade and pulse to chop the walnuts coarsely. Set the nuts aside. Remove the steel blade and wipe the bowl clean with a paper towel. Add the butter. Microwave on 100% (high) for 40 seconds, until melted. Refit the processor bowl with the steel blade.

3. Add the sugar and eggs to the processor bowl. Process for 30 seconds, until creamy. Add the lemon zest, lemon juice, lemon extract, and milk. Pulse 2 or 3 times to blend.

4. In a small bowl, combine the flour, baking powder, and salt. Stir to blend. Remove the lid of the processor bowl and spoon the dry ingredients over the batter. Process with 1 or 2

on-off turns just to combine. Stir in the walnuts and any dry particles using a rubber spatula. Pour the batter into the prepared pan. Bake on the middle rack of the preheated oven for 50 minutes to 1 hour, until a toothpick inserted comes out clean or with a dry crumb. Remove to a rack.

5. To prepare the lemon syrup, in a 4-cup microwavable measure, combine the lemon juice and sugar. Stir well. Microwave on 100% (high) for 2 minutes. Stir to dissolve any remaining sugar crystals.

6. With a skewer, poke holes all the way through the hot lemon bread. Pour the syrup over all. Allow the syrup to soak into the bread for about 30 minutes. Cool the bread to room temperature and remove from pan. To store, wrap in a plastic bag and refrigerate for up to 2 weeks, or freeze for up to 6 months.

CRANBERRY-ORANGE NUT BREAD

Makes one 9-inch loaf
20 minutes to prepare
1 hour to 1 hour and 10 minutes to bake
9½ × 2¾-inch loaf pan

Crisp cranberries and crunchy walnuts floating in an orange sweet crumb will sweeten your morning with this fruity loaf. It is best to let this loaf sit for 24 hours before trying to slice it so it will not tear.

    2 cups whole fresh or frozen cranberries
    ¾ cup walnut halves
    6 tablespoons (¾ stick) unsalted butter
    2 large eggs
    1¼ cups sugar
    ¼ cup sour cream
    ¾ cup fresh orange juice
    3 tablespoons minced orange zest
    1 teaspoon orange extract
    2½ cups unbleached all-purpose flour
    1 teaspoon baking soda
    1 teaspoon baking powder
    1 teaspoon salt

(continued)

Sweet Breads, Pancakes, and Waffles 253

Old Spice

When doing spring cleaning or when cleaning out kitchen cupboards, don't toss the old spices, such as allspice berries, stick cinnamon, cloves, and apple chips. Add them to a bag along with last year's dusty potpourri and some old dry lemon or orange rind. Store the bag near the fireplace. When you light a fire, add a handful or two of spice mixture to the fire, and your house will be filled with the sweet scent of spices and citrus.

1. Preheat the oven to 350° F. Coat one 9½ × 2¾-inch loaf pan with cooking spray.

2. Fit the processor bowl with the steel blade. Add the cranberries and chop coarsely. Set aside in a large bowl. Wipe out the processor bowl with a paper towel. Add the walnuts and chop coarsely. Add to the cranberries.

3. Remove the steel blade and add the butter to the bowl. Microwave on 100% (high) for 50 seconds, until melted. Refit the processor bowl with the steel blade. Add the eggs and sugar to the butter in the processor bowl. Process for 30 seconds, until creamy. Add the sour cream, orange juice, orange zest, and orange extract. Process for 10 seconds to blend.

4. In a medium bowl combine the flour, baking soda, baking powder, and salt. Stir to blend. Remove the lid of the processor bowl and spoon the dry ingredients over the batter. Process with 2 or 3 on-off pulses, just to combine. Scrape the batter into the bowl containing the cranberries and nuts. Fold the cranberries and nuts and any remaining dry particles into the batter using a rubber spatula. Spoon the batter into the prepared pan.

5. Bake the batter on the middle rack of the preheated oven for 1 hour to 1 hour and 10 minutes, until a toothpick inserted comes out clean or with a dry crumb. Cool in the pan on a wire rack for 20 minutes. Carefully run a knife around the edge of the pan and shake the bread loose onto the rack to finish cooling. Serve at room temperature or chilled. To store, wrap in aluminum foil. This bread keeps well refrigerated for 1 week or frozen for 2 months.

KATHIE'S WHOLE WHEAT BLACK WALNUT–BANANA BREAD

Makes one 8-inch loaf
20 minutes to prepare
30 to 45 minutes to bake
8 × 4-inch loaf pan

Quick breads made with whole wheat flour are more dense, moist, and nutritious than those made with all-purpose flour. The bananas in this bread add the flavor and moistness that will keep this bread in tip-top shape in the refrigerator for up to 2 weeks. An added bonus is the low cholesterol count.

Black walnuts are our favorite nut in banana breads and cakes and are usually broken in pieces when we buy them; however, if they are not available in your area, substitute English walnuts.

½ cup packed light brown sugar
½ cup (1 stick) margarine, softened
  Juice of 1 lemon
3 firm, ripe medium bananas
1½ cups whole wheat flour
½ cup wheat germ
½ teaspoon salt
½ teaspoon baking powder
½ teaspoon baking soda
1 cup black walnut pieces or English walnuts halves, chopped
  coarsely in food processor

1. Preheat the oven to 375° F. Coat one 8 × 4-inch loaf pan with cooking spray.

2. Fit the processor bowl with the steel blade. Add the brown sugar and margarine to the processor bowl. Process for 30 seconds, until creamy. Break the bananas into several pieces, and add them and the lemon juice. Process until the batter is smooth and no banana chunks are visible, about 30 seconds.

3. In a small bowl, combine the flour, wheat germ, salt, baking powder, and baking soda. Stir to blend. Remove the

(*continued*)

The Best Pans

The best pans for baking quick breads have anodized aluminum or dark metal interiors to help absorb heat and give the breads well-browned crusts. A shiny metal pan can be "seasoned," or darkened, by heating it for 4 to 5 hours in a 350° F oven.

lid of the processor bowl and spoon the dry ingredients over the batter. Process with 3 or 4 on-off turns just to combine. Stir in the nuts and any dry particles using a rubber spatula.

4. Spoon the batter into the prepared pan. Bake on the middle rack of the preheated oven for 30 to 45 minutes, until a toothpick inserted comes out clean or with a dry crumb. Remove to a rack to cool for 15 minutes. Carefully run a knife around the edge of the pan and shake the bread loose onto the rack to finish cooling. Serve at room temperature or chilled. To store, wrap in aluminum foil. This bread keeps well refrigerated for up to 2 weeks or frozen up to 4 months.

PAN CAKES

Makes eight 4-inch cakes to serve 4
15 minutes to prepare
10-inch skillet or griddle

After a simple supper of soup and salad, here's a dazzling, easy dessert that may look a bit like your breakfast pancakes, but is lighter, more tender, more golden, more flavorful, more . . . you'll say, "I want more."

Place a pair of these golden cakes on a dessert plate. Roll them around fresh fruit of the season or your favorite all-fruit preserve, top with a dusting of confectioners' sugar or a dollop of whipped cream.

2 large eggs, separated
½ teaspoon cream of tartar
½ cup sour cream
½ cup water
½ teaspoon baking soda
⅞ cup cake flour
1 tablespoon granulated sugar
¾ teaspoon baking powder
½ teaspoon salt
2 tablespoons butter
  Fresh fruit of the season or jam
  Confectioners' sugar

1. Using the wire whisk, steel blade, or beater attachment to the processor, beat the egg whites until frothy, then add cream of tartar and beat until soft peaks form (see pages 19–20). Remove to a medium bowl and set aside.

2. In the bowl of the food processor fitted with the steel blade, process the egg yolks until frothy, then with the motor running add the sour cream, water, and baking soda. Process, counting to 20.

3. Open the lid and sprinkle in the flour, sugar, baking powder, and salt. Close the lid and process, counting to 20.

4. Melt the butter in a 10-inch skillet or griddle over medium heat. Pour the fat into the batter and pulse to mix. Replace the skillet or griddle on the stove to preheat.

5. Open the processor lid and fold the beaten egg whites into the mixture with a rubber spatula.

6. Pour 2 cakes onto the hot skillet or griddle in 4-inch rounds. Cook, turning once, until golden brown on both sides. Set aside on a hot plate in the oven until serving time, while you cook 2 more.

7. To serve, roll the cakes around fresh fruit of the season or jam, and place 2 fruit rolls on each dessert plate. Dust with confectioners' sugar and serve.

How to Cook Perfect Pancakes

• Preheat a dry skillet or griddle over medium heat, then add butter or oil and turn the pan to coat the bottom. Pour out any excess oil.

• Use a ½-cup measure or soup ladle to pour the thin batter onto the preheated skillet or griddle. Tilt the skillet to cover evenly.

• Cook, watching to see bubbles rising through the batter. When the bubbles are evenly distributed just under the top surface (about 2 minutes), flip the cake and cook the second side, about 2 more minutes. Set aside on a warm plate in the oven.

• If you're cooking a lot, separate the cakes with sheets of waxed paper.

There are a couple of caveats to making a Dutch Baby. Although easy as pie to a Dutch cook, they're tricky, in that the idea is to create a puffed and airy oven-baked pancake, and you have to have a hot oven to start, the right pan to cook in, and people willing to wait so that you can serve the hot pancake to them instantly once it's out of the oven because it collapses fast.

We find we have the best luck baking them in a 10-inch cast-iron skillet. Make sure your oven is really hot. Also make sure you mix the batter up quickly.

DUTCH BABY

Serves 4
About 20 minutes to preheat
5 minutes to prepare
25 to 30 minutes to bake
10-inch cast-iron skillet

It's kind of a toss-up whether these puffed pancakes are best for dessert or for brunch. We know one Dutch Baby convert who likes them so well, she serves these pancakes to her family for dinner with maple syrup and link sausage.

3 large eggs
3 tablespoons granulated sugar
Few grains of salt
1 cup milk
1 cup unbleached all-purpose flour
2 tablespoons butter
Freshly grated nutmeg
Confectioners' sugar
Lemon-peel curls
Fresh berries of the season (optional)
Jam (optional)

1. At least 10 minutes *before* you do anything else, preheat the oven to 425° F with a 10-inch cast-iron skillet inside.

2. Once the skillet has preheated, working quickly, make the batter in the food processor fitted with the steel blade by whirling the eggs with the sugar and salt, then with the motor running, pouring in the milk through the feed tube and finally the flour. Process just a moment. Now melt the butter in the hot skillet, then pour the batter into the hot butter and pop the skillet back into the oven.

3. Bake in the preheated oven until the pancake is puffy and well browned, about 25 to 30 minutes. Sprinkle it with freshly grated nutmeg, then dust confectioners' sugar onto it through a strainer. Serve straight out of the oven in wedges with lemon-peel curls, fresh berries, if you have them, or jam, if desired.

WAFFLE SURPRISE

If you get caught flat-footed with company coming and no dessert, one quick and easy solution is to make waffles on the spot. Black & Decker provided us with a heart-shaped waffle iron we adore that creates a perfect dessert shape. Pile the heart with fresh fruit, and give it a shot of whipped cream. It's dessert.

You can also make waffles early in the day at your convenience, then hold them until dinnertime. Pop them in the toaster to heat and crisp them, then add fruit and whipped cream.

If your waffle iron doesn't have a nonstick surface, coat the grids with cooking spray before you preheat the iron. And remember not to peek at the waffles while they're baking until the light goes out. Otherwise, you're likely to have a disembodied waffle to contend with.

We find the easiest tool for removing waffles from the iron after baking is a common wooden skewer. You can pierce the waffle, and usually it will lift right off the iron. On the waffle irons we use, the "down" side is the serve side. Take a look at both sides of the waffles you make as they come off the griddle. Place the toastiest, best-looking side UP on the plate. All recipes given here serve 8 for dessert, but the recipes can be halved if you need fewer servings. Conversely, as written, they'll serve 4 people for brunch or for a sweet-main-dish supper.

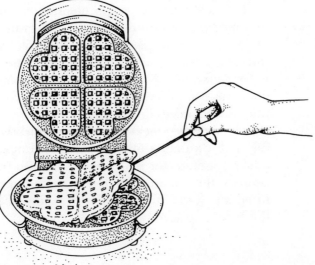

Lemon-Buttermilk Waffles

Makes 4 waffles to serve 4
10 minutes to prepare
Waffle iron

When time permits, treat your guests to the wonderful aroma and taste of fresh, tangy homemade buttermilk waffles.

1 large egg
1 cup buttermilk
3 tablespoons unsalted butter, melted and cooled slightly
1 cup unbleached all-purpose flour
1 tablespoon lemon zest
1 tablespoon packed light brown sugar
½ teaspoon baking soda
Pinch of salt

1. Preheat the waffle iron and grease it lightly. Fit the food processor with the steel blade. Combine the egg and buttermilk in the food processor bowl and process for 2 minutes. With the machine running, pour the butter through the feed tube and process for 10 seconds.

2. In a small bowl, stir together the flour, lemon zest, brown sugar, baking soda, and salt. Spoon the dry ingredients on top of the egg-buttermilk mixture. Pulse 3 or 4 times just to combine.

3. Bake the waffles in the waffle iron until crisp and golden. Cool on a rack to preserve crispness.

WAFFLE-CONE CORNUCOPIAS WITH BERRIES AND LEMON CUSTARD

Serves 6
20 minutes to prepare
1 hour to chill
4-cup glass measure

A light and lovely luncheon dessert napped with fresh lemon custard—line the outside of the dessert plates with intertwined twigs of fresh mint for a breathtaking presentation.

3 cups fresh ripe sliced strawberries, blueberries, or raspberries or a combination of all 3, hulled
¼ cup sugar or to taste
1½ teaspoons minced grated lemon zest
2 tablespoons Grand Marnier

LEMON CUSTARD

5 tablespoons fresh lemon juice
6 large egg yolks
⅓ cup sugar
3 tablespoons plus ⅓ cup whipping cream, chilled
6 waffle cones, sugar cones, waffle ice-cream cups or waffles
Fresh mint leaves, for garnish

1. Mix the berries, sugar, lemon zest, and Grand Marnier in a medium bowl. Refrigerate for 1 hour.

2. Meanwhile, prepare the lemon custard. In a 1-quart microwavable mixing bowl combine the lemon juice, egg yolks, sugar, and 3 tablespoons of whipping cream. Whisk to combine. Microwave on 70% (medium) for 2 minutes. Whisk. Microwave on 70% (medium) for 1 minute. The mixture should now be thickened. If not, microwave on 70% (medium) for an additional 30 seconds. Cover with plastic wrap and refrigerate for 45 minutes to chill. Just before serving, process the remaining whipping cream in the food processor fitted with a steel blade until stiff, about 30 seconds. Fold into the lemon custard.

3. To serve, place 1 cone, waffle cup, or waffle on each plate. Stuff or top each with ¼ cup lemon custard. Spoon the berry mixture over the custard. Garnish with fresh mint leaves.

*S*PONGE-CAKE WAFFLES

Makes four 9-inch waffles to serve 8 for dessert
10 minutes to prepare
15 minutes to bake
Waffle iron

Here's a great strawberry-shortcake base. Make these waffles early in the day, then heat them in the toaster at dessert time, and top with freshly sliced strawberries and whipped cream scented with Chambord.

5 eggs, separated
2 tablespoons fresh lemon juice
1 cup sugar
1 cup cake flour
1 teaspoon baking powder
½ teaspoon salt
½ cup finely chopped pecans
½ cup (1 stick) butter, melted
Zest of ½ lemon

1. Preheat the waffle iron. Place the egg whites in the food processor bowl fitted with the steel blade (see pages 19–20). Process until foamy, then add the lemon juice and process until soft peaks form.

2. Meanwhile, in a large mixing bowl, whisk together the egg yolks and sugar. Over this, sprinkle the flour, baking powder, and salt and whisk in. Add the pecans, melted butter, and lemon zest. Whisk. Fold in the beaten egg whites.

3. Bake the waffles in the preheated waffle iron, then hold them in a warm oven until serving time.

Be a Picky Pumpkin Picker

Choosing the right pumpkin for the kid's Jack-o'-Lantern is a matter of choice and how much Dad can lift, right? Choosing the right pumpkin for cooking is a little easier. Ask your produce manager for a "sugar" pumpkin. A sugar pumpkin has a sweeter, less stringy flesh and fewer seeds. Sugar pumpkins are smaller than the giants being sold for Jack-o'-Lanterns. Look for a 3- to 4-pound pumpkin for making pumpkin puree. A 3-pound pumpkin, washed, cut into chunks, cooked in water, and drained will yield 2 cups of pumpkin puree.

PUMPKIN-PECAN WAFFLES

Makes four 9-inch waffles to serve 8 for dessert
10 minutes to prepare
15 minutes to bake
Waffle iron

In the fall, using canned pumpkin puree or your own homemade, these luscious bright-orange waffles are good for Sunday brunch as well as dessert. Try them with pure maple syrup and crème fraîche or sour cream. A jot of blueberry preserves is gorgeous here.

    3 eggs, separated
    1 tablespoon fresh lemon juice
1¾ cups milk
    ½ cup (1 stick) butter
    ½ cup pumpkin puree, canned or homemade (see sidebar, page 287)
    2 cups cake flour
    1 tablespoon plus 1 teaspoon baking powder
    1 teaspoon salt
    1 teaspoon ground cinnamon
    ¼ teaspoon freshly grated nutmeg
    ¾ cup chopped pecans

1. Preheat the waffle iron. Place the egg whites in the food processor bowl fitted with the steel blade (see pages 19–20). Process until frothy, then add the lemon juice through the feed tube and continue processing until soft peaks form. Set aside.

2. Meanwhile, in a large mixing bowl, whisk the egg yolks with the milk. Microwave the butter at 100% (high) until melted, about 20 seconds, then pour it into the egg-milk mixture along with the pumpkin. Whisk together.

3. Sprinkle the cake flour, baking powder, salt, cinnamon, and nutmeg onto the egg-milk-pumpkin mixture and thoroughly whisk together. Fold in the beaten egg whites. Pour the batter onto the hot waffle iron just until it nearly reaches the edges. Sprinkle each waffle with 3 tablespoons of pecans. Bake each waffle until the light goes out. Don't peek.

4. Place 8 dessert plates in the oven to warm, and as the waffles are cooked, transfer them to the warm oven.

GINGERBREAD WAFFLES

Makes four 9-inch waffles to serve 8 for dessert
10 minutes to prepare
15 minutes to bake
Waffle iron

If you have a Mickey Mouse waffle iron, here's the perfect kid dessert. Serve with a scoop of vanilla ice cream.

2 egg whites
1 tablespoon fresh lemon juice
2 cups cake flour
1 teaspoon salt
1¼ teaspoons baking soda
2½ teaspoons ground ginger
1¼ teaspoons ground cinnamon
¼ teaspoon ground cloves
1 cup molasses
½ cup buttermilk
⅓ cup vegetable oil
1 large egg

1. Preheat the waffle iron. In the food processor bowl fitted with the steel blade, process the egg whites until foamy. Then add the lemon juice through the feed tube and beat until soft peaks form. Remove to another large mixing bowl.

2. Replace the steel blade in the food processor and combine the flour, salt, baking soda, ginger, cinnamon, and cloves. Pulse to mix. Now add the molasses, buttermilk, oil, and whole egg, and pulse to mix, about 10 times. Fold the mixture by thirds into the beaten egg white.

3. Bake each waffle, then hold in a warm oven until serving. Place 2 waffle quarters (or a Mickey face) on each plate.

If some of your pie pans are old
family friends handed down from
aunts, grandmothers, and mothers and show the full life they've
led with nicks and scars, you can
dress them up by setting the pie
inside a lined basket made beautiful with fabric, a doily, or a colorful napkin. Present the pie as a
gift, and the lucky person who re-
ceives the pie also gets a basket to
keep after the pie is just a memory.
But tell them you want your mama's pie pan back.

Tuck fresh flowers of the season
in around the edge of the basket, or
if the pie is fruit, add the same
whole fruit to the basket for a
mouth-watering garnish.

SWISS FRUIT FLAN

Makes one 10-inch deep-dish pie
30 minutes to prepare
40 minutes to bake
10-inch deep-dish glass pie pan

A sweet yeast dough topped with custard and fruit then baked into a
gorgeous sweet-tart deep-dish pie, this plays well after a souper supper.

Although the directions may look daunting, this is easier to make
than it is to describe. Basically, you make a yeast piecrust, mix up a
custard, and top it with the fruit you like best. Bake the whole thing
together, and you get a wonderful yeasty aroma, silky smooth custard,
and sweet-tart fruit all in one bite.

SWEET YEAST DOUGH

2 cups bread flour
½ teaspoon salt
2 tablespoons nonfat dry milk
2 tablespoons granulated sugar
2½ teaspoons (1 package) 50% faster active dry yeast
2 tablespoons unsalted butter
1 large egg
½ cup water

CUSTARD

2 large eggs
1 cup half-and-half
3 tablespoons granulated sugar
½ teaspoon ground cinnamon

2 cups fruit of your choice, mix and match: sour cherries, cran-
     berries, pears, blueberries, apples, plums, clementines, pome-
     granates
Confectioners' sugar

1. Preheat the oven to 350° F. Spritz a 10-inch deep-dish
glass pie pan with cooking spray. Set aside.

2. Make sweet yeast dough in the food processor. Add to
the food processor bowl fitted with the steel blade the flour,
salt, nonfat dry milk, sugar, and yeast. Pulse to mix.

3. With the motor running, add the butter through the feed tube and process 10 seconds. Break the egg through the feed tube and process 5 seconds, then pour the water through the process until the mixture forms a ball that rides the blade around. Machine knead for 60 seconds.

4. Remove the dough and blade. Hand knead the dough a few seconds on a lightly floured board, then form it into a ball. Punch a hole in it with your thumbs to form a doughnut shape and replace it in the food processor bowl. Cover with plastic wrap and prepare to micro-rise.

5. To Micro-Rise, place an 8-ounce glass of water in the back of the microwave, and reduce the power to 10% or the appropriate microwave setting (see page 244). Place the bowl of dough in the microwave. Heat 3 minutes. Rest 3 minutes. Heat 3 minutes. Rest 6 minutes. The dough will be doubled in bulk.

6. Remove the dough from the microwave, punch it down on the lightly floured board. Form it into a ball, cover it with the food processor bowl, and let it rest for 10 minutes. Roll it out into a 12-inch circle, arrange it in the 10-inch pie pan, and let it rise 10 minutes or so in a warm, draft-free place.

7. Meanwhile, whip up the custard in the food processor bowl fitted with the steel blade by mixing the eggs, half-and-half, sugar, and cinnamon. Set aside.

8. Cut up the fruits of your choice. Remember to peel and seed them first.

9. Once the dough is puffy and light, pour the custard into the piecrust, top with the fruit, and bake in the preheated oven for 40 minutes, until the custard has set. Remove to a rack to cool. Dust the top with confectioners' sugar and cut into thick wedges.

11
HALF-TIME HOLIDAY DESSERTS

f there was ever a season when the cook ran out of time, it's the holiday season. And that age-old dilemma comes roaring forth. You're out of time. You want to make a great celebration dinner. You certainly don't have time or energy to devote to an elaborate dessert. But you still want one.

What can you do short of making a visit to the bakery? Try some of the dessert concoctions we've learned to make—mostly from necessity and having our backs to the wall.

A Fast Holiday Trifle that makes use of winter fruits and store-bought cake can go into your prettiest clear glass straight-sided bowl, then add homemade microwave pudding, and you'll get oohs and aahs from the company before they even taste it. A real chance to feast with the eyes.

Our old-fashioned faux cherry pie, a recipe that came from depression days when cranberries were abundant and cheap, is an easy, tart red crumble that goes together fast and makes a homey finish to Thanksgiving.

Some of the rarest desserts we saved for special occasions and put in this chapter: Black-Bottom Thimble Cakes, Valentine Parfait Fools, and Halloween Candy-Apple Cake, Babka, Hamantashen.

These are all desserts that deliver.

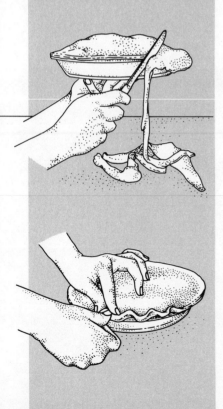

PRESIDENTS' DAY SOUR CHERRY PIE

Serves 6 to 8
20 minutes to prepare
45 to 50 minutes to bake
9-inch glass pie pan

With an easy-to-handle prepared piecrust and a microwavable filling, cherry pie is now a delight to prepare at home.

  1 cup sugar
¼ cup cornstarch
  2 16-ounce cans pitted tart red cherries, drained, with ¾ cup juice reserved
  2 prepared 9-inch piecrusts, unbaked
  2 tablespoons unsalted butter
¼ teaspoon almond extract
  1 teaspoon fresh lemon juice
    Pinch of salt

1. Preheat the oven to 425° F. In a 2-quart microwavable mixing bowl, combine the sugar and cornstarch, mixing well. Stir in the ¾ cup reserved juice from the cherries. Microwave at 70% (medium) for 9 minutes, stirring with a wooden spoon every 3 minutes. The filling should now be thickened. If not, microwave at 70% (medium) for an additional 2 minutes.

2. Add the well-drained cherries to the thickened juice and stir. The cherries will dilute the thickened juice a little. Microwave at 70% (medium) for 6 minutes, stirring after every 3 minutes with a wooden spoon.

3. Meanwhile, gently place 1 prepared piecrust in the bottom of a 9-inch glass pie pan. Remove the cherries from the microwave and add the butter, almond extract, lemon juice, and salt. Stir to melt the butter. Pour the cherry filling into the prepared pan.

4. Place the second piecrust over the top of the pie. Trim and flute the edges. Make 3 or 4 slits in the top crust to allow steam to escape.

5. Bake the pie on the middle rack of the preheated oven for 10 minutes. Reduce the heat to 375° F and bake for an additional 35 to 40 minutes, until the crust is brown and juice bubbles through the slits. Cool to room temperature.

$\mathcal{V}$ALENTINE PARFAIT FOOLS

Serves 4
20 minutes to prepare
2 tall 10-ounce parfait glasses

The light mixture of cream, liqueur, and cranberries is all mixed and finished in just 20 minutes. Serve store-bought chocolate truffles on the side, pop a romantic CD in the player, and you're all set.

¾ cup homemade whole-berry cranberry sauce (recipe is on the back of the cranberry bag) or canned whole-berry cranberry sauce
2 cups whipping cream, chilled
2 tablespoons confectioners' sugar
2 tablespoons Grand Marnier
1 kiwi, for garnish

1. In a small bowl, with a whisk break up any large chunks of cranberry sauce. Set aside.

2. Pour the cream into the processor bowl fitted with the steel blade. Process until the cream holds medium peaks when tested with a spoon. Gradually add the sugar through the feed tube and process for 15 seconds. Add the Grand Marnier and continue beating until the cream has tripled in volume, is fluffy, and forms stiff peaks.

3. Add half of the whipped cream to the cranberries and very gently fold the two together. Do not overmix. The mixture will be pink with streaks of white.

4. In tall 10-ounce parfait glasses, alternate layers of cranberry mixture and whipped cream. Peel and slice the kiwi and then cut each slice in half. Garnish each parfait with a half slice of kiwi. Serve each parfait glass on a doily-lined saucer with an antique iced-tea spoon if you have them.

MRS. O'BRIEN'S IRISH CREAM SMOOTHIE

Serves 8
15 minutes to prepare
2 hours to chill

In Ireland, St. Patrick's Day is a sacred religious holiday. The faithful attend church throughout the day, which leaves them little time for major meal preparation. However, there is time afterward for a shot or two of Irish cream liqueur. We padded it a bit and serve it in Waterford brandy snifters. Pass around a tray of best quality store-bought truffles (or see page 102 for Katherine's Faux Truffles) and dessert is done.

6 large eggs
1/3 cup sugar
1 1/2 cups Irish cream liqueur
3 cups milk
1/2 teaspoon freshly grated nutmeg
2/3 cup whipping cream, whipped
2 cups vanilla ice cream, softened
Freshly grated nutmeg

1. In a large 3-quart mixing bowl beat the eggs until foamy at medium speed with an electric mixer. Gradually add the sugar, beating until thick and lemon colored, about 5 minutes. Reduce the speed to low; gradually add the liqueur, milk, and the 1/2 teaspoon of ground nutmeg. Beat just until combined. Chill thoroughly or for at least 2 hours.

2. To serve, slowly blend in whipped cream and softened ice cream. Pour into individual stemware and sprinkle with additional nutmeg.

AMANTASHEN

Makes 24 Hamantashen
20 minutes to prepare
12 minutes to bake
Large baking sheet

Traditional Purim pastries filled with prune or poppy-seed filling you can buy in a can are made easy with food processor short paste. In 40 seconds you're ready to roll. Cut the circles of dough with a mason-jar lid, add prepared filling, then pinch the dough into the traditional 3-cornered hat.

Purim parties, held in early spring, celebrate the Purim story as related in the Book of Esther. Jewish young people dress up as characters in the story, and Hamantashen, named for Haman—the story's villain—are exchanged as gifts as well as being served as part of the refreshments.

PASTRY

½ cup (1 stick) unsalted butter
2 large eggs
½ cup sugar
2 tablespoons ice water
1 teaspoon vanilla extract
Zest and juice of 1 lemon
½ teaspoon baking soda
½ teaspoon baking powder
⅛ teaspoon salt
3 cups unbleached all-purpose flour

FILLING

1 12-ounce lekvar (prune butter) or prune pastry filling or poppy-seed filling or 1¼ cups pureed cooked pitted prunes
Zest and juice of 1 lemon
½ cup coarsely chopped walnuts
½ cup crushed cornflakes
½ cup mild honey

(continued)

1. Preheat the oven to 375° F. Coat a large baking sheet with cooking spray and set aside.

2. To prepare the pastry, microwave the butter in a glass measure at 100% (high) until melted, about 45 seconds. Set aside.

3. In the food processor bowl fitted with the steel blade, process the eggs with the sugar, melted butter, water, and vanilla.

4. Using a zester, remove the zest from the lemon and add it to the food processor bowl. Squeeze and strain the lemon juice into the bowl. With the motor running, add the baking soda, powder, salt, and flour. Process just until the mixture forms a ball, about 20 seconds. Turn out onto plastic wrap. Squeeze the dough into a ball, twist the plastic wrap, and chill in the freezer for 10 minutes.

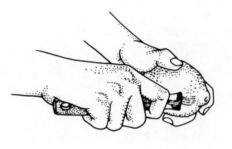 

5. Meanwhile, to make the filling, combine the lekvar or prune pastry filling or poppy-seed filling, or pureed prunes with the zest and juice of the lemon. Stir in the chopped nuts and cornflakes. Mix well.

6. Roll out the dough on a lightly floured board to a thin ⅛-inch-thick layer. Cut circles of dough by dipping a jar lid or 5-inch-round cookie cutter into flour, then cutting out circles. Cut the circles as close together as possible. Pull up the extra dough strips, re-form, then reroll, and recut.

7. Place a heaping teaspoon of filling onto each dough circle. Flip 2 sides of the circle over the filling, then flip up the bottom to make a 3-cornered hat. Pinch the dough edges together, then lift the pastry with a spatula onto the prepared baking sheet. Once you have formed all the pastries, drip a little honey onto the top of each one.

8. Bake in the preheated oven for 12 minutes, until golden. Remove from the oven and let the pastries cool on the baking sheet on a rack for 5 minutes, then with a spatula carefully transfer them to a rack to cool completely.

Getting the Most from Your Lemon

To remove more juice from a cold lemon, pierce the lemon several times with the tip of a sharp knife or stab it with a fork and then microwave at 100% (high) for 30 seconds before squeezing. The warm lemon will give more juice.

BABKA

Makes one 9-inch tube cake
20 minutes to prepare
1 hour and 30 minutes to rise
35 minutes to bake
9-inch kugelhopf or a 10-inch bundt pan

This Polish Easter cake is made especially easy using the Micro-Rise method. Bake it in the traditional 9-inch kugelhopf pan or, barring that, in a nonstick bundt cake pan. No icing's required. Just a simple sprinkling of confectioners' sugar, and you have a cake to serve at Easter or any other time.

¾ cup (1½ sticks) unsalted butter
½ cup granulated sugar
    Zest of 2 medium lemons
½ teaspoon salt
 6 egg yolks
 1 cup golden raisins
¼ cup rum
 3 cups cake flour
 2 cups bread flour
2½ teaspoons (1 package) 50% faster active dry yeast
 1 cup milk
    Confectioners' sugar

1. In the food processor bowl fitted with the steel blade place the butter, sugar, lemon zest, salt, and egg yolks. Process until completely mixed, about 30 seconds.

2. Combine the raisins and rum in a 2-cup glass measure. Cover tightly with plastic wrap. Microwave at 100% (high) until the rum boils, about 45 seconds. Set aside.

3. Open the processor lid and sprinkle the flours and yeast on top of the butter–egg yolk mixture. Process until thoroughly blended, about 15 seconds.

4. Place the milk in a 2-cup glass measure and microwave at 100% (high) until it's about 115° F, about 45 seconds. With the processor motor running, pour the hot milk through the feed tube. Process 1 minute. Remove the steel blade from the processor bowl, cover the bowl with plastic wrap, and prepare to Micro-Rise.

You can, if need be, use 5 cups of all-purpose flour for Babka if you don't have both bread and cake flours, but the results may be heavier. (See pages 20–21 for more discussion of specialty flours.)

5. Place an 8-ounce glass of water in the back of the microwave oven. Place the covered processor bowl of batter in the oven. Lower the microwave to 10% power or the appropriate Micro-Rise power (see page 244). Heat for 3 minutes, rest 3 minutes, heat 3 minutes, and rest 6 minutes.

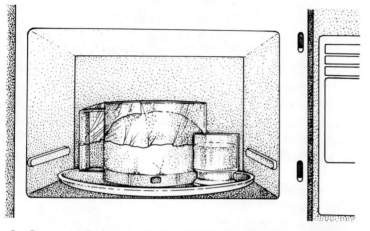

(see page 244)

6. Generously butter the 9-inch kugelhopf pan or 10-inch bundt pan. Adjust the oven rack one-third up from the bottom. Preheat the oven to 400° F.

7. Drain the raisins of any remaining rum, then fold them by hand or rubber spatula into the batter. Pour the batter into the prepared baking pan. Smooth the top with a rubber spatula. Cover with well-buttered plastic wrap and set aside in a warm, draft-free place to rise until it reaches to the top of the pan. In the center, you'll notice the cake will have risen slightly above the tube. This rising may take more than an hour.

8. Bake in the preheated oven for 5 minutes, then lower the temperature to 350° F and continue to bake 30 minutes longer. Remove the cake to a rack and let it cool in the pan for 10 minutes. Then cover with a rack and flip it over. Lift off the baking pan. Cool the cake completely, then dust with confectioners' sugar. The cake is best if it's served the second day. It freezes well.

Anjou, available from October to May, are lovely egg-shaped light green or yellow-green pears that are sometimes more difficult to ripen than others. These are best when eaten fresh, but are also wonderful in crisps, pandowdies, and pies.

Bartletts, available from August to December, are both yellow and red and shaped like a bell, and terrific for eating fresh or used as a garnish on top of a cake or focaccia. Bartletts are frequently canned. In France they are called "Williams."

Bosc, available from September to May, these dusky brown pears with long tapered necks are so gorgeous you may be tempted to use them for decoration. They are also ideal cooking pears, whether baked, broiled, or poached. Their flesh is tender, buttery, and aromatic.

Comice, available from October to March, have been made famous by mail-order houses such as Harry & David and Pinnacle. They are greenish chubby pears that when ripened are so good and tender you could eat them with a spoon—which is what many people do. They also can be used in baking because they are super sweet and peary tasting.

Seckels, available from August to January, are little bite-sized green pears with a red blush. As they ripen the red and green colors intensify. The flesh is a warm light ivory color. These are best eaten fresh.

SANDY DOWLING'S PASSOVER CREAM PEARS

Serves 6 to 8 people
30 mintures to prepare
24 hours to chill

Sandy won $500 with this recipe several years ago in a local cooking contest. She peels the pears after they have been poached in the vanilla syrup. However, if you have beautiful red Comice or red D'Anjou pears available, we suggest leaving the skin on as it will turn a deep, rich ruby red and look something like a still life from an Old Master painting. This light dessert is perfect to serve after any heavy meal.

1 quart water
2 cups sugar
1 vanilla bean, split
6 large pears, cored, or 8 small pears, cored
1 8-ounce package cream cheese, room temperature
1/3 cup powdered sugar
1/2 teaspoon almond extract
3 tablespoons roasted almonds, finely chopped
1 10-ounce package frozen raspberries in syrup
2 tablespoons Chambord (raspberry liqueur)
1 lemon, cut in half (optional)
8 fresh mint leaves (optional)

1. Combine water, sugar, and vanilla bean in a large 3-quart saucepan and bring to a boil. Add the pears and reduce the heat to low. Cook gently just until tender, about 10 to 15 minutes depending on the ripeness of the pears. Cool the pears in the syrup until room temperature and then refrigerate, covered, for 24 hours.

2. In the food processor bowl fitted with the steel blade, add the cream cheese, powdered sugar, and almond extract. Process until smooth and well combined. Add the chopped almonds and pulse 2 to 3 times just to incorporate.

3. Press the raspberries and syrup through a sieve and discard the pulp and seeds. Add the Chambord to the raspberry syrup and refrigerate until serving time.

4. To serve remove the pears from the syrup and pat dry. (If you decide to peel the pears, rub them with the cut side of the lemon to prevent darkening.) Using one finger, gently stuff the pears with with cream cheese mixture. This mixture may also be piped in using a pastry bag with a large decorative tip. Spoon a pool of raspberry syrup onto each dessert plate to cover the bottom. Place each pear upright in the raspberry syrup. Pour a few more drops of the raspberry syrup on the top of each pear and garnish with a fresh mint sprig if desired. Pass more raspberry syrup when serving.

Crème de Framboise

Deep garnet red raspberries are the base for the liqueur Crème de Framboise. Chambord is one of many brands available in the United States. The raspberry's intense flavor is a favorite throughout Europe. Belgium uses it to flavor creme centers for chocolates, and the French use it to intensify the fruit sauces served with wild game, poultry, and pork.

*H*APPY BIRTHDAY ORANGE PASTRY CREAM WITH RASPBERRIES, PUFF PASTRY, AND CARAMEL SAUCE

Serves 4
30 minutes to prepare
1 hour to chill
10 to 12 minutes to bake
Large heavy baking sheet

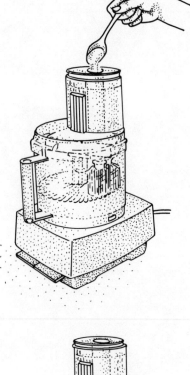

We are big fans of classic French dessert recipes. What could be better for a birthday party dessert? This recipe is our adaptation of a famous recipe served in the French Room of the Adolphus Hotel in Dallas, Texas. Don't make puff pastry and caramel sauce from scratch. Frozen puff pastry sheets work fine, and we found a wonderful gourmet caramel sauce in the ice-cream section of the grocery made with real cream and butter. The pastry sheets and orange pastry cream can both be made in advance and will hold for several hours. In a real pinch, eliminate the pastry sheets and substitute split best-quality croissants.

Serve these to guests on your prettiest china and be prepared for compliments.

ORANGE PASTRY CREAM

⅓ cup granulated sugar
1 tablespoon cake flour
1 tablespoon cornstarch
1 cup whole milk
2 large egg yolks
1 tablespoon Grand Marnier
½ teaspoon vanilla extract
½ teaspoon minced orange zest

½ pound (1 sheet) frozen puff pastry, partially thawed
1 cup confectioners' sugar
¼ cup whipping cream
12 ounces best-quality caramel sauce made with real cream and butter
2 cups fresh raspberries or unsweetened frozen raspberries, thawed or 2 cups fresh strawberries, quartered
Fresh mint leaves (optional)

1. For the orange pastry cream, in a 1-quart microwavable mixing bowl, combine the sugar, cake flour, and cornstarch. Mix well. Whisk in the milk. Microwave on 100% (high) for 3 minutes. Meanwhile, in a small bowl, lightly beat the egg yolks. Slowly pour half the hot milk mixture into the egg yolks and whisk. Return the egg yolk–milk mixture to the hot milk. Whisk. Microwave on 90% (medium-high) for 1 minute. Whisk in the Grand Marnier, vanilla, and orange zest. Cover the top of the bowl with waxed paper and chill for 1 hour.

2. Preheat the oven to 450° F. Carefully unfold the well-chilled puff pastry sheet. The sheet may crack in the folds; that's ok. Prick the pastry sheet gently with a fork. Cut the sheet into 9 equal 3-inch-square pieces. Place the pastry squares on a heavy ungreased baking sheet, 2 inches apart. Bake on the middle rack of the preheated oven for 10 to 12 minutes, until puffed and golden. Cool the pastry on the baking sheet for 5 minutes and then carefully slide a spatula underneath the squares and remove them to a rack to cool completely. The recipe may be completed up to this point several hours in advance.

3. Just before serving, preheat the broiler. Place the cooked pastry squares on a heavy baking sheet and sprinkle generously with the confectioners' sugar. Broil about 6 inches from the heat until the sugar is glazed, about 30 seconds. Watch them carefully.

4. In the bowl of the food processor fitted with the steel blade, process the whipping cream until it begins to thicken and is stiff (see page 17). Fold the processed cream into the pastry cream.

5. Microwave the caramel sauce on 100% (high) until hot, but not boiling, about 1 minute. The heat will thin the sauce and make it pour like liquid gold.

6. To serve, place 1 pastry square on each of 4 plates. Top each pastry square with ¼ cup orange pastry cream. Top the pastry cream with ½ cup raspberries or strawberries. Cover the berries with the remaining orange pastry cream. Top with an additional pastry square. Save the leftover pastry square for a snack. Pour warm caramel sauce around the base of the bottom pastry square. Garnish with mint leaves if desired. Serve immediately.

Lone Star Lickin'

Makes 1¼ cups to serve 1

If there's still room for a toddy after puff pastry and orange cream, why not try a Lone Star Lickin'? Delicious!

3 tablespoons bourbon or brandy
1½ teaspoons dark brown sugar
Pinch of ground cinnamon
1 cup strong hot coffee
¼ cup whipped cream

In a tall mug, combine the liquor of choice, brown sugar, cinnamon, and coffee. Stir. Top with whipped cream. Serve immediately.

Chocolate-Dipped Strawberries with Nuts

Makes 24 strawberries to serve 8 to 10

8 ounces (8 squares) semisweet chocolate or 1⅓ cups chocolate chips
24 fresh ripe strawberries with stems, washed and dried
2 cups finely chopped pecans, walnuts, almonds, or pistachios

Line a large baking sheet with waxed paper. Microwave the chocolate on 100% (high) for 4 minutes. Stir to melt any remaining bits. Dip the bottom ¾ of each strawberry into the chocolate. Roll the strawberry in the chopped nuts. Place the finished berries on the waxed paper and allow them to cool until set.

JULY FOURTH'S RED-STAR TART

Serves 10
25 minutes to prepare
15 to 20 minutes to bake
11 × 16-inch baking sheet

A unique and very pretty tart that brings good cheer to a holiday gathering—this is a dessert the entire family will enjoy!

CRUST

½ cup (1 stick) unsalted butter
1 cup sugar
1 large egg
2 cups unbleached all-purpose flour
1 teaspoon baking powder
½ teaspoon vanilla extract
¼ cup milk

FILLING

12 ounces cream cheese, room temperature
1 teaspoon vanilla extract
½ cup sugar

TOPPING

6 cups fresh ripe strawberries, hulled
Fresh mint leaves

1. Preheat the oven to 375° F. Spray an 11 × 16-inch baking sheet with cooking spray. For the crust, in the bowl of the food processor fitted with the steel blade, combine the butter, sugar, egg, flour, baking powder, and vanilla. Process to combine thoroughly, about 30 seconds. With the processor running, add the milk through the feed tube. Process just until the dough leaves the sides of the bowl and masses together.

2. With well-floured hands, press the dough into the bottom of the prepared pan. Bake on the middle rack of the preheated oven until lightly browned, 15 to 20 minutes. Set aside to cool to room temperature.

3. Meanwhile, wipe out the processor bowl with a paper towel and place it back on the processor base fitted with the steel blade. Add the cream cheese, vanilla, and sugar. Process until well blended and smooth. When the crust has cooled to room temperature, about 20 minutes, spread it with the cream-cheese mixture. Top with the strawberries. Garnish with fresh mint if desired, and serve. This tart may be made and refrigerated 1 day before serving.

*R*ASPBERRY CHEESECAKE FOR HOLIDAYS AND ENTERTAINING EVENINGS

Makes one 9- or 10-inch cheesecake to serve 12 to 14
20 minutes to prepare
2 hours to bake 10-inch cake; 2 hours and 15 minutes to bake
9-inch cake
4 hours to chill
9- or 10-inch cheesecake or springform pan

Diana freezes raspberries in July, at least 3 or 4 flats, to be used in December for making this gift cake. The cheesecake is very moist, not the drier New York style. If fresh berries are available, use them to garnish the top of the cake.

Blueberries and coarsely chopped fresh peaches can be substituted for the 1½ cups of frozen raspberries in the filling. Replace the raspberry sauce with our Blueberry Sauce (see sidebar, page 210) and let it run down the sides of the cake, forming a blue pool that gently naps each bit of peach and smooth, creamy filling. Served on a white footed serving piece or on individual white milk-glass plates, this cake is breathtaking. Garnish with mint or clean peach leaves.

CRUST

2 cups ground (about 18) shortbread-pecan cookies
½ cups pecans (optional)
¼ cup (½ stick) unsalted butter

(continued)

> We call for a cheesecake pan in this recipe, which is a little different from a springform pan. A cheesecake pan has no spring clip on the side; instead, the bottom just slips out through the top. If you frequently make cheesecakes, you may want to invest in this specialized pan. The acid from raspberries or citrus will not eat through the sides of the cheesecake pan as easily as it will in some of the less expensive springform pans, resulting in a cake with a metallic taste and an off color on the sides.

Half-Time Holiday Desserts   281

FILLING

4 8-ounce packages cream cheese or light cream cheese
1½ cups granulated sugar
4 large eggs
1 teaspoon vanilla extract
½ cup whipping cream
3 cups fresh raspberries, divided or 1½ cups frozen unsweetened raspberries
½ cup sour cream
Fresh mint leaves (optional)

RASPBERRY SAUCE

3 cups fresh raspberries or 10-ounce package frozen, sweetened raspberries, thawed
2 teaspoons cornstarch
2 teaspoons butter
2 teaspoons fresh lemon juice

1. With cooking spray coat the bottom and sides of a 9- or 10-inch cheesecake pan or springform pan. Preheat the oven to 300° F.

2. For the crust, fit the food processor with the steel blade and add the ground cookies and the pecans, if desired, to the work bowl. Process until the mixture is ground into fine crumbs.

3. Place the butter into a microwavable 2-cup measure and microwave at 100% (high) for 30 seconds, until just melted. With the machine running, slowly add the butter to the crumbs through the feed tube.
Process for 5 seconds.

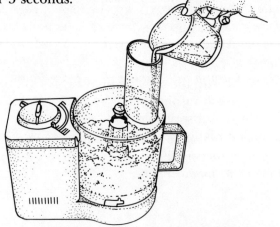

Place the crumbs in the prepared pan and press evenly over the bottom. Set aside.

4. For the filling, in the clean bowl of the food processor fitted with the steel blade, process the cream cheese until light. Remove the lid and add the sugar. Process until smooth. Remove the lid and add the eggs, vanilla, and cream. Process until smooth. Pour ⅔ of the filling into the pan and sprinkle with 1½ cups fresh or frozen raspberries. Pour the remaining filling over the berries and smooth with the back of a spoon.

5. Prepare the cheesecake pan to bake in a water bath. Place the pan on a large piece of aluminum foil and fold up the sides of the foil around the pan to keep the water out when the pan is placed in the water bath. Trim off any excess foil that might hang down over or into the filling. Place the pan in a larger pan and place both pans on the middle rack of the preheated oven. Very carefully fill the larger pan with 1 inch of water (a plant-watering can makes this easy). Bake a 9-inch cake for 2 hours and 15 minutes and a 10-inch cake for 2 hours, until the middle is just set (the cheesecake will jiggle just a bit in the middle, not be soupy). Remove the cake from the oven and remove the foil. Place the cake on a wire rack to cool completely before removing the outside of the pan. Refrigerate at least 4 hours or overnight.

6. Meanwhile, prepare the raspberry sauce. With the back of a spoon, press the raspberries through a strainer, reserving the juice. Discard raspberry seeds and skins. (If fresh raspberries are not available, the strained juice from a thawed 10-ounce package of frozen sweetened raspberries may be used for sauce.) Add the cornstarch to the juice and stir well. Place the juice in the microwave and heat on 50% (medium-low) for 1 minute. Stir and heat on 50% (medium-low) for 1 more minute. Remove from the microwave and add the butter and lemon juice. Cover and chill.

7. To serve, place the cheesecake on a serving plate and whisk the sour cream to remove any lumps. Spread the top of the cheesecake with the sour cream. Garnish with the remaining 1½ cups fresh raspberries, if available, and sauce or just with the sauce and sprigs of mint. The cake may be made 2 days ahead, up to the point of adding the sour-cream topping, and may be kept covered in the refrigerator for 1 week.

Mailing Thimble Cakes

These cakes are moist yet hold their shape wonderfully. They are good to mail in the cool months if a few guidelines are followed.

Wrap them separately or recycle your clean paper egg cartons. Place 2 or 3 cakes in each of the 12 egg holders and cover with a sheet of plastic wrap. Close the lid and secure it. Place the egg carton in a packing box padded with crumpled or shredded paper and ship.

BLACK-BOTTOM THIMBLE CAKES

Makes 48 mini-cupcakes
20 minutes to prepare
20 minutes to bake
2 miniature-muffin tins

Far and away this is Diana's favorite sweet to make in large batches at holiday time or for school or church functions. The 2-bite cakes do, however, require special equipment. Muffin tins that are small, about 1½ inches in diameter, are needed, plus muffin or candy paper liners to fit. Both of these items are available in most cookware specialty shops. Buy at least 2 small pans so you can bake much faster. These are beautiful on a Halloween buffet table, served in a large basket lined with orange tissue paper and tied with a black ribbon.

CUPCAKE BATTER

1½ cups unbleached all-purpose flour
1 cup sugar
¼ cup unsweetened cocoa
1 teaspoon baking soda
½ teaspoon salt
1 cup water
⅓ cup vegetable oil
1 tablespoon white wine vinegar
1 teaspoon vanilla extract

FILLING

1 8-ounce package cream cheese, room temperature
1 large egg
⅓ cup sugar
⅛ teaspoon salt
12-ounces (1 bag) mini–chocolate chips (regular chips are too big)

1. Preheat the oven to 350° F. For the cupcake batter, in a large 8-cup glass measure with a lip, combine the flour, sugar, cocoa, baking soda, and salt. Stir. Add the water, oil, white wine vinegar, and vanilla and whisk thoroughly. The batter will be thin. Set aside.

2. For the filling, in the processor bowl fitted with the steel

blade, add the cream cheese, egg, sugar, and salt. Process until smooth and creamy, about 20 seconds. With a rubber spatula, stir in the bag of chocolate chips.

3. Place cupcake liners in 2 miniature-muffin tins. Pour into each muffin cup 2 teaspoons of batter, or enough to fill the cup half-full with cupcake batter. Then drop ½ teaspoon of the filling onto the top. Bake the cupcakes on the middle rack of the preheated oven for 20 minutes, until lightly browned around the edges. Remove the cupcakes from the oven and tins to cool. Repeat step 3 until all of the cupcakes are filled and baked.

*H*ALLOWEEN CANDY-APPLE CAKE

Serves 8
10 minutes to prepare
1 hour and 10 minutes to bake
10-inch tube or bundt pan

Combine everything in one bowl and mix this festive apple cake with a spoon. Prepare the cake 1 day ahead and store covered at room temperature to allow the flavors to blend. Spoon prepared caramel sauce over the cake, or serve it in a pool of luscious sauce.

2 cups unbleached all-purpose flour
1 cup sugar
1 teaspoon baking soda
1 teaspoon baking powder
   Pinch of salt
1 teaspoon ground cinnamon
½ teaspoon freshly grated nutmeg
1 teaspoon vanilla extract
1 20-ounce can apple pie filling
½ cup vegetable oil
2 eggs, lightly beaten
⅔ cup chopped walnuts
½ cup golden raisins
12 ounces best-quality caramel sauce made with real cream and
      butter

(continued)

1. Preheat the oven to 325° F. With cooking spray coat a 10-inch tube or bundt pan.

2. In a large bowl combine the flour, sugar, baking soda, baking powder, salt, cinnamon, nutmeg, vanilla, apple pie filling, oil, and eggs. Mix well with a wooden spoon. Fold in the walnuts and raisins.

3. Spoon the mixture into the prepared pan. Bake on the middle rack of the preheated oven for 1 hour and 10 minutes, until a tester inserted in the center comes out clean. Cool to room temperature in the pan on a rack, cover, and store for 24 hours to allow the flavors to blend.

4. To serve, remove the cake from the pan and place on a serving plate. Spoon the caramel sauce into a 4-cup glass measure and microwave on 100% (high) until hot but not boiling, about 1 minute. The heat will thin the sauce and make it pour like liquid gold. Pour the sauce over the cake and serve immediately.

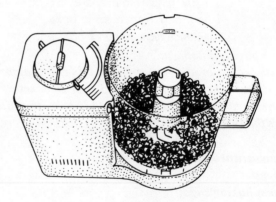

MINCEMEAT-PUMPKIN PIE

Serves 6 to 8
15 minutes to prepare
45 to 50 minutes to bake
10-inch pie pan

This Thanksgiving pie showcases 2 holiday favorites baked together. The velvety pumpkin custard has a fascinating, subtle flavor all its own as it envelops the rich, spicy mincemeat—it's luscious!

1 prepared 9-inch piecrust or ⅓ recipe (1 crust) Bride's Crust Revisited (see page 63), unbaked
1 cup pumpkin puree, canned or homemade (see sidebar)
1 large egg, lightly beaten
¼ teaspoon salt
⅓ cup sugar
1 teaspoon pumpkin-pie spice, homemade (see sidebar) or store-bought
¾ cup evaporated whole milk
2 cups prepared mincemeat

1. Preheat the oven to 400° F. Fit the piecrust into a 10-inch pie pan. Trim and flute the edges. In a medium mixing bowl combine the pumpkin puree, egg, salt, sugar, pumpkin-pie spice, and milk. Blend well.

2. Spread the mincemeat over the bottom of the piecrust. Spoon the pumpkin mixture over the mincemeat layer. Bake on the middle rack of the preheated oven for 45 to 50 minutes, until a knife inserted halfway in the middle of the pie comes out clean. Cool on a rack. Serve at room temperature or chilled.

Homemade Pumpkin-Pie Spice

Prepare this spice mixture in advance to flavor your favorite pumpkin pie or squash pie. Remember to label the jar. Otherwise, you're going to look at that jar full of tan dust some morning after you've dredged it from the back of the pantry and wonder, What on earth can that be?!

5 teaspoons ground cinnamon
2½ teaspoons ground nutmeg
2½ teaspoons ground ginger
1¼ teaspoons ground cloves

Combine all the spices well and store them in a small baby-food jar or other container with a tight-fitting lid. Use just 1 teaspoon of Pumpkin-Pie Spice per pie for flavoring.

❖   ❖

Pumpkin Puree

Preheat the oven to 325° F. Coat a large baking sheet with shallow sides with cooking spray. Wash the pumpkin in a dishwashing solution and rinse well. Cut the pumpkin into large chunks and scrape off the seeds. Place the pumpkin, shell side up, on the baking sheet. Bake for 1 hour, until the flesh is easily pierced with a fork and scraped from the skin. Puree in the food processor fitted with the steel blade, or pass through a food mill. Cooled puree may be frozen for up to 3 months.

Spread the seeds and stringy membranes on sheets of newspaper and dry in the sun for several days. Serve to your feathered friends.

For an extra festive holiday drink to serve with this or other holiday desserts why not try an old Southern drink: iced tea. Yes, we do drink plain old Lipton's all yearround. And, for special occasions we sometimes jazz it up a bit.

• **Fruit Tea**   Stir cranberry juice into iced tea and serve in a fluted champagne glass
• **Celebration Iced Tea**   Add a splash of champagne, ginger ale, or fruit flavored seltzer water to a tall champagne flute of iced tea
• **Sangria Tea**   Cut up fresh seasonal fruits such as oranges, pomegranates, sweet Texas pink grapefruits, grapes, strawberries, apples and/or oranges. Add them to tea and let them steep for a couple of hours. To serve, pour into a footed wineglass half full of Fruit Tea, splash with seltzer, and serve over ice. Add a jaunty sprig of mint to the top of the wineglass.

MARILOU ROBINSON'S DEEP-DISH FAUX CHERRY PIE WITH OAT-CRUMBLE CRUST

Makes one 9-inch pie
15 minutes to prepare
40 minutes to bake
9-inch pie pan

A recipe that began in the depression when cranberries in Oregon were as common as the proverbial pigs' tracks. Then, Thanksgiving feasts were finished with such homey desserts. We like the pie so well, we stock up on cranberries in the fall, throwing sacks of them in the freezer for use all year long

We also find this crust to be a perfect foil for other fall fruits. Pears and raisins, apples and walnuts. Use your imagination. That's how this pie was invented in the first place. Necessity being the mother of . . .

CRUST

½ cup roasted peanuts
1½ cups rolled oats (not instant)
¼ cup unbleached all-purpose flour
¾ cup firmly packed dark brown sugar
2 teaspoons ground cinnamon
½ teaspoon ground nutmeg
¼ teaspoon salt
½ cup (1 stick) unsalted butter or margarine, softened

FILLING

2 cups fresh or frozen whole cranberries
¾ cup granulated sugar
1 tablespoon unbleached all-purpose flour
1 teaspoon almond flavoring
1½ teaspoons butter or margarine

Vanilla ice cream

1. Preheat the oven to 475° F.

2. To make the crust, first grind the peanuts in the food processor using the steel blade or blender, then combine with the rolled oats, flour, brown sugar, cinnamon, nutmeg, and salt. Blend thoroughly, then cut in the butter or margarine and process until the mixture resembles coarse meal, about 10 seconds. Press half the crust mixture into a 9-inch pie pan.

3. To make the filling, place the cranberries in the pie plate over the oatmeal crust. Combine the sugar and flour and sprinkle the mixture over the berries. Sprinkle the almond flavoring on top, then dot with butter or margarine.

4. Pour the remaining crust mixture on top, smoothing out as much as you can. Bake in the preheated oven for 10 minutes, then reduce the heat to 425° F and bake for 30 minutes more, until the crust is bubbly and brown.

5. Cool thoroughly, then scoop out servings onto dessert dishes and top with vanilla ice cream. Don't expect perfect wedges. They don't call it a crumble crust for nothing.

"The man is a common murderer."
"A common murderer, possibly, but a very uncommon cook."

—SAKI (1870–1916)
The Blind Spot, *Beasts and Super-Beasts*

"Prune" is the name given to certain varieties of plums with a high sugar content that can be dried for longer shelf life. Plums can be successfully sun dried at home in warm, dry climates, including those of southern California, Arizona, and New Mexico. In cooler, more humid climates, they must be dehydrated in ovens or in dehydrators.

If you are interested in sun drying or dehydrating the plums in your area, check with your local county extension agent for safety procedures to be followed.

*P*UCKERED-PLUM TART WITH COGNAC

Serves 6 to 8
30 minutes to prepare
1 hour and 10 minutes to bake
9-inch tart pan with removable bottom

Little Jack Horner won't be the only one with a Christmas pie. For this recipe, plumped prunes are baked on top of a succulent filling of almonds, butter, and more prunes. A splash of cognac and a deep, rich cup of espresso are the only finishing touches needed.

Some sort of weights are needed to weigh the crust down so it won't puff up and look like the foothills of Vesuvio. We use commercially made pie weights, which are available in most kitchen specialty stores. Look for a brand that is for the conventional oven or the microwave and is washable. These weights conduct heat evenly from the top down on your pastry while your oven is cooking the bottom of your pastry. If you don't have pie weights, you can use dried beans; however, after 2 or 3 uses, the bean skins will start to flake off and float around in your oven. Puhleeze, look for pie weights or put them on your Christmas list and let someone else search for them.

  2 cups water
  2 pekoe tea bags
1¾ cups pitted prunes, divided
  ½ pound (1 sheet) frozen puff pastry, thawed
  ½ cup (1 stick) unsalted butter, softened
  1 cup confectioners' sugar
  2 large eggs
  1 cup blanched slivered almonds
  2 tablespoons cognac

1. In a 1-quart microwavable mixing bowl, microwave the water on 100% (high) until it comes to a boil, about 3½ minutes. Add the tea bags and 1¼ cups of the prunes. Set aside.

2. Preheat the oven to 375° F. Lightly coat the bottom of a 9-inch tart pan with a removable bottom with cooking spray.

3. On a piece of waxed paper, roll out the prepared puff pastry dough to a square that measures 11-inches square. Turn the pastry into the pan. Press it into the bottom of the pan,

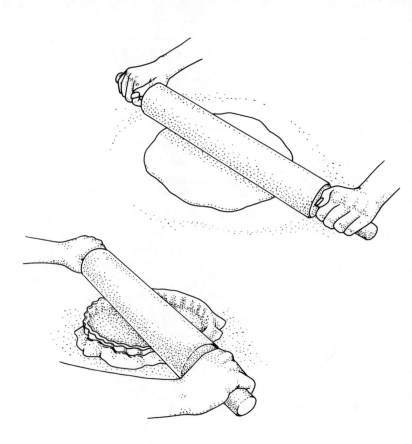

and trim the edges even with the pan. Prick the bottom and the sides with the tines of a fork. Line the pastry with foil and weight with pie weights or dried beans. Bake on the middle rack of the preheated oven for 15 minutes. Remove the foil and weights. Bake for an additional 5 minutes, just until the pastry begins to brown.

4. Meanwhile, prepare the filling. In the bowl of a food processor fitted with the steel blade, combine the butter, sugar, eggs, almonds, and the remaining ½ cup of prunes. Process until the prunes are chopped and the ingredients are combined thoroughly.

5. Spread the butter-prune filling into the bottom of the partially baked crust. Drain the soaking prunes, discarding the tea and tea bags, and cover the top of the filling with the prunes, cut side down. Bake until the filling is set and the crust is well browned, about 50 minutes. Cool to room temperature and sprinkle with the cognac. Serve at room temperature. May be made up to 4 hours before serving.

We buy pecans in the shell in bulk
and crack them ourselves to save
money. October or November is the
best time to buy, as you will be
getting a new crop and the price
will be lower. Five pounds of un-
shelled pecans will yield about 2½
pounds of nut meats. One pound
of nut meats is a volume measure
of about 4½ cups. Store the nuts
in airtight containers in the refrigerator for up to 9 months or in the
freezer for up to 2 years.

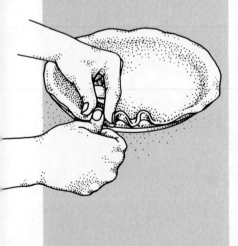

CAPRICE'S HOLIDAY CARAMEL-PECAN PIE

Serves 8
15 minutes to prepare
1 hour to bake
9-inch glass pie pan (only a glass pie pan will work with this recipe)

*A rich caramel holds the pecans together in this dense filling. Pecan
lovers everywhere will appreciate the change from the standard soft
filling used in most pecan pieces. If you're short on time, a prepared
piecrust works just fine; however, if time allows, please try this pie
made with our Shortcut Processor Crust.*

½ recipe (1 crust) Shortcut Processor Crust (see page 59), un-
    baked or 1 prepared 9-inch piecrust
2 large eggs
1 cup sugar
1 cup dark corn syrup
½ teaspoon unbleached all-purpose flour
¼ teaspoon salt
1 teaspoon vanilla extract
¼ cup unsalted butter, melted
1 cup broken or coarsely chopped pecans
1 cup pecan halves

1. Preheat the oven to 350° F. Fit a 9-inch *glass* pie pan
with our Shortcut Processor Crust, or a prepared piecrust.
(Freeze the remaining crust for later use or keep it in the
refrigerator for up to 1 week.) Trim and flute the edge of the
crust.

2. In the processor bowl fitted with the steel blade, add the
eggs, sugar, corn syrup, flour, salt, vanilla, and melted butter.
Process for 15 seconds, until smooth. Add the pecans and,
with a rubber spatula, stir to blend. Pour the filling into the
prepared crust.

3. Bake the pie on the middle rack of the preheated oven
for 1 hour, until the edges of the pie are lightly browned and
the top is puffed. Remove the pie to a rack and allow to cool
to room temperature completely. Serve immediately, or the
pie may be stored at room temperature for 2 to 3 days, if you
can keep it around that long.

ℱ︎AST HOLIDAY TRIFLE

Serves 6
25 minutes to prepare
1 hour to chill
2-quart glass trifle or other serving bowl

On Diana's sideboard this past Christmas, she served trifle in a beautiful, footed glass trifle bowl and Chocolate Mighty Mousse (see page 112) in stemmed goblets. Both desserts were made the day before in an hour and refrigerated until Christmas Day to be served. Although formal enough for the holidays, the trifle is easy enough to leave the cook relaxed.

> **1 10-ounce best-quality pound cake or ½ recipe (1 loaf) Harriet and David's Pound Cake (see page 42)**
> **1 cup Amaretto**
> **¾ cup raspberry jam or sauce**
> **3 cups fresh or individually quick-frozen raspberries, unsweetened without syrup**
> **1 recipe Vanilla Princess Pudding (see sidebar, page 199), warm**
> **1½ cups whipping cream**
> **2 tablespoons confectioners' sugar**
> **Slivered almonds, for garnish**
> **Fresh mint leaves, for garnish**

1. Cut the pound cake crosswise into ½-inch-thick slices. Lay the slices flat on a large baking sheet. Sprinkle the slices generously with the Amaretto. Spread each one with 1 tablespoon of jam or sauce. Line the sides and bottom of a 2-quart glass trifle or other serving bowl with the slices of pound cake, jam or sauce side facing inside the bowl.

2. Into the middle of the bowl pour 1½ cups of the fresh or frozen raspberries. Pour half of the warm vanilla pudding over the berries. Repeat with the remaining berries and pudding.

3. Fit the processor bowl with the steel blade and add the whipping cream. Process until thickened, about 30 seconds. Gradually add the sugar through the feed tube and process until stiff. Spread the whipped cream on top of the trifle. Garnish with slivered almonds. Refrigerate for at least 1 hour and garnish with mint leaves just before serving. This may be made a day ahead if kept covered and refrigerated.

Store all nuts in clean, dry containers with tight lids to protect them from insects and dust. We like to use glass jars with tight lids or polybags tightly closed. The secret to storing in-shell nuts and nut meats is to keep them cool. Refrigerate or freeze them as soon as possible after purchase. The lower the temperature the longer the nuts will keep. Refrigerated nuts keep for about 9 months; frozen nuts for about 2 years.

Never chop or grind nuts until you are ready to use them. This causes the nut oils to come to the surface, and they may go rancid if not used right away. Coarsely chopped nuts will not sink to the bottom in a batter that is rather thick or contains other ingredients such as chocolate chunks or fruit. For delicate cake batters, finely chop the nuts so they will be distributed evenly (the food processor is a pro at this) and not sink to the bottom.

CRANBERRY-TANGERINE CHRISTMAS COBBLER

Makes 1½ quarts to serve 6 to 8
20 minutes to prepare
25 minutes to bake
1½-quart shallow glass baking dish

With all the sweet sweets prepared for the holidays, it's nice to have something a little more tart and refreshing. Bubbling ruby-red cranberries, juicy tangerines, and the crunch of fresh walnuts, covered with the tender crumb of dumplings, provide the sights and smells of Christmas all in one dish.

FILLING

2 cups whole fresh or frozen cranberries
1 cup coarsely chopped walnuts
1 cup raisins
½ cup sweet small seedless tangerine sections
¾ cup sugar
2 teaspoons cornstarch
½ teaspoon ground allspice
1 cup fresh orange juice

DUMPLINGS

1 cup unbleached all-purpose flour
2 teaspoons baking powder
2 tablespoons sugar
¼ teaspoon salt
¼ cup (½ stick) unsalted butter
½ cup milk

Vanilla ice cream (optional)

1. For the filling, in a large microwavable mixing bowl, combine the cranberries, walnuts, raisins, tangerines, sugar, cornstarch, allspice, and orange juice, and stir thoroughly. Microwave on 100% (high) for 5 minutes, until the mixture boils (this time will vary depending on whether frozen or fresh cranberries are used).

2. When the filling comes to a boil, remove the mixing bowl from the microwave and whisk. Return the mixture to the microwave and continue to cook on 100% (high) for 2 to 4 minutes, until the cranberries begin to pop and the mixture thickens slightly. Pour into a shallow 1½-quart shallow glass baking dish. Preheat the oven to 400° F.

3. For the dumplings, in the bowl of the food processor fitted with the steel blade, combine the flour, baking powder, sugar, and salt. Pulse once to mix. Cut the butter into 4 chunks, open the lid, and scatter it evenly over the flour in the machine. Pulse 5 to 6 times, until the butter is the size of small peas. Add the milk through the feed tube to the dry ingredients and pulse 3 to 4 times, until the dough masses around the blade. Drop spoons of batter over the hot filling. Bake on the middle rack of the preheated oven for 25 minutes, until golden. Serve warm over vanilla ice cream.

Frozen Cranberries

Cranberries freeze better than any berry we know of. They stay nice and firm and don't turn to mush when thawed. Cranberries are available year-round in the frozen-food section of our market. To freeze fresh ones, pack them into an airtight bag and remove any excess air. Freeze. They will keep for a almost a year. When using them in a recipe, do not defrost.

Due to a shortage of cranberries, the cranberry industry recently changed its standard bag size. We used to buy a 16-ounce bag and now the standard size is 12 ounces. Amounts called for in older recipes may need to be checked if the recipe calls for "1 bag of cranberries."

PANETTONE

Makes 1 large coffee cake
45 minutes to prepare
1 hour to bake
10-cup charlotte mold or two 1-pound coffee cans

Italian Christmas is not complete without the high-domed cylinder of fruit-studded sweet bread the apocryphal baker named for himself. The bread begins with a brioche-type dough, and one story has it that a baker named Tony invented this sweet bread to present to his sweetheart for a Christmas present.

Here's your chance to try out our Micro-Rise process and make a sweet bread that's lovely to have on hand for impromptu Christmas get-togethers as well as for gifts. You can make the bread in a charlotte mold, or two 1-pound coffee cans you've greased and floured. For gifts, even small Campbell's soup cans would be great. Adjust cooking times down for smaller containers. This makes a great gift packed in a tin.

2 cups bread flour
1¾ cups cake flour
⅓ cup granulated sugar
½ teaspoon salt
5 teaspoons (2 packages) 50% faster active dry yeast
¼ teaspoon freshly grated nutmeg
⅔ cup (1 stick plus 3 tablespoons) unsalted butter or margarine, cut into bits
¼ cup milk
½ cup water
1 teaspoon vanilla extract
2 large eggs
2 egg yolks
  Zest of ½ orange
½ cup golden raisins
¼ cup Marsala
⅓ cup slivered candied cherries
⅓ cup diced mixed candied fruits
¼ cup pine nuts
  Confectioners' sugar

1. In the processor bowl fitted with the steel blade, combine the flours, sugar, salt, yeast, and nutmeg. Pulse to mix. Now cut the butter or margarine into pieces and arrange them on the top. Pulse to blend so that they almost disappear.

2. Combine the milk and water in a glass measure. Microwave at 100% (high) to 120° F, about 40 seconds, then with a fork, whisk in the vanilla, eggs, and egg yolks.

3. With the processor motor running, *drizzle the liquids very slowly into the flour mixture.* Process 60 seconds. Add the orange zest and pulse to mix. Remove the blade from the processor bowl and prepare to Micro-Rise. Cover the food processor bowl loosely with a damp tea towel or plastic wrap.

4. Place an 8-ounce glass of water in the back of the microwave. Lower the microwave to 10% power or the appropriate Micro-Rise setting (see page 244). Place the dough in the microwave. Heat for 3 minutes. Rest for 3 minutes. Heat for 3 minutes. Rest for 6 minutes, until the batter has risen to about double in bulk. It will look bubbly and light.

5. While the dough is rising, soak the raisins in the Marsala.

6. Stir the batter down, then stir in the raisin mixture, cherries, candied fruits, and pine nuts until well distributed in the batter (you may find it's easier if you transfer the whole business to a large mixing bowl and use a wooden spoon).

7. Generously grease and lightly flour a 10-cup charlotte mold (about 7½ inches in diameter and 4 inches deep) or two 1-pound coffee cans. Cut a parchment-paper circle to fit the bottom of the pan or each can and add it, dusting and flouring it as well. Preheat the oven to 325° F. Spoon the batter into the mold or cans, press down slightly, then raise in a warm, draft-free place until nearly double in bulk, about 30 minutes. Just before you pop it in the oven, cut an X in the top of the loaf with a razor. Italian bakers add a blob of butter to the cut.

8. Bake in the preheated oven for 1 hour, until evenly browned and a skewer stuck in the center comes out clean. Remove immediately to a rack to cool; then 15 minutes later, slide the cake out of the pan or cans and lay it on its side to continue cooling. Dust all over with confectioners' sugar while warm. Wrap in plastic to store.

INDEX

Equivalent Imperial and Metric Measurements

American cooks use standard containers, the 8-ounce cup and a tablespoon that takes exactly 16 level fillings to fill that cup level. Measuring by cup makes it very difficult to give weight equivalents, as a cup of densely packed butter will weigh considerably more than a cup of flour. The easiest way therefore to deal with cup measurements in recipes is to take the amount by volume rather than by weight. Thus the equation reads:

1 cup = 240 ml = 8 fl. oz.   ½ cup = 120 ml = 4 fl. oz.

It is possible to buy a set of American cup measures in major stores around the world.

In the States, butter is often measured in sticks. One stick is the equivalent of 8 tablespoons. One tablespoon of butter is therefore the equivalent to ½ ounce/14 grams.

Liquid Measures

Fluid ounces	U.S. measures	Imperial measures	Millimeters
	1 tsp	1 tsp	5
	2 tsp	1 dessertspoon	10
½	1 tbs	1 tbs	14
1	2 tbs	2 tbs	28
2	¼ cup	4 tbs	56
4	½ cup		110
5		¼ pint or 1 gill	140
6	¾ cup		170
8	1 cup		225
9			250 or ¼ liter
10	1¼ cups	½ pint	280
12	1½ cups		340
15		¾ pint	420
16	2 cups		450
18	2¼ cups		500 or ½ liter
20	2½ cups	1 pint	560
24	3 cups		675
25		1¼ pints	700
27	3½ cups		750
30	3¾ cups	1½ pints	840
32	4 cups or 1 quart		900
35		1¾ pints	980
36	4½ cups		1000 or 1 liter
40	5 cups	2 pints or 1 quart	1120
48	6 cups		1350
50		2½ pints	1400
60	7½ cups	3 pints	1680
64	8 cups or 2 quarts		1800
72	9 cups		2000 or 2 liters
80	10 cups	4 pints	2250
96	12 cups or 3 quarts		2700
100		5 pints	2800

Solid Measures

U.S. and Imperial measures		Metric measures	
ounces	pounds	grams	kilos
1		28	
2		56	
3½		100	
4	¼	112	
5		140	
6		168	
8	½	225	
9		250	¼
12	¾	340	
16	1	450	
18		500	½
20	1¼	560	
24	1½	675	
27		750	¾
28	1¾	780	
32	2	900	
36	2¼	1000	1
40	2½	1100	
48	3	1350	
54		1500	1½
64	4	1800	
72	4½	2000	2
80	5	2250	2¼
90		2500	2½
100	6	2800	2¾

Suggested Equivalents and Substitutes for Ingredients

all purpose flour—plain flour
coarse salt—kitchen salt
confectioners' sugar—icing sugar
cornstarch—cornflour
granulated sugar—caster sugar
sour cherry—morello cherry
unbleached flour—strong, white flour
vanilla bean—vanilla pod
zest—rind
heavy cream—double cream
baking sheet—oven tray
cheesecloth—muslin
parchment paper—greaseproof paper
plastic wrap—cling film

Oven Temperature Equivalents

Fahrenheit	Celsius	Gas Mark	Description
225	110	¼	Cool
250	130	½	
275	140	1	Very Slow
300	150	2	
325	170	3	Slow
350	180	4	Moderate
375	190	5	
400	200	6	Moderately Hot
425	220	7	Fairly Hot
450	230	8	Hot
475	240	9	Very Hot
500	250	10	Extremely Hot

Any broiling recipes can be used with the grill of the oven, but beware of high-temperature grills.